D1202067

SHOPPING CENTERS: U.S.A.

SHOPPING CENTERS: U.S.A.

Edited by George Sternlieb and James W. Hughes

Center for Urban Policy Research
Rutgers, the State University of New Jersey
P. O. Box 489
Piscataway, New Jersey 08854

Published in the United States of America
by the Center for Urban Policy Research
Building 4051 - Kilmer Campus
New Brunswick, New Jersey 08903

The preparation of *Shopping Centers: U.S.A.* was aided by a grant
from the U.S. Department of Housing and Urban Development,
Office of Policy Development and Research

The statements and conclusions contained herein are those of the authors and do not necessarily
reflect the views of the U.S. Government in general nor particularly the U.S. Department of
Housing and Urban Development. Neither the Federal Government nor the Department of
Housing and Urban Development makes any warranty, expressed or implied, or assumes
responsibility for the accuracy or completeness of the information herein.

Library of Congress Cataloging in Publication Data
Main entry under title:

Shopping centers, USA.

    Bibliography: p.
    Includes index.
    1. Shopping centers--United States--Addresses,
essays, lectures. I. Sternlieb, George. II. Hughes,
James W.
HF5430.3.S47   381'.1'0973   80-21702
ISBN 0-88285-068-7

Cover Design by Francis G. Mullen

Contents

Notes on the Contributors

Claude Ballard
Vice President
Real Estate Investment Department
Prudential Insurance Company
Newark, New Jersey

Brian J. L. Berry
Williams Professor of City and
Regional Planning
Graduate School of Design
Harvard University
Cambridge, Massachusetts

Philip Brous
President
Miller- Wohl Company, Inc.
Secaucus, New Jersey

Martin Cleary
Vice-President
Teachers Insurance & Annuity
Association
New York, New York

Stephen H. Cowen
Vice President, Retail Development
Hartz Mountain Industries, Inc.
Secaucus, New Jersey

Michael Fix
Research Associate
The Urban Institute
Washington, D.C.

Jack Gould
President
HSG/Gould Associates
Washington, D.C.

Howard L. Green
David L. Huntoon
President and Vice President
Howard L. Green & Associates

Charles M. Haar
Louis D. Brandeis, Professor of Law
Harvard University Law School
Cambridge, Massachusetts

Bruce Hayden
President
Hayden Associates
Bloomfield, Connecticut

Howard E. Kane
Elizabeth L. Belkin
Senior Partner and Attorney
Jenner & Block
Chicago, Illinois

Marshall Kaplan
Office of Community Planning and
Development
U.S. Department of Housing and
Urban Development
Washington, D.C.

Michael F. Kelly
President
Dayton Hudson Properties
Minneapolis, Minnesota

Peter D. Leibowits
President
Cadillac Fairview Shopping
Centers, Ltd.
White Plains, New York

Daniel R. Mandelker
Stamper Professor of Law
Washington University in St. Louis

Thomas Muller
Principal Research Associate
The Urban Institute
Washington, D.C.

Foster Sears
President
International Retail Institute
New York, New York

Frank H. Spink, Jr.
Editor, Dollars and Cents of
Shopping Centers
The Urban Land Institute
Washington, D.C.

Albert Sussman
Executive Vice President
International Council of
Shopping Centers
New York, New York

Ray Trieger
Vice President, Property Development
R.H. Macy Properties
New York, New York

Grady Tucker
Senior Vice President
Larry Smith & Company, Ltd.
Rockville, Maryland

Clifford L. Weaver
David T. Hejna
Attorneys
Ross, Hardies, O'Keefe, Babcock
and Parsons
Chicago, Illinois

The White House
Washington, D.C.

Margaret S. Wirtenberg
Urban Planner
New York, New York

Introduction:
The Uncertain Future
of Shopping Centers

GEORGE STERNLIEB
JAMES W. HUGHES

It is nearly sixty years since the first beginnings (1923) of a significant integrated suburban shopping center—Kansas City's Country Club Plaza, nearly thirty years since the East Coast pioneer enclosed mall at Framingham, Massachusetts filed for bankruptcy, largely as a result of the inadequacy of its leasing mechanisms and basic design flaws. At the very least, after faltering beginnings, the full coming into being of the regional and subregional shopping center as a dominant form of general merchandise retailing activity has been with us for a full generation.

The constituents of shopping centers have changed radically, indicating the vital shifts that have taken place in their role and function. The increase, for example, in nonmerchandise retailing activity, such as food and entertainment facilities, indicates the changing set of functions. Yet, just as the highway-oriented facilities seem to have clearly seized dominance in general merchandise distribution in the United States, serious issue is being raised as to their future. Despite its importance, the literature of substance on the topic is remarkably sparse. Academic research and analysis tend to follow rather than proceed major marketing changes.

In attempting to provide insight into this vital area, it is important that perspective be secured as to the elements which made for the enormous rapidity of growth of the major suburban shopping center—and now raise the issues of whether it has become a relatively mature form of organization with limited growth potential for the future.

DYNAMICS AND TRENDLINES

The second energy crisis and the emerging phenomenon of stabilizing or declining real incomes have brought the issues of future center development front and center. Relative stagnation of shopper goods (department store type merchandise) sales volume in the face of increased consumer outlays for housing and energy related expenses has been observed since the early 1970s, but was barely reflected in developers' patterns of shopping center production.

The shopping center industry has long enjoyed the virtues of bringing into being a new product and of catching up with latent demand—the latter enhanced by the new growth settings of the United States—within a context of a seemingly ever expanding national economy. As the 1980s begin, however, Grady Tucker's observation that it must now move into a phase of replacement and maintenance of supply, within a reduced growth rate national economy, is clearly urgent.

A knowledge of history is viewed as much more a luxury than a necessity in periods of ebullience. It becomes a far more serious requirement in eras of potential crisis. This certainly is the case in reviewing the development of shopping center patterns within the United States. At its simplest, major retailers were very slow to move en masse into suburbia. At least until the beginning of the 1950s, there remained a distinct downtown orientation in the nation's retail structure. It was that decade, however, that spawned the initial development of the regional shopping center in concept and application, together with a number of very important support structures—strategies of leasing and advertising which made the format increasingly aggressive—which fostered its multiplication.

The 1960s were characterized by the increasing size of regional shopping centers and inclusion of a broader variety of merchandizing approaches, as well as the coming into being of developers whose scale permitted easy replication of a standardized development format at wide ranging geographic settings. Based upon the latter, shopping centers experienced multidimensional expansion. This was also a period in which increasing sophistication was gained in successfully repackaging an idealized urban form into the suburban milieu. The decade of the 1960s thus ended with the dominance of a standardized shopping center product predicated on its appeal to a vast monolithic middle-class market.

The 1970s represented a period of transition. The superregional center emerged in the earlier part of the decade; this time frame also witnessed the emptying of the pipeline of large scale untapped markets and with it the conceptual apparatus of belief in the unique center-of-the market pulling power that lay behind regional centers. A desperate search for untapped markets, sometimes of a scale that in palmier days would not have seen developer interest, came into being at mid-decade, i.e., the emergence of the so-called mid-market focus. In the last several years of the 1970s, the reemergence of downtown and select in-town areas as loci of shopping center development had made tentative, but significant, beginnings.

Thus the shopping center industry begins the 1980s with an immediate historical momentum increasingly characterized by diversity and market segmentation. The industry as a whole now has a much more diversified product line: of center configuration, marketing approach, and locational elements, than was heretofore the case. A much greater degree therefore of sophistication of development—and developers—is now required.

Critical to the decade in progress is the recognition of the market segmentation that has been a corollary to the shifts in America's social geography. The multinodal, multiconnected social systems that dominate our national landscape offer a wide variety of environments. As Brian Berry suggests:

> What has become important today are relative qualities of amenities and externalities within the whole rather than relative access to a historical center . . . The older hierarchies of retail centers were a product of access-constrained market orientation of facilities of different scales. As access variables have declined in relative significance, the advantages of specializing to meet the particular needs of particular local markets, or of particular metropolis-wide market segments, has increased. As the metropolis has spread and differentiated, so have retail and service opportunities.

In turn, successful developers in the future must be capable of servicing a range of consumer needs. As Bruce Hayden points out, the day of the superregional—the five- and six-department store center of 1.5 million square feet or more—has come, is here, and is starting to wane. The diversity emerging at the end of the 1970s may just have been a preview of the many directions that new retail development will follow in the 1980s.

Some of the relative stagnancy in total national department store type merchandise sales during the past decade was obscured by the regional shifts which have taken place. The growth nodes of Florida and the southwest, for example, seemed capable of absorbing endless new development. Their very conspicuousness, however, has resulted in a near saturation. The market research snake dance of consultants' reports following the obvious led everyone to the same market opportunities—and limited their yield. There is some issue, as expressed by a number of contributors to this volume, that relative ease of financing, given the shopping center's preferred status as a nominally inflation-proof instrument, may lead to some very costly excesses within this context.

Regardless of this latter stipulation, there is a largely finite future in terms of the demographics that must be serviced.

Markets and Demographics

The evolving demographic parameters of American society have received a level of scrutiny by both the popular and learned media that would bewilder the observer of a decade ago. While the current tendency is to ascribe a host of unexplained phenomena—and their virtues and demerits—to "shifting demographics," it is difficult to overestimate their significance to impending changes in the nation's retailing structure. Certainly, the physical dimensions of the prime demographic-market targets can be discerned:

1. The maturing baby boom generation will bulk ever larger as the prime market for retailers in the 1980s, while the trailing baby bust cohorts will define a shrinking of those age-related (15 to 24 years of age) sectors underpinning some critical markets of the 1970s.

2. The 55-to-65 years and over population will also gain critical mass in the present decade, creating a somewhat unique market target.

3. Household configurations—the growth of the single person households as well as two-worker households—also must be factored into the basic retail equation.

While a host of other demographic "shapes" can be outlined, a more difficult task involves the forecasting of the associated shifts in expenditure patterns and consumption desires. Failure to properly anticipate the latter, particularly in the context of broader economic events, has been exemplified by the stagnation of the supermarket industry and currently by the problems of domestic automobile manufacture. Is this a harbinger for general merchandise retailing and the shopping center industry? What must be confronted are the internal dynamics of the segmented demographic sectors. Foster Sears, for example, has speculated on some concerns attendant to the baby boom tide:

They represent the arrival of a new generation of adults with new lifestyles, objectives, opportunities and problems. They will have smaller families—two-worker families—and they may have difficulty maintaining the rising lifestyle that their parents took for granted . . . They are likely to develop new values, keyed more to quality than to quantity—more in keeping with the values of their grandparents than those of their parents. They will have more sophisticated tastes.

Clearly, substantial adjustments will be required to cope with the complex challenges of market segmentation emanating from demographic trendlines.

Principles and Parameters:
The Entrepreneur's View

In the latter context, it has been suggested that the fundamental principles on which shopping centers are located have not altered, but some of the bounding factors which affect development are changing significantly. Certainly, the historic parameters of optimum site location—of maximum trade area accessibility—of retail and service shifts characteristically following those of people and incomes and similar factors still prevail. But the search for new locations has become more intense and more competitive, demographic ramifications have yet to be fully comprehended, and retailing technology may be poised on a period of rapid evolution.

Since there are many players involved in the process of shopping center development, forecasts of several of the component entities are virtually mandatory. In the very effort of attempting this, however, the limits of the art form are all too evident. While the major demographic market sector profiles are largely fixed over the next decade, their morphology—how they live, work and play, their total lifestyles—is far from immutable. The issue of what, in the future, Americans will do to justify their historically high standards of living are far from resolved. And certainly the ingenuity of man is not confined to present retailing forms.

Within these areas of uncertainty it is evident that the old full-line department store, which has been the locomotive—the dynamic pulling power—of major center developments, both in central business districts as well as in highway-oriented facilities, is in a struggle for distinctiveness.

The decline of the broad circulation magazine may very well have its parallel in the problems that the relatively characterless, omnibus retail institutions may have in the future.

If we may use an analogy, there is room for "tigers," i.e., stores with a very rigorous cutting edge of character, with unique characteristics that generate saliency and pulling power, and "elephants," i.e., other stores that can survive in the very sense of carrying more of everything than anyone else. Institutions in between them are destined to fade.

Separate from this, however, is the declining significance of specific metropolitan area site locations to the major chains. In the last twenty years, we have seen a very vigorous growth in national and near-national department store chains at the expense of localized entities. This provides a level of flexibility in terms of choice of financial outlet and development type. But this is not the end of the cycle. The increased sophistication of management that is essential to make larger organizations viable may yield (and indeed already has) a capacity to view the business much more as the management of financial assets—much less a confinement to traditional large-store retailing—or for that matter general department store type merchandise distribution as such. A dozen years ago, it would have been sacrilegious to have thought that Sears Roebuck would secure the bulk of its income from insurance rather than retailing. The latter case, while perhaps at the moment unique, may forecast startling changes in the future.

The national specialty chain operations, initially stunned by the decline of the old downtown 100-percent location (and many of the most familiar names of a generation ago disappeared through failure to make the transition to the suburban shopping mall), have been rejuvenated. Indeed, most of the major national chains presently engaged in specialty retailing either emerged concurrently with the advent of regional shopping centers or were completely reorganized in its wake. As elaborated by Philip Brous, several factors spurred their development.

1. The tremendous expansion of bank credit cards permitted the small merchant to secure the same credibility and advantages as the large department store.

2. The homogenous environment of the enclosed regional mall established a retail setting far superior to the limited facilities occupied by chain stores in downtown locations. The sharp differentiation in the quality of space between downtown department and chain stores virtually disappeared with regional mall facilities.

Properly managed specialty store chains have attained substantial vitality and growth power by using as a vehicle the rapid expansion of regional shopping facilities—living parasitically off the research done by the anchors or majors (department stores) in the centers in which they enter, depending on the majors to generate traffic at mall locations. Their rapid growth was made possible by employing standard facility design formats. As a result, even a cursory comparison of operating results in the last decade between the department store chains and the specialty store operators confirms the greater vigor of the latter in adapting to changing circumstances and new opportunities.

A number of the most successful chains, however, have owed their success to the unique baby-boom generation, specializing in merchandising for this powerful group of new consumers. There is some issue as to their adaptive capacity in the future. Further, much of their growth has not been within the same units but is a tribute to ease of expansion. It has been external expansion rather than internal optimization (though the latter is far from meaningless in this regard) which has been the keystone. Can they compete within a much less expansive world?

But that assumes that the age of shopping center expansion will slow down. Much clearly depends upon the attitudes of lenders and the heavy retail players—the major department store chains. The latter have not yet exhausted the potential of market extensions (particularly to metropolitan areas where they are not represented) and the filling of voids between existing branches, both currently undertaken despite the risk of market saturation. And what has not yet been addressed adequately by retail strategists is the effect of takeovers by major chains of regional department store operations. Where there are weak regional chains, new suburban shopping center opportunities may be very significant. Conversely, however, the diversification of department store chains into specialty and discount operations—as typified by Dayton-Hudson—may constrain the generation of new department store units to rates far below that of the immediate past, in turn limiting the number of anchors for new regional center development.

The future guidelines are beginning to take shape. But our minds are still conditioned by the past in terms of the composition and nature of the players and the dynamics of the process in which they are involved. It is chastening to realize that within a teenager's lifetime Kresge's, a near bankrupt variety store chain using a form of general merchandise distribution unheard of ten years before its changeover, emerged as the second largest retailer in the United States. And the end of the wheel of retailing is not yet in sight.

The Evolving Economics of Retailing

There is a radical shift taking place between the economics of erecting new facilities (typically capital intensive) and the rehabilitation and reshaping of older plants (typically a labor-intensive activity). For more than a generation, it is the former, in the United States, whose economy has been characterized by relatively inexpensive money, which have dominated the scene. Whether in the provision of housing or in retailing facilities, however, it is the latter—rehabilitation and reshaping—which is an increasingly competitive alternative. In attempting to forecast a profitable future for retailing facilities, these rival dynamics are clearly brought to the fore.

The casual purchase of redundant space within shopping centers was only made possible by the relatively low costs of operating within these contexts, combined with a belief in future expansion of real sales. Neither of these conditions hold in the present. Even in the absence of clear-cut limits on future real sales expansion, the increasing costs of developing and operating retail facilities combined with the costs of money would necessarily weight the balance toward smaller, more efficient facilities.

These trends have been evolving with increasing clarity over the last several years. In part they have been obscured by an unbundling of occupancy costs. The definition of developers' responsibilities in terms of facility finish and operating costs has become more limited over time—the elements for which the individual retailer is responsible, increasing in a complementary fashion. The concept of building an excess-sized facility in order to preclude competition, i.e., overbuilding for a specific market, is a perilous strategy given the new cost matrices. The penalties that have occurred for similar strategies in the supermarket industry are all too chastening. Retailers, in turn, as they see their basic maintenance charges exceeding base rents in magnitude, must redesign stores to optimize space utilization and minimize unproductive footage if they are to profitably survive.

The challenge of doing so while preserving a maximum level of flexibility with which to meet the demography of the 1980s is evident. The enormous, long-term concentration on various facets of the baby-boom generation, for example, has permitted the growth (and sometimes enormously successful growth) of a variety of chains dedicated to one or another segment of this element. The issue of whether they will prove to be "one-shot" successes or whether they will have a capacity to adapt to the new market realities is far from determined. But at the very least much of this adaptation will require a flexibility of space use, a capacity for completely altering image and offerings, which may well make the comparative inflexibility of present day leasing techniques obsolete in the future.

THE SEARCH FOR NEW LOCATIONS

The basic emphasis of shopping center locational strategy has been both to follow and to proceed (but not by too much!) the equivalent migration of resident population. As earlier indicated, however, the number of players in the development game and the sheer vigor of expansionism which has taken place has raised the demand for alternative approaches. What are the evolving configurations and rationales?

The Central-City Alternative

The central city as a future locus for major shopping center development can be viewed in three overlapping yet largely alternative roles:

1. As a set of sites with a relatively limited potential for the future. In a few isolated cases, there are opportunities, but even among this handful they are of relatively unique character;

2. The central city may provide a significant potential to complement suburban development. The beginnings of population and job stability in central cities is forecastible, in large part through a decline in housing-buying power, new demographic profiles and potential job revitalization. Given government aid—particularly Urban Development Action Grants (UDAG) or equivalent activity—a substantial (if not overwhelming) set of opportunities will become both available and highly desirable to developers in the future.

3. The centrifugal forces which have dominated American development patterns, certainly since World War II, are coming to an end; the future will be marked by a return to dominance of central locations. The core cities will regain a substantial part of their past functions as the focal point, particularly of services, and within those sets of services, bulking ever increasingly in significance, will be retailing. The exurban center, which has rapidly come into being over the last decade, may very well be a dinosaur reflecting a previous ecology. The new energy realities are so harsh that they will impose a true return-to-the-city movement.

Regardless of which of these scenarios appropriately gauges the future, there is a very clear-cut and striking interest in the potential of utilizing the techniques and technology which have evolved in the suburban shopping center as basic to central-city revitalization efforts. Thus, in many cities in the United States, sometimes aided by federal funding and sometimes utilizing private funding solely, the equivalent of the suburban mall is being constructed.

The problems of dealing with the older, extant retail ecology while this change is being accomplished have not been fully examined. One can look back to the early days of urban renewal with New Haven as a striking prototype. An old balance of retailing was destroyed through massive land clearance; ultimately the principal major stores downtown were attenuated by the loosening of retail linkages and the clienteles that had grown around them—leaving a partial vacuum downtown. Nearly a generation has passed and this gap is still far from filled. Do we risk similar problems in the new excitement of revitalization? Even if we assume a renewed vigor of downtown activity, is the replication of the highway-oriented mall an appropriate technological response?

The question of whether the focal points of redevelopment in a number of major cities (the names are so well known as to indicate the singularity of the phenomenon as yet, i.e., Society Hill, Capitol Hill, Brooklyn Heights, etc.) are forerunners of the future or are relatively unique in and of themselves is as yet unanswered. There are forecasters, however, who envision a primary central-city market which will become increasingly attractive to developers as prime suburban locations are rendered unavailable—or their market potential split between too many players.

Yet there are other market sectors to be considered. The daytime work force of central cities, at least those with a strong service base, is still a very vital and powerful factor. Over the past generation, it has been increasingly composed of suburbanites who in turn shop on evenings and weekends near residence place rather than workplace. As family structures evolve in America, there is a potential for a reversal of this pattern—central cities capturing a much greater market penetration via mid-day and postwork retailing activity. But in order to secure this market potential, clearly the downtown will have to be a much more effective, much more aggressive factor than is presently the case with few exceptions.

And yet the very functions of our central cities are changing very rapidly following new lifestyles. The rise of the tourist industry, both internationally and nationally as well, has bred new life into a number of our downtowns. While generalizations based on short time periods are highly dangerous, the renewed vigor of New York City's department stores, particularly those catering to the more affluent clientele, is in substantial part a tribute to that city's renascent role as a worldwide tourist magnet. New interest in historic preservation in central cities is inspired and paralleled by a broad consumer interest in the same phenomenon. Those cities which have been able to accomplish meaningful restorations have seen them bring in their wake new forms of retail vigor. The Charleston Harbor Redevelopment has many equivalents elsewhere in America. The Faneuil Hall Market revitalization may signal yet increased interest in this type of unique cutting edge with which to pique consumer interest.

The incredible growth in the convention industry is only in part focused on "logical" locations—in many cases, it is a thinly disguised form of tax-free perquisite. Cities cognizant of this reality are beginning to upgrade their elements of distinction—and of pulling power. The resulting retail impact can be most meaningful.

Just as the suburban centers increasingly project their businesses into the entertainment area, both as a source of sales—but perhaps equally important as an element of distinctiveness—so central cities, or at least those which can both hold and perhaps grow entertainment elements, may find these generators of traffic are highly complementary to increased retail volume.

Any visitor to Denver's Larimer Square or the Ghirardelli Square complex of San Francisco is immediately aware of the intimate relationship between providing a combined food and entertainment complex—and this within a unique setting—as a means to secure broader consumer interest.

Not all downtowns are the same; the dangers of casually attempting to replicate the format of suburban centers within each of them are evident. Subject to that stringency, however, there are some clear-cut prototypes which have evolved. The early interest in pedestrian malls has left a residue of disenchantment in most cases, but also a continued interest in attempting an approach which has been so uniquely successful in European cities. The new megastructures which dominate our major cities, i.e., the Galleria in Houston, or the Citicorp Center in New York, have incorporated within them significant retailing complexes, as has the latter city's World Trade Center.

There has been nearly a generation of experience in the design of linkages between major downtown retailers through the development of mall equivalents. Rochester's Midtown Plaza, for example, has now had nearly twenty years of seasoning. By incorporating extant major downtown facilities, a support structure of flagship department stores has been assured, often at a scale that none of the suburban centers can match. But much of the success or failure of such developments depends upon the vitality not only of the central city within which they are located, but of its broader trading area. In a zero sum environment even the most unique of central-city retail complexes may find its profitability marginal at best.

Mid-Market Focus

As large suburban regional markets are built out, increasing attention has been captured by so-called middle-market areas. In essence, these are locations whose population densities are so thin or limited in absolute and growth dimensions as to have been by-passed by the initial wave of development. While not confined to nonmetropolitan areas, they typically are focused there.

The basic development rationale is that though the population densities peripheral to projected centers may be relatively limited, their sheer pulling power in the face of generally small town, relatively obsolete competing facilities enables them to secure an adequate market yield.

There is, however, a very real danger when marketing people adopt a concept: in the very making of virtue out of necessity, they may exaggerate the scale and scope of the phenomenon in question.

Regardless of its real potential, the middle-market expansion brings to the fore the issue of preservation of central business districts in smaller cities. In major metropolitan areas, the level of attrition which has been accomplished through competition has largely reached some form of equilibrium. In the relatively unexploited areas of middle-market development, this is not the case.

New political opposition pressures are forming both on the state and national levels. A most significant case is the frustration of efforts to build Vermont's first major enclosed mall outside of Burlington, which, at least at this writing, has been halted by the opposition of the city.

The Twilight Zone

There is a broad new category of development that, while certainly not unique to the last several years, has secured enhanced interest: in-fill or twilight-zone development. In major metropolitan areas there are substantial geographic stretches which are less than adequately serviced by major shopping facilities. This is particularly the case in some of the older, peripheral ethnic areas in major cities or their in-lying "trolley-car" suburbs. While site location is far from simple the potential rewards are most substantial. Chicago's Brickyard is a prime example of such a development on a site whose features had seemingly left it beyond development.

Even though the conventional clear-cut, clearly defined market potentials of yesteryear may have largely disappeared, the sheer drive of competitive forces of major retailers, desperate for a share of the market, and investors, perhaps overly casual or overly hungry to partake of the shopping center boom, will continue to enable strong expansion efforts.

The issues of whether, in relatively saturated markets, this may yield a level of competition which will be self-defeating for the retail players and, not least, raise a variety of governmental interventionary efforts are still to be fully heard. Certainly, however, as indicated by the new federal policy on major commercial installations as well as the rumblings of discontent in many state capitals, the latter are well on their way.

But the very act of limiting development by government raises the value of new successful development aside from enhancing the prospects of existing centers. Thus the front-end costs of site approval may soar, limiting the number of developers capable of accepting the risk, but the rewards of success will further be enhanced by a narrowing of the competition.

Re-Merchandising and Repackaging Existing Centers

There is a clear and imminent danger that the shopping center is in the process of moving from a revolutionary, consumer-exciting, new form of retailing and recreational activity to much more of a staple commodity entity. The sheer growth in number of centers, their increasingly consistent physical appearance and the lack of unique merchandising or crowd-pulling competence of individual centers in competitive areas may require much vital reshaping and repackaging for the future.

There is a clear and prevalent danger in assuming that depreciation charges are strictly a gift from IRS rather than reflecting some functional reality. *Passive shopping centers in the future will be losers.* The 1980s must see the recycling of first-and second-generation regional shopping centers if they are to maintain their market position.

While it is evident that the number of new major regional centers to be developed in the future will be limited because of site requirements as well as strictures in terms of total market demand, the basic marketing picture of the United States has never remained static. New forms of retailing endeavor, many of them anti-center, show surprising vitality. The catalog store and mail-order retailing, for example, are increasing their share of the market. The very competition between center-type merchandise and other forms of consumer expenditure should not be overlooked in this context. The sheer growth of parasite operations adjacent to or intersecting the traffic flows of centers is evident.

Shopping center developers and major merchants must be alert to the requirements, not only for much more hard-hitting forms of merchandising old offerings, but the necessities for new sales-generating elements as well—using the shopping center as a focal point for the creation of a true central market place. And certainly there are clear signs of a gathering of new functions within or peripheral to some of our major centers.

At this writing the flows of population to exurbia, upon which so many forecasts have been predicted, has yet to meet the tests of our present recession and generalized economic uncertainty. But clearly the set of retail players presently in existence even if there were no newcomers, given the decline of real income, would find an increased level of internal competition. The efforts of central-city governments, in conjunction with federal support, to secure retail revitalization will not disappear. They will rather increase. Thus the domino of competition to the older, first-tier suburban centers and from them to the exurban regionals will become ever fiercer.

Will the shopping center serve as a focal point for intraregional development? Howard Green, for example, speculates that many of the functions that we think of as downtown will agglomerate around the extant major regionals. And certainly one of the most important development resources of our time is the redundant acreage presently provided for one-level parking. Increased potential development opportunities may more than overweigh the costs and inconvenience of multideck facilities—thus liberating significant developable assets immediately peripheral to centers. The possible consequences of this in generating a completely new format are far from theoretical. There are some indications that the process is presently taking place.

Specialty Centers and
the Limited Sophistication
of America's Retailers

Until fairly recently America's major retailing giants were far more specialized in the kinds of businesses they pursued than their European peers. In the latter case relatively small markets had led entrepreneurs to diversify in the kinds of merchandise offerings—and institutions—which they included under their corporate umbrellas. Thus one finds major food retailers, specialty store operations, department stores, etc., conventionally grouped and operated by single organizations in France or Germany, and very successfully so. This process has just begun to be paralleled within the United States. Major U. S. department store chains were just that—their specialty store equivalents equally limited, etc. The growth of the discount-house movement broke down some of these barriers and there has been a generalized blurring of specialized operations within the United States. This process, which in turn has generated a much greater level of retail sophistication and much greater competence at analyzing a diversity of retail opportunities for investment, may be just the beginnings of what is required in the future as the changing consumer moves ever more rapidly in terms of spending patterns. *The emphasis here clearly must be on spending patterns rather than on conventional store retail expenditures per se.* The fast-food phenomenon will have many descendants. And the forms and substance of the physical structures which have housed classic approaches to retailing may have to be shifted with equal vigor.

The very definition of shopping center may well change in the future as saliency becomes essential; a very clear-cut, if by necessity narrow, penetration of consumer consciousness will become an increasing necessity. Thus one can easily envision, as Martin Cleary does, the rise of *specialty centers*. In a sense the beginnings of development of retailing as part of the theme park on the one hand, or the center dedicated to one strata of society on the other, represent some prototypes.

The difficulties of appraising these from a credit point of view are particularly illustrative of one of the reasons that shopping center development has been so very rapid—and why its future may well prove to be so hazardous. Once the shopping center structure became recognized and accepted, financing quickly became available. The latter, however, was largely predicated upon the major department store or major lessee of the center being 1) credit-worthy and 2) having a track record which showed successful market research. Thus lenders really depended upon the market savvy of the lessees. Some of the specialty centers of the future may not, by their very definition, incorporate such credit-worthy stalwarts. The impact upon lending mechanisms and the relative casualness with which credit has been available to conventional centers may require substantial revision.

Specialty centers by their very definition are one of a kind. They will require much more in the way of individual analysis and financial "set-up costs" than the relatively tested and consistent format of the conventional center. The transferability of technique and approach in specialty centers is much more limited than is sometimes understood. A Ghiardelli Square or Faneuil Hall's success may be a tribute to unique settings, or, for that matter, a reward, on a national level, for an original idea. Continuous emulation, however, may prove disastrous. The "Ghiardelli Squaring of America," midwifed by federal funding in scores of downtown settings, may yield highly costly platitudes, not economic revitalization.

Retail distribution in the United States is accomplished with greater efficiency than anywhere else in the world, a tribute to the adaptability and rationalization of systems which have historically characterized the field. The pressures of the future, however, may require even greater exertion if they are to be adequately met. The classic regional shopping center, given insightful, imaginative development, may evolve into a true community center, serving as a basic node for a variety of intensive developments, enhancing lifestyles and providing a true systems efficiency. The purely "retail" center may prove to be a relatively transient phenomenon.

The extrapolation of short-run history, as suggested earlier, often is a meaningless exercise, but a longer perspective can provide insight to a number of dangers, both from an areal perspective as well as in terms of institutional format. The days of the great jobber/wholesalers dominating the distributional patterns of the United States are nearly a century old and have left little remnant behind them. Less far back, morever, are the great department store edifices of yesteryear—the old downtown Wanamaker's of New York and the Siegel-Cooper establishment, once billed as the country's largest department store. They are now remarked only by students of the history of urban architecture.

Adaptation to change has been the rule, not the exception, and certainly America's retailers have shown a greater capacity in this direction than perhaps holds true in some of our classic areas of industrial activity. The increasing pressures driving toward multifaceted optimization, not merely the satisfying of consumer demand in the classic frameworks, but also within a broad range of societal imperatives as characterized by the new limitations that loom for development patterns, require developers, planners and merchants of real vision. We cannot go back in time, but given the capacity for creative evolution shown by the field in the past—and its continuance in the future—the generation of the better life for Americans, the justification of free enterprise marketing, is still deliverable.

SECTION I

Trends and Realities

Preface

Forecasting the future sites and configurations of American general merchandise retailing is of enormous importance. A new major retail shopping center can easily cost in excess of $100 million. Its impact upon lifestyles, economics and expenditures within its market region sets in motion a broad ripple impact, submerging older focal points on the one hand and creating new, desirable additional areas on the other.

The pipeline of development is a very lengthy one; not uncommonly six or eight years may elapse between an initial proposal and its coming into fruition. The viability of any new major capital investment in facilities to provide the broad cornucopia of services which we inadequately capsulize under the title "Shopping Center" requires a payback period that can outlast a generation. Thus, forecasting the future is far from a luxury; it is rather a necessity of the field.

The inputs, however, are enormously complex, involving as they do not merely retail distribution but rather a vast web of sociological and economic factors. The contrast with major industrial installation provides insight into this element. The latter generally are predicated on a much faster return of investment. For example, in some areas of the chemical industry new facilities must meet the test of a three-year period. While certainly the requirements of environmental safety and economic reality are equally substantial in these latter cases, the areas of uncertainty, and most particularly the time frame within which they must be positively resolve, is far more limited.

The penalties for being wrong in terms of both location and the kind of amenity that is provided are enormous. The decline of a number of the major national supermarket chains gives insight into these factors. The "losers" are those who stayed with a pattern of development in terms of scale of store (6,000 to 12,000 square feet) that was too small to meet the

new competition, those who remained in obsolete locations (many in the
central city and/or older suburbs) for too long, and those who did not
structure their growth parallel to the major regional surges which have
overtaken America. The very homogenization which has overtaken the
shopping center industry, despite follow-up efforts at distinguishing individual centers, makes their locational attributes bulk ever larger in their
future success.

Awareness of potential weaknesses and, indeed, the vulnerability of
the field, has led to perhaps more scientific analysis of location in this industry than holds true in many others. Much of this however, is proprietary—the available literature is all too limited. Further complicating
the old rules of the game lurk some of the new realities of energy constraints, of limitations on income, and the slowing of population growth
which increasingly dominates the American scene. Perhaps as a result of
these factors—but certainly of enormous potency in and of itself—is the
new element of the Community Conservation Guidelines (Community
Conservation Guidance). The federal government and, increasingly,
local governments as well, are going to bulk far more significantly in
terms of future locational decisionmaking than has heretofore been the
case.

In this first section of this volume the basic trends and realities of the
shopping center industry are reviewed. In addition, the importance of the
federal guidelines is of such great potential and possibly may have such an
enormous impact upon the field as to require separate cognizance.

The final paper included in this section—"Community Conservation
Guidance"—contains the official policy guidelines emanating from the
White House. It is this document that provides a reference base for many
of the statements in this volume.

*In the first essay of this section Professor Brian J. L. Berry, of Har-
vard University, describes the foundation of the evolution within which
the future of retailing and shopping centers will occur:*

1. Since World War II, there has been a breakdown of the nation's
traditionally core-oriented settlement patterns on two scales:

   a) Intraregionally, the center city is withering *vis a vis* the suburbs
   and the rural periphery.
   b) Interregionally, the heartland-hinterland organization of the
   economy as a whole is now giving way to a preeminence of the Sunbelt.

2. This shift is a result of the changing location of industry and of

jobs. In turn, job shifts have been accompanied by population shifts. As a result, nonmetropolitan areas are now growing more rapidly than metropolitan areas and central cities are declining, especially within the largest metropolitan regions.

3. Retail and service shifts have characteristically followed those of people and incomes; such is the nature of market-oriented economic activity. Where markets are growing—in the Sunbelt, in smaller towns and cities, in new suburbs and in nonmetropolitan areas—the trade and service sector is expanding. Where markets are static or declining—in the Frostbelt and in larger central cities and older suburbs—the trade and service sectors move in parallel.

4. As a result, in many markets major new enclosed shopping malls have replaced traditional central business districts as the retail foci of rapidly dispersing metropolitan regions.

5. What has emerged is a new scale of low-slung, far-flung metropolitan regions and a new force of counter-urbanization: the transfer of the locus of new growth to some of the most remote and least urbanized parts of the country. Today's urban systems appear to be multinodal, multiconnected social systems sharing in national growth and offering a wide variety of environments.

6. What have become important today are relative qualities of amenities and externalities within the whole rather than relative access to a historical center. Already there has been a retail response beyond the enclosed superregional mall; theme centers are multiplying in special locations; older structures are being rehabilitated for use as specialty centers: and, where conditions are right, some CBDs are being privately regenerated. And, contrary to common expectation, energy fears have not slowed traditional shopping center development.

7. To be sure, many markets are saturated today, and developers are looking for such things as by-passed in-fill opportunities. There is an increasing emphasis on mixed use—including recreation, community and cultural services, art, music, and food—catering to evening and weekend activities in appealing enclosed environments.

8. An important principle of retail and service development is thus illustrated. The old hierarchies of retail centers were a product of access-constrained market orientation of facilities of different scale. As access

variables have declined in relative significance, the advantages of specializing to meet the particular needs of particular local markets, or of particular metropoliswide market segments, has increased. As the metropolis has spread and differentiated, so has the retail and service opportunity.

9. Yet the thrust of the White House urban conservation statement is that the most market-dependent sector of the economy should become the instrument of neighborhood and inner-city revival. If only new shopping center developments can be contained, the argument apparently assumes, central business districts will once again assume their proper role as the hearts of high-density cities, the centers of innovation and control, and the middle class will once again want to live in the city.

10. The mismatch between federal concept and retail reality is likened to one of the policymaker, blissfully unaware that things have changed, looking for barn doors to close to prevent the horses from escaping some time after the barn has been demolished to make room for a new subdivision.

In the following contribution, Dr. Grady Tucker, Senior Vice President of Larry Smith & Company, Ltd., focuses on the new economics of shopping center location and scale within this broader societal evolution:

1. The fundamental principles on which shopping facilities are located and scaled have not changed, but some of the socioeconomic factors which affect development are changing significantly.

2. The trends of population growth and distribution point to fewer new large-scale, regional-center development opportunities. The search for new locations has become more intense and more competitive.

3. The demographic trends and competition for development opportunity will increase the activity in smaller center development in small and middle-size markets.

4. The absolute market potential limitations of small markets will tend to create higher-risk situations for small store tenants and put pressure on the developers' profit.

5. The increasing costs of developing and operating retail facilities will tend to reduce store size and require higher productivity. Competi-

tion among centers has tended to increase design standards so as to enhance the retailing ambiance in order to extend the shopper's visit.

6. Development will be considered in more inner-city sites where public funds will provide for infrastructure. If market support is not available and adequate, retail facilities will not be successful.

7. More multi-use projects will be developed to spread costs and utilize more expensive sites.

8. Controls and regulations are going to become more complex and stringent. They have already lengthened the development period from two to three years to up to five to seven years.

9. The shopping center development industry has experienced the combined effects of developing a new product, a catch-up effect, and a growing national economy. It is now moving into a phase of replacement and maintenance of supply and a national economy with a reduced growth rate. National economic policy and direction is going to have a most important impact on the future of the industry.

10. Public policy which is not aligned with the economic fundamentals of shopping facility development will result in ineffective use of public funds, and an erosion of the private sector effectiveness.

Moving from this base, Jack Gould, President of the HSG/Gould Associates, examines the emerging markets of the 1980s for alternative shopping center developments:

1. The examination of emerging markets in the 1980s will focus principally on those shopping environments that make a major statement in their marketplace—ranging from theme centers to massive-scale regional facilities.

2. In contrast to the past thirty years, it is difficult to foresee the emergence of a single dominant geographic locus for shopping center developments. The 1980s will witness a more or less balanced mix of areas upon which the industry will focus its efforts.

3. A recent trend has been the attention centered on small and medium markets—the mid-market focus. Actually, these markets have

been around for a long time. They have simply been ignored as a major thrust for development opportunity.

4. The difference, however, is that the psychological fog that has obscured sparsely populated territories as well as inner-city areas is lifting. We are basically looking at the same landscape that has been with us for a long period of time.

5. The vogue of the mid-market focus probably resulted from the maturation of many small areas in the rapidly growing Sunbelt to the point where their population levels justify the development of an appropriately scaled center. However, for every new market of this type in the Sunbelt, there have been three or four long-standing markets of similar size in the Frostbelt.

6. In addition, there is an abundance of opportunity even in large markets with little or no population growth—the Northeast and North Central states.

7. An important guide to the future is the evolutionary pattern of retailing development over the past thirty years.

a) Historically, until the beginning of the 1950s, the nation's retail structure had a very distinctive downtown orientation.
b) The 1950s then spawned the initial development of the regional shopping center in concept and application.
c) The 1960s witnessed the increasing sophistication of the regional shopping center as an urban form very successfully repackaged.
d) The 1970s will be remembered as a period of transition which started with the super-regional center, saw the emphasis shift to smaller markets in the middle part of the period, and finally witnessed the reemergence of downtown and selective in-town areas for development at the end of the period.

It is highly probable that the diversity of the 1970s is a preview of the many directions that new retail development will follow in the 1980s.

8. Joining forces with the preceding elements will be a very substantial number of older facilities which will assume new forms and greater competitive dimensions. Thus the 1980s will see the recycling of first-and second-generation regional shopping centers in order to maintain their market position.

9. Retail developments, then, will not be restricted in terms of form, size, or market; the 1980s will be a period of diversity. Opportunities will abound in:

a) new market areas as well as aging market areas,
b) very large market areas as well as smaller ones,
c) the Frostbelt as well as the Sunbelt,
d) downtown and in-city areas, suburban areas and nonmetropolitan areas, and
e) suburban superregional facilities, in-city regional centers, the expansion of older centers, theme centers of all types and downtown redevelopment packages.

10. In addition, a final market option awaits in what can be labeled the "twilight zone"—that area that lies between the central business district and the first suburban tier of regional shopping centers in our ten largest metropolitan areas (which contain over 27 percent of the nation's population).

Subsequently, Howard L. Green and David L. Huntoon—President and Vice President, respectively, of Howard L. Green and Associates, Inc.—sketch out the issues that will shape the regional shopping center industry in the 1980s:

1. In locational terms, the coming decade will be a period in which metropolitan areas stabilize rather than spread outward—the area we now have settled will remain relatively fixed and will become more dense.

a) Energy costs will be a major factor in this regard, decreasing the mobility of the American population. As a function of rising costs, people will desire to minimize the cost of travel to work, to shopping, to entertainment, etc.
b) There is no alternative form of transportation available as a substitute for the automobile in our low-density, suburban living pattern.
c) Many of the functions that we used to call central-place functions—shopping, working, meeting, entertaining, or dining—are now an integral part of suburbia.
d) New housing, to satisfy the continuing surge of new households in the 1980s, will be clustered around existing shopping centers and office complexes in order to minimize the costs of travel to the preceding functions. As a result, metropolitan areas will continue to become more

multinucleated, characterized by a number of "downtowns"; the latter in many cases will be centered on regional shopping centers in conjunction with the office and service complexes associated with them.

2. Within this spatial context, new shopping centers are most likely to be clustered with already existing, successful shopping centers while the expansion of existing centers will become an increasingly viable option. There is, and will continue to be, more potential in our largest metropolitan areas for this kind of clustering than for the searching out of new trade areas to fill unmet needs, such as we had in the 1970s.

3. The original downtown (CBD) retail function will continue in the 1980s to serve four groups: a large population of daytime workers, those who chose to live near the central-city downtown, those who have access to some form of mass transportation, and, in selected cities, tourists and conventioneers. Innovations in downtown shopping centers will ensue, but will represent only one segment of regional mall activity.

4. A number of growing and changing markets will need to be served in the 1980s:

a) The basic overall market will be defined by basic shifts in expenditures, which will influence tenant mix in regional shopping centers.
b) The maturing baby-boom generation will bulk larger as the prime market for retailers in the 1980s.
c) Also significant will be the emerging critical mass of the fifty-five-to eighty-years of age population.
d) A fourth growth segment has been, and will continue to be, the single-person-household phenomenon.

These markets imply shifting tenant mixes in regional shopping centers as adaptions are made to the new market contours.

5. Retailers will be on short-term leases and will remain within centers only if they meet the consumers' expectations; they will be eliminated or precluded from new centers if they fail to keep pace with the changing desires and wants of the marketplace.

Albert Sussman, Executive Vice President of the International Council of Shopping Centers, takes direct issue with federal involvement and/or interference with the preceding market tendencies:

1. The new federal guidelines, at the very best, may only harass, delay, and create problems (particularly, cost) for real estate and retail developers. At worst, they can seriously damage continued suburban development, particularly shopping center development.

2. The guidelines appear to be predicated on the notion that one of the best ways to help cities is to cut off all, or virtually all, support to the suburbs, thereby forcing people downtown. This view overlooks reality. Urban areas will not be aided by trying to stop suburban development.

3. The members of the International Council of Shopping Centers (I.C.S.C.) are fearful of the level of governmental interference these guidelines represent; they are distrustful of government and distrustful of bureaucrats.

4. Yet the downtowns that deserve to be saved, and need to be saved, have many alternative remedies. An affirmative, positive federal pro-urban development policy would be much more preferable than an anti-suburban shopping center one.

5. In order for cities and downtowns to be successful, they have to understand that in the partnership that must exist between the private and public sectors, the municipality has its responsibilities and its obligation to provide all the incentives that will bring a developer downtown—incentives that will make building inside the city as attractive as it now is in the suburbs.

6. The I.C.S.C. wants to move forward on a positive program to aid downtowns. It does not think the present federal policy will help the program in any substantial way.

Defending the federal policy is Marshall Kaplan, Deputy Assistant Secretary for Urban Policy of the U. S. Department of Housing and Urban Development:

1. Despite complex socioeconomic changes influencing the evolving functions of central business districts and urban areas, knowledge relative to the probable impact of pending federal actions is crucial prior to initiating such actions. Securing such knowledge is the primary thrust of the Community Conservation Guidelines.

2. Contrary to the criticism from some in the industry, the guidelines

will not vastly expand the power of the federal government to restrict the construction of planned large scale developments outside central cities.

3. In the past, the federal government has been correctly criticized for initiating inconsistent actions and/or actions which inadvertently exacerbate urban problems. The guidelines direct federal agencies to prepare brief analyses of the urban impact of their respective actions, if such actions are likely to lead to a commercial development, and if requested to do so by an elected official.

4. Federal, and indeed private, actions are rarely neutral. Clearly, Congress and the American people have a right to expect this or any administration to evaluate the impact of federal actions before they occur and to develop mitigating options if the anticipated results run contrary to public policy and/or the public interest.

5. There is a visible tie between the vitality of a community's central business district and the health and vitality of the community at large—the link between people and place. The guidelines draw attention to the problems of people, and places within broad urban areas prior to initiating federal action likely to impact them.

6. Underlying the guidelines are the following rationales:

a) Large commercial developments on the urban fringe have drained economic vitality from existing central business districts in distressed small, medium and large communities.
b) HUD studies have shown that shopping centers in many communities lead rather than follow population. In addition, mall development in a diminished aggregate market may negatively affect some communities. At a metropolitan level, regional mall sales growth in these areas typically results in reduced sales somewhere else.
c) There is also a significant relationship between inner-city workers and large-scale planned developments. Job markets, particularly for low-income unskilled and minority workers, are relatively narrow and bounded by distance from place of residence. Thus shifting retail (and other types of) employment has a deleterious effect on urban area residents.

Conceptual Lags in
Retail Development Policy
or
Can the Carter White House
Save the CBD?

BRIAN J. L. BERRY

I can best liken the mismatch between federal concept and retail reality to one of the policymaker, blissfully unaware that things have changed, looking for barn doors to close to prevent the horses from escaping some time after the barn has been demolished to make room for a new subdivision. As Figures 1 and 2 show, central business districts had already been declining as the primary retail foci of metropolitan America for more than twenty years when, in 1970, the Congress declared that the urban problem still was one of rapid urbanization and rural decline:

> The rapid growth of urban population and uneven expansion of urban development in the United States, together with a decline in farm population, slower growth in rural areas, and migration to the cities, has created an imbalance between the Nation's needs and resources and seriously threatens our physical environment . . . The Congress . . . declares that the national urban growth policy should—favor patterns of urbanization and economic development and stabilization which offers a range of alternative locations . . . help reverse trends of migration and physical growth . . . treat comprehensively the pro-

blems of poverty and employment . . . associated with disorderly urbanization and rural decline.[1]

Indeed, it has taken another decade for an awareness that the nature of urban growth has changed to be finally admitted. As the White House's 1978 urban policy statement says:

> Three major patterns of population change can be traced in the Nation today: migration from the northeastern and north central regions of the country to the south and west: the slower growth of metropolitan areas and the movement from them to small towns and rural areas; and movement from central cities to suburbs . . . Today's widespread population loss in the Nation's central cities is unprecedented . . . the thinning out process has left many people and places with severe economic and social problems, and without the resources to deal with them . . . Our policies must reflect a balanced concern for people and places . . . to achieve several broad goals: (to) preserve the heritage and values of our older cities; maintain the investment in our older cities and their neighborhoods; assist newer cities in confronting the challenges of growth and pockets of poverty . . . and provide improved housing, job opportunities and community services to the urban poor, minorities, and women . . . If the Administration is to help cities revitalize neighborhoods, eliminate sprawl, support the return of the middle class to central cities, and improve the housing conditions of the urban poor it must increase the production of new housing and rehabilitation of existing housing for middle class groups in cities . . . We should favor proposals supporting: (1) compact community development over scattered, fragmented development; and (2) revitalization over new development.[2]

And just as in 1970 there was a reactive response to try to reverse rural-to-urban migration and rapid urban growth, so today there is a reaction to outmigration and urban decline. We find the following in the White House's proposed Urban Conservation Policy:

> The primary objective . . . is to encourage through appropriate Federal, State and local action, the redevelopment and or development by the private sector of healthy central business districts in distressed communities (and to) reduc(e) insofar as possible the liklihood (sic) that major Federal actions will directly and strategically lead to the construction of large commercial developments that clearly weaken established central business districts in distressed communities or promote unnecessary urban sprawl.[3]

Growth, it appears, is to be inhibited when urban impact analyses show that older central business districts are unable to withstand the competitive impact of proposed new regional shopping centers.

Yet we must be prepared to admit that the current White House urban conservation policy is as perceptually laggard and, indeed, as conceptually bankrupt, as were the declarations of the 1970 Housing Act. If this

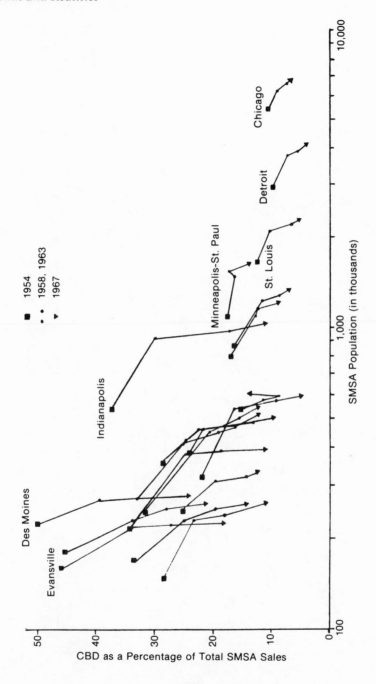

Figure 1.   *Decline of the CBD as a Retail and Service Nucleus of Midwestern SMSA between 1954 and 1967.*

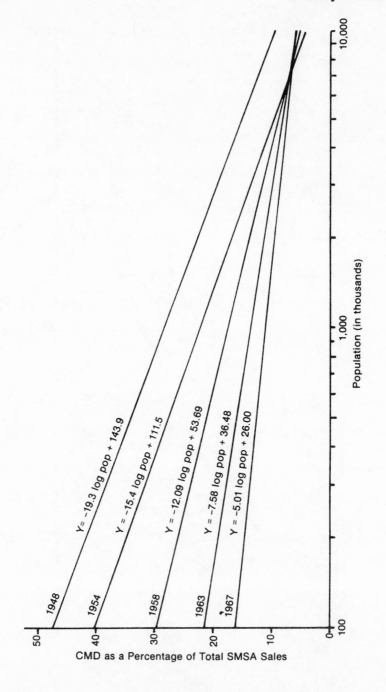

Figure 2.   Regression relationships reveal the Nationwide Trend of
                 CBD Decline.

is the case, and I believe it to be so, implementation of the policy will once again be the wrong thing in the wrong place at the wrong time. In what follows I therefore propose to do three things: (a) to review the changes in the nation's settlement patterns that are unfolding today; (b) from this, to propose an alternative concept of spatial organization to the CBD - focused model that apparently remains central to the White House policymakers' mindset; and (c) to suggest the emerging patterns of commercial organization that are consistent with this alternative concept. We can then return to the key question of the proposed urban conservation policy: will the attempt to undergird central business districts in distressed communities work?

Changing Settlement
Patterns: The Evidence

Since World War II there has been a breakdown of the nation's traditionally core-oriented settlement patterns on two scales. Interregionally, the heartland-hinterland organization of the economy as a whole is now giving way to a preeminence of the Sunbelt. Intraregionally, the center city is withering *vis a vis* the suburbs and the rural periphery.

This is, first of all, a result of the changing location of industry and of jobs. For the first half of the twentieth century, the northeastern manufacturing belt accounted for some 70 percent of the nation's industrial employment. Between 1950 and the mid-1960s, manufacturing jobs continued to grow in the Northeast, but the growth was more rapid in other regions of the country and the manufacturing belt's relative share fell to 56 percent. By 1970, relative decline had been replaced by absolute losses. From 1969 to 1977, the manufacturing belt lost 1.7 million industrial jobs, almost exactly the job growth of the former hinterlands. Similar shifts have taken place intraregionally. Between 1947 and 1958, to cite a few examples, central cities of the New York region lost 6 percent of their manufacturing jobs, whereas the suburbs gained 37.2 percent. In other heartland cities comparable figures were: Chicago, city-18.5 and suburbs 49.4 percent; Philadelphia, -10.4 and 16.4; St. Louis -21.1 and 41.7. Continuing from 1958 to 1967, the figures are: New York, -10.3 and 36.0; Chicago, -4.0 and 51.6; Philadelphia, -11.6 and 30.0; and St. Louis, -14.9 and 41.4.

Traditionally, the major central cities of the manufacturing belt were the centers of innovation. They were able to introduce new industries to offset losses of standardized industries to cheap-labor areas elsewhere. But this is no longer the case. The economy's rapid growth industries (electronics, aerospace, scientific instruments, etc.,) are dispersed throughout the former interregional and intraregional peripheries; it is the older slow-growth industries that remain in the former cores. Employment in these remaining industries is extremely sensitive to cylical change in the economy, which compounds the distress of northeastern central cities when the economy is in recession. But what is even more critical is that the central cities of the former manufacturing belt appear to have lost their traditional seedbed function. The locus of innovation and growth has shifted elsewhere.

Job shifts have been accompanied by population shifts. Following the bulge in the population pyramid formed by the post-World War II baby boom, there has been a decline in fertility rates to less than replacement levels. As natural increase has diminished, migration has become an increasingly important source of population change. This growing importance of migration as a factor of growth has been intensified by the movement of the baby-boom cohort into its most mobile years. In all urban-industrial countries, a certain minimum amount of geographical mobility is a structured part of the lifecycle, with the greatest rates associated with the stage at which young adults leave the parental home and establish an independent household shortly after formal schooling is completed. The baby-boom cohort is now passing through this stage, and the subsequent period in which spatial differences in real wage rates and in employment opportunities provide signals that encourage economically motivated migration. This migration not only increases the well-being of the movers themselves, but also results in improved resource allocation. Thus, the job shifts in a period of maximum potential mobility have resulted in increased net migration from manufacturing belt to periphery, for both majority and minority members of the U. S. population. The South has experienced a dramatic and accelerating migration reversal. Within regions the balance of migration flows is away from central cities to suburbs and exurbs, and from metropolitan to nonmetropolitan areas. Throughout the nation, migrating workers have left jobs located in major metropolitan cores for workplaces in smaller urban areas, suburbs, and nonmetropolitan America. Since 1970, the Northeast as a whole has lost population, a result of decreasing natural increase and of the net migration reversal; in the South, continued high levels of growth have occurred despite declining natural increase because of increasing in-migration.

As a result, nonmetropolitan areas are now growing more rapidly than metropolitan areas and central cities are declining, especially within the largest metropolitan regions. Thirty of the nation's fifty largest cities have lost population since 1970; one in five registered a loss of at least 10 percent between 1970 and 1975. Because the incomes of outmigrants were greater than those of immigrants, the income loss of metropolitan areas (gain of nonmetropolitan areas) was over $17 billion between 1975 and 1977 alone.

Retail and service shifts have characteristically *followed from* those of people and incomes; such is the nature of market-oriented economic activity. Indeed, the high mobility rates characteristic of the retail and service sectors of the economy make these sectors extremely sensitive barometers of changing market conditions and of shifts in business organization and practices. Where markets are growing—as in the Sunbelt, in smaller towns and cities, in new suburbs and in nonmetropolitan areas—births of new businesses and expansions of existing ones exceed deaths and business contractions, and the trade and service sector is expanding. Where markets are declining—as in the Snowbelt, and in larger central cities and older suburbs—deaths and contractions exceed births and expansions, and the trade and service sectors are declining.

It is in growing markets, in particular, that increasing concentration of business in larger establishments has been occurring. Chain stores and nationally advertised franchise businesses have been better able to respond to the changing market opportunities by combining with real estate developers to use new planned business centers as instruments for structuring new residential growth. To them accrue the advantages of better corporate planning, national advertising, easier financing, and ability to withstand temporary market perturbations. In many markets major new enclosed shopping malls, housing mainly chains and franchisees, have indeed replaced traditional central business districts as the retail foci of rapidly dispersing metropolitan regions, and have been used to set the tone for surrounding residential areas. Meanwhile, traditional shopping streets and classical unplanned business centers continue to wither away in older urban neighborhoods as populations dwindle and the relative incomes of those left behind decline. Yet the thrust of the White House urban conservation statement is that the most market-dependent sector of the economy should become the instrument of neighborhood and inner-city revival. If only new shopping center developments can be contained, the argument apparently continues, central business districts will once again assume their proper role as the hearts of high-density cities, the centers of innovation and control, and the middle class will once again want to live in the city.

New Forms of Spatial Organization

This is, surely, to get the cart before the horse. The job shifts have joined with a successful national housing policy oriented toward promoting household wealth through home ownership, improved living conditions via new construction, and increased efficiency by means of mobility, to facilitate the emergence of a new scale of low slung, far-flung metropolitan regions and to a new force of counter-urbanization—the transfer of the locus of new growth to some of the most remote and least urbanized parts of the country. The settings where this growth is now occurring are exceedingly diverse. They include regions oriented to recreation in northern New England, the Rocky Mountains, and the upper Great Lakes; energy supply areas in the northern Great Plains and southern Appalachian coal fields; retirement communities in the Ozark-Ouachita Uplands; small manufacturing towns throughout much of the South; and nonmetropolitan cities in every region whose economic fortunes are intertwined with state government or higher education. Other factors contributing to these shifts appear to be changes in transportation and communications that have removed many of the problems of access that previously served to constrain the growth prospects of the periphery, permitting decentralization of manufacturing on the inexpensive land and benefiting from the low wage rates of nonmetropolitan areas, the trend toward earlier retirement which has lengthened the interval during later life when a person is no longer tied to a specific place by a job, and an increased orientation at all ages toward leisure activities, caused in part by rising per capita income and centered on amenity-rich areas outside the daily range of metropolitan commuting.

These are but symptoms of the more profound forces that are at work, however. The concentrated industrial metropolis only developed because proximity meant lower transportation and communication costs for those interdependent specialists who had to interact with each other frequently or intensively. One of the most important forces contributing to counter-urbanization thus is the erosion of centrality by time-space convergence. Virtually all technological developments of industrial times have had the effect of reducing the constraints of geographical space. Developments in transportation and communications have made it possible for each generation to live farther from activity centers, for these activity centers to disperse, and for information users to rely upon information sources that are spatially more distant yet temporarily more immediate.

In other words, large, dense urban concentrations are no longer necessary for the classical urbanization economies to be present. Contemporary developments in communications are supplying better channels for transmitting information and improving the capacities of partners in social intercourse to transact their business at great distances at great speed. The time-eliminating properties of long-distance communication

and the space-spanning capacities of the new communication techno-
logies are combining to concoct a solvent that has dissolved the ag-
glomeration advantages of the industrial metropolis, creating what some
now refer to as an urban civilization without cities. The edge of many of
the nation's metropolitan systems have now pushed 100 miles and more
from declining central cities. Today's urban systems appear to be
multinodal, multiconnected social systems sharing in national growth and
offering a variety of lifestyles in a variety of environments. And what are
being abandoned are those environments that were key in the traditional
metropolis-driven growth process: the high-density, congested, face-to-
face, center-city settings that are now perceived as aging, polluted and
crime ridden, with declining services and employment bases, and
escalating taxes.

In contemporary theories of land use, three sets of variables are joined
to explain the bid-rents of potential occupants that ultimately set the
pattern of land values and create the land use map. The first of these is accessibility, traditionally measured in the mindset of the early industrial
metropolis as distance from the CBD. It is one of the distressing features
of contemporary urban economics that the models taught to new students
seldom stray from this particular case.

The second set of variables relates to qualities of the site itself. The
case is clearest in Ricardian theories of land use, but also is relevant in urban land use, as observers from Hurd to Hoyt have emphasized, although
not independently of the third set, externalities. To the extent that traditional centrality has been eroded by time-space convergence, variables in
these other two sets—environment and amenity—have increased in importance in determining the structure of the emerging metropolis. What
is important today are relative qualities of amenities and externalities
within the whole rather than relative access to a historical center. Hence
the multinodal, multiconnected quality of contemporary urban systems.

The Retail Response

Already there has been a retail response, far ahead of White House
thinking. Theme centers are multiplying in special locations; older structures are being rehabilitated for use as specialty retail centers, as in Utica
where the former UNIVAC building (now Charlestown) has been
transformed into a mall housing factory outlet shops; and, where conditions are right, some CBDs are being privately regenerated. And, contrary to common expectation, energy fears have not slowed shopping
center development. *Shopping Center Digest* reported earlier this year
that sixty-three new malls with over 400,000 square feet of gross leasable

area will have opened during 1979, seventy-seven more are scheduled for opening in 1980, and 100 are already committed for 1981 and beyond.

To be sure, many markets are saturated today, and developers are looking for such things as by-passed in-fill opportunities. Much of the current exploration relates to possibilities for reconstructing deteriorating suburban CBDs or older downtown areas with viable surrounding trade areas. There is an increasing emphasis on mixed use, including recreation, community and cultural services, art, music, and food, catering to evening and weekend activities in appealing enclosed environments.

Some industry spokesmen suggest that at least 10 percent of new mall activity will be in older central business districts in the next few years, and in this it is clear that the industry is way ahead of the White House. Unfortunately, however, the Carter conservation policy's focus on communities in distress precludes the cases where private market activity will be significant, thus perpetuating Gresham's Law of Urban Policy, with which we are all too familiar. But meanwhile, in certain metropolitan areas—those where too great an excess supply of new housing has not been created, and where a modern office sector has created new jobs for young professional members of the post-World War II baby-boom generation—private market reinvestment has been taking place in certain older neighborhoods and has supported specialized retail and service growth.

The essence has again been on the demand side. What are determining are the housing preferences of new higher-income young homeowners not pressed by child rearing, with two workers, one or both of whom may be a professional, seeking neighborhoods in the inner city with geographic clusters of housing structures capable of yielding high quality services, a variety of public-good amenities within safe walking distance of these areas, such as a scenic waterfront, parks, museums, or art galleries, universities, distinguished architecture, and historic landmarks or neighborhoods, and range of high quality retail facilities and services, including restaurants, theaters, and entertainment.

These preferences follow directly from lifestyle and compositional shifts. First, continued development of American society has resulted in increased economic parity for women; this enables them to have the option of roles other than those of housewife and mother. In consequence, men and women lead more independent lives and are able to exercise more options in life-course transitions. Increasing numbers of couples live together without the formal ties of marriage. The direct and opportunity cost of childrearing is rising, birth control technology has improved, and abortion laws have been liberalized; hence, the birth rate is dropping.

There are increasing numbers of families with two or more workers and more working wives than ever before.

Revitalization, then, has been taking hold first in superior neighborhoods in those metropolitan areas which have the tightest housing supply and which also have a sizeable cluster of professional jobs that support the youthful, college-educated labor force most likely to evidence lifestyle shifts. Because smaller households require less space, because the fluidity of households and the looser legal links among their members is contrary to the rigidity of tenure associated with ownership, because the maintenance of such a house and its grounds is time consuming and because, with most people working, time for domestic work becomes scarce and costly, there is a preference for apartments, or row or town houses and innovative forms of design, as well as experimentation with such forms of tenure as condominiums and cooperatives, which preserve some of the tax advantages of ownership but provide greater liquidity, and increases in new forms of contracting arrangements for the operation and maintenance of housing. Increasing attractiveness of more central locations in the core city and the older suburbs follows, for it is there that there is an appropriate stock of housing and access to services as well as locational convenience for the journey to work. Since many of these households have no children, the racial factor of school integration does not act as it did in the white flight to the suburbs. And, out of the new lifestyle being created in old neighborhoods, a new environment of opportunity for retail growth has occurred and is being realized.

An important principle of retail and service development is thereby illustrated. The older hierarchies of retail centers were a product of access-constrained market orientation of facilities of different scales. As access variables have decline in relative significance, the advantages of specializing to meet the particular needs of particular local markets, or of particular metropoliswide market segments, have increased. As the metropolis has spread and differentiated, so has the retail and service opportunity. And, as for the years to come, as long as a high degree of mobility is maintained, there will be a continuing responsiveness to the changing nexus of opportunities, and indeed, of constraints. If there is a principle at work, it is that of opportunity seeking and constraint avoidance, which leads directly to the conclusion that the negatively formulated Carter conservation plan can only result in everyone becoming worse off. A creative policy shifts incentives, creating attractive market opportunities that, if realized, also achieve the sought-after goals. Such has been the example of the nation's housing policy for the last fifty years. Negatively formulated systems of regulation, on the other hand, lead only to avoidance, and avoidance by private developers of distressed communities can ony deepen the malaise that afflicts the CBDs that the White House conservation policy is supposed to alleviate.

Notes

1. Quoted from Section 702 of Title VII of the Housing and Urban Development Act of 1970 (Public Law 91-609, 84 Stat. 1791; 42 U.S.C. 4501)

2. Quoted from President Carter's Urban and Regional Policy Group's March 1978 report *A New Partnership to Conserve America's Communities. A National Urban Policy.*

3. Quoted from a White House staff paper entitled "An Urban Conservation Policy" circulated in the fall of 1979.

The New Economics
of Shopping Center
Location and Scale

GRADY TUCKER

The fundamental principles of shopping center development presented here can be viewed as a background for evaluating the Community Conservation Guidance policy as well as the expectations of the 1980s. They are not new principles. They have been in development and refinement for more than twenty years since the planned, integrated shopping center concept, based on the automobile, began. These principles embody private enterprise utilizing an infrastructure provided to meet the needs of the public. They present the perspective of the decision-making processes of shopping center development.

The ideal shopping center location optimizes access to maximum market potential for the tenant merchants, or, conversely, access to merchandise for the shopping public. This fundamental underlies the inception of the shopping center concept.

A center is scaled to provide optimum profitable marketing impact, or customer attraction. The stores must be large enough to cover a significant sector of the merchandise spectrum and numerous enough to provide the choice which is an essential element in comparison shopping. The sales productivity of the stores must be high enough to provide profitable operation for the merchant and allow for enough rent within normal merchandising expense structure to cover the cost of producing the facility.

These principles have also continued to operate throughout the evolution of the shopping center.

The rationale, or the calculus, of shopping center development involving these fundamental principles of location and scale has not changed. The values of some of the parameters in the formula are changing.

A shopping center is a highly localized phenomenon. Even a regional center with a trade area radius of twenty five to fifty miles is an expression of an infinitesimal areal segment of the national market. This localization is an expression of the convenience of the shopping center to its supporting population and implies that the center is intricately woven into the fabric of the community. This relationship subjects the center to local and national economic changes.

The historic pattern of shopping center development is the product of the availability of a highly flexible personal transportation system utilizing relatively cheap energy and the desire of the public to live in low-density residential areas of single-family detached houses. Changes in these socioeconomic factors are now impinging on the fundamentals of shopping center development to an observable extent.

Market Potential

This existence of adequate market potential is a necessary condition for the successful development and operation of a shopping center. It is a function of the number of people in a trade area that can logically be served by the facilities and the average annual per capita expenditure by that population for the types of merchandise which are presented in the center.

Change in the number of people arises primarily from two types of sources: natural increase, which is the excess of births over deaths and the ultimate source of population, and migration, which is the shift of the population in response to several stimuli.

Natural increase is a sociologically complex phenomenon which is the result of the forces and factors which influence birth rates and death rates. Death rates have primarily reacted to advancing medical technology and improved health conditions, and show a relative non-volatile trend of slow decline.

Birth rates have been on a long-term decline almost for the last generation. During the 1950s and into the early 1960s, the rate of natural increase for the national population was on the order of 12 to 15 per thousand population. In 1978 it is slightly above 6; it has been in single digit figures since 1966. During the 1950s the net change in national population annually was about 3 million persons. Since 1972 it has been about half that number. It is significant that the national population is still growing on the order of about 1.5 million persons per year. At the threshold level of support for a regional shopping center, the annual increase is the equivalent of support for fifteen small regional centers a year. The long-term trend in this factor, however, indicates a limit for the increasing demand for shopping center facilities and a change in the rates of development from those reflected in the catch-up years of the 1960s.

Migration, the second population change factor, and the one which has been most important in generating new shopping center markets, is continuing in its general trends but may be displaying some new variations, and may be most subject to change with the introduction of new economic forces, especially that of increasing costs of energy.

Historically, the most massive interregional migrations began occurring during the era of World War II and continued, particularly into California and Florida, into the 1960s. Simultaneously, there occurred intrametropolitan area migrations from central areas to suburbs, which further intensified the growth of suburban shopping center markets and created the opportunity for new centers.

The intrametropolitan area migration streams have slowed down. These have been influenced by public policy expressed through growth management programs, sewer moratoria, and land use controls. In some instances these factors have created more distant outward spread of suburban development. A part of the newly identified growth in nonmetropolitan areas is in part a statistical aberration resulting from the definition of metropolitan areas. The growth has been pushed into counties beyond the statistical delimitation but is still in an adjacent tier of counties outside the metropolitan areas. This type of population movement or residential development pattern is continuing to develop opportunities for new centers even in metropolitan areas where overall growth has stopped or total population may be declining. Generally, this is operative only in major metropolitan agglomerations.

The reverse migration trend into the inner cities is not of the same order of magnitude and represents a relatively minor change in the location of market potential. In most instances the number of dwelling units available to be rehabilitated and gentrified will not result in major infusions of market potential into inner-city areas for some time to come.

There appears to be a new variant in the migration patterns oriented to middle-and smaller-sized cities. This is creating opportunities for small centers, some in markets of about 100,000 population.

The most publicized migration is into the Sunbelt. In many counties in Florida, over 50 percent of the population growth since 1970 is represented by in-migration. Climatic amenity and economic opportunity, especially centers of energy production, continue to attract migrants. Houston is one of the better recognized and developed examples. Development in these areas can only continue in accord with the market potential generated, and as the major sources of in-migrants are drained of population, this inflow will tend to slow down.

Retirement income obviates the need for economic opportunity in those areas which are attractive to retirees. A significant part of the immigration into southern New Jersey and into Florida falls in this category. The source of these flows is declining and the market created may evidence relatively weak purchasing power.

Per Capita Expenditures

The per capita expenditures of the population served by a shopping center are circumscribed by the total income. On a national basis per capita personal income increased in 1967 dollars at a rate of about $83 per year from 1958 to 1978. In current dollars, in contrast, per capita personal income increased at the rate of $154 per year from 1958 to 1970, and $493 per year from 1970 to 1978. The inflated current-dollar figure tends to have considerable significance from the standpoint of shopping center development because of the percentage rent relationship in modern shopping center leases.

The allocation of income among the categories of personal consumption expenditures since 1960 indicates a relatively steady share of expenditure in the categories of merchandise most prominent in regional shopping centers. The trend has been one of near stability or slight decline. Housing, utilities, medical care, transportation and recreation show trends of absorbing increasing shares of the personal consumption expenditures.

Analyses of a number of metropolitan areas indicate that per capita sales in shopper goods, the merchandise categories most significant in shopping center development, have been increasing at a rate of about 5 percent per year during the 1970s. The expenditure trends and competition appear to have somewhat countered the growth of per capita expenditure, but the continued increase in per capita expenditures has resulted in the growth of potential even in markets with relatively slow population growth, to the extent that the expansion of existing shopping centers can be justified after the competitive development in a market has been stale for ten to fifteen years.

The increasing cost of energy expressed through increasing utility costs and transportation costs is expected to influence the allocation of personal expenditures further and probably erode the per capita expenditure in shopping goods. This will tend to aggravate the slowdown in the growth of market potential in combination with slower population growth.

The localized nature of shopping center trade areas and the continuing migration of population can still create new concentrations of market potential which afford the possibility of center development.

Development Economics

The rent which the merchant tenants of a shopping center can pay within the normal expense structure of their operations is a function of the productivity, measured in annual sales per square foot, of the stores. The availability of adequate rent is one primary element in determining the feasibility of developing a center. The counterclaim of the cost of developing the facilities is, in simplistic terms, the other determinant in feasibility.

The term "rent" may not be synonymous with occupancy cost, since in modern shopping center leases the rent, made up of a guaranteed minimum element and a percent-of-sales element, is combined with costs such as utility costs, common area maintenance charges and taxes which are passed directly through to the tenant.

The rent factor *per se*, which is a percentage of sales after sales productivity passes the break point in the rent formula, maintains a constant relative position with sales. With per capita income increasing at the rate of about 8 to 9 percent per year, particularly during the 1970s, and with expenditures in shopping goods remaining a relatively constant share of expenditure, sales potential increases at about the same rate as income. Without changes in competitive facilities, therefore, absolute rental income would tend to maintain its position relative to per capita personal income. The operating cost element in occupancy cost, however, marches to a different drummer. Energy cost increases, for instance, do, and will continue to, generate increasing pressure on the tenants' occupancy cost.

The cost of providing shopping center facilities varies significantly from project and with location. Cost has generally moved up, with an underlying annual increase in construction costs of about 7 percent to 8 percent per year. This same approximate rate is reflected in the capital costs reported in Urban Land Institute's *Dollars and Cents of Shopping Centers*, 1968, 1974, 1977.

Shopping center site costs have been increased by increasing land costs reflecting inflation as well as the decreasing availability of sites. As the rate of spread of suburban population declines, there are fewer and fewer opportunities to acquire peripheral sites the success of which will be secured by outward growth. Consequently, the search for sites has turned to fill-in locations. Land use controls and growth management plans have aggravated a shortage of sites.

Controls and regulations have lengthened the development period from two to three years up to five to seven years. In addition to delaying development of the project, this time is frequently spent in negotiating the control mechanisms with the use of numbers of experts and specialists designing and redesigning projects, analyzing economic and fiscal impacts and preparing environmental impact analyses.

Competition among centers has also engendered the thrust of increased standards within centers with plans and designs intended to create enhanced ambiance to extend the shopper's visit.

The effect of the increasing cost of facilities and the increasing operating costs has been to encourage more intensive use of space and for most merchants an attempt to utilize smaller stores. In the 1960s, sales productivity of $60 per square foot was a relatively common design standard for department stores. In the 1970s this standard increased to about $100 per square foot. Mall shop sales performance has also increased from about $80 to $100 per square foot to $150 to $175 per square foot for design standards, and performance requirements of $200 per square foot are becoming relatively common.

The development of shopping centers in the late 1950s and 1960s was at a rate faster than the growth of population and market potential. This was a catch-up phase in the production cycle of a new concept for the final link in goods distribution. The convergence of this trend with the gradual slowdown in the growth of population and the potential slowdown in the rate of spread of population has gradually limited the opportunities for center develoment. As a consequence, the search for and competition for new locations has become more intense and more competitive. This situation has been aggravated by land use controls. This has resulted in renewed consideration of sites which are well inside the periphery of urban development (where fringe property surplus over the developing requirements of the shopping center is not available), where parking has to be provided in structures, and in the consideration of expanding older centers which may have a surplus of property.

The search for new development opportunities has also spread to the middle and smaller markets which, in conjunction with the recent trend of population growth in smaller-sized cities, has resulted in new small-market opportunities. The centers built in these markets have to be sized to the market and, consequently, are smaller centers.

A third area of new development consideration is the inner city, including central business districts (CBD). Some of the CBD projects have a history going back to the now inoperative federal urban renewal program which originated with the 1949 Housing Act. New sources of public funds are encouraging this trend. In the inner cities, particularly in large metropolitan conglomerations, air-right sites and other in-fill locations are being developed with the help of public funds.

Conclusions

The fundamental principles on which shopping facilities are located and scaled have not changed, but some of the socioeconomic factors which affect development are changing significantly.

The trends of population growth and distribution point to fewer new regional center development opportunities.

The demographic trends and competition for development opportunity will increase the activity in smaller center development in small markets.

The absolute market potential limitations of small markets will tend to create higher risk situations for small-store tenants and put pressure on the developers' profit.

The increasing costs of developing and operating retail facilities will tend to reduce store size and require higher productivity.

Development will be considered in more inner-city sites where public funds will provide for infrastructure. If market support is not available and adequate, retail facilities will not be successful.

More multi-use projects will be developed to spread cost and utilize more expensive sites.

Controls and regulations are going to become more complex and stringent.

The shopping center development industry has experienced the combined effects of developing a new product, a catch-up effect, and a growing national economy. It is now moving into a phase of replacement and maintenance of supply and a national economy with a reduced growth rate. National economic policy and direction is going to have a most important impact on the future of the industry.

Public policy which is not aligned with the economic fundamentals of shopping facility development will result in ineffective use of public funds and an erosion of the private sector effectiveness.

Emerging Markets in the 1980s

JACK GOULD

The objective of this paper is to examine emerging markets in the 1980s for alternative shopping center developments. First, however, it is necessary to clearly identify those types of shopping centers that will be discussed subsequently. For the purpose of this particular discussion we will focus principally on those shopping environments that make a *major statement* in their marketplace. The boundaries of this definition range from small-size theme centers, which attract specialized patronage from a limited sector of the total market in which they are located, to massive regional shopping centers, which draw trade from a definable but much broader sector of the total market. Now what are and where are the markets of the 1980s?

In the 1950s and 1960s, suburban shopping centers multiplied at the expense of traditional downtown areas. In those years development opportunities were certainly one-sided—the suburbs represented the dominant arena for shopping center development. Today, and in the years ahead, it is difficult to foresee the emergence of a single dominant geographic locus for shopping center development. Instead, and for the very first time since the advent of the shopping center, a more or less balanced mix of areas being available and selected for the development of shopping centers will emerge.

This conclusion is basically set forth despite the current vogue of the shopping center industry—the small and medium-size market focus. Actually these markets have been around for a very long, long time. They have simply been ignored as a major thrust for development opportunity. It is true that many small markets in the rapidly growing Sunbelt have only recently obtained a population level that justifies the development of an appropriately scaled center. However, for every new market of this type in the Sunbelt, there have been three or four long-standing markets of similar size in the Frostbelt.

For instance, in 1974, my firm conducted three studies for new centers in small markets, i.e., those with a total trading-area population of 110,000 to 140,000 people. By 1979, we had completed fifteen studies in markets of this size. The amazing thing is that twelve of these fifteen markets were in the Northeast; and of the twelve markets in the Northeast, not one had experienced a population growth of more than 4 percent since 1970. The point to be made by this example is simple. The present and future development landscape is not particularly characterized by many new components. Instead, we are basically looking at the same landscape that has been with us for a long, long time. The difference, however, is that the psychological fog that has obscured sparsely populated territories as well as inner-city areas is lifting. Both developers and retailers are taking a more rational look at all parts of the landscape. These development opportunities are not limited to the Sunbelt or to explosive growth areas such as Houston. There are an abundant number of opportunities that are available in our older cities experiencing little or no growth.

For some time we have heard that the older, larger metropolitan areas in the Northeast and North Central states, characterized by stagnant population levels, offer little development opportunity. It is now time that we put this particular myth to rest. For example, let us consider four of our large metropolitan areas. They are all old-line industrial areas in the Frostbelt: Chicago, the third largest metropolitan area; Philadelphia, the fourth; Pittsburgh, the thirteenth; and Baltimore, the fourteenth largest metropolitan area. Since 1976, six major regional centers have opened in Chicago and at least five new ones are planned for the immediate future. In addition, six new department stores will be added to existing centers within the next two years. Also, since 1976, two major in-city developments have opened—the prestigious Water Tower Place and the Brickyard, a major suburban-type regional center. Yet population growth in the broader Chicago market since 1970 has been less than 1 percent.

In Philadelphia the development pace is also rapid and diverse. One major regional center opened in 1977, as did the Gallery, a major downtown retail development. The market's oldest center is now in the process of being redeveloped and at least three new regional centers are planned that will encompass, at a minimum, a total of eleven major department store units. Yet since 1970 the Philadelphia market has experienced population losses.

Across the state of Pennsylvania, in Pittsburgh, the retail landscape is also changing. In 1979, one major suburban center opened and at least three new major regionals are planned. Two of the market's largest centers are planning expansion and this year the city's first major theme center opened in an old railroad station. Also, in recent years, a new Saks Fifth Avenue store opened downtown. This development activity took place in a market that has been losing population since 1970.

The Baltimore metropolitan area is also experiencing strong development activity. The area has had a modest population growth of less than 4 percent since 1970. Yet, at the present time, four regional shopping centers are being planned, each with at least three department stores, and a major theme-type center is being built in the downtown area (or close to the downtown area).

Now, despite all this development activity, the four metropolitan areas since 1970 have seen a decline in their collective population total of more than 21,000 persons. The message here is simple. There is an abundance of opportunity, even in large markets with little or no population growth.

At the other end of the population scale, it is possible to cite two completely different types of development opportunities in much smaller markets. In 1970 the population of metropolitan Pittsfield, Massachusetts totaled 149,000 persons. By 1977 the population had declined to approximately 142,000 people. Yet, despite the small size of the market and despite the population decline, a major downtown multidepartment store shopping center is planned (there is no major suburban center in the market). In contrast, Sarasota, Florida had a population of approximately 120,000 persons in 1970. In 1977, the population had increased to approximately 167,000 people. Nonetheless, at present, the downtown retailing area has died while a major new center has recently opened in the suburbs. Thus, here is a surprising example of two contrasting development types in two contrasting market situations.

An important guide to the future of retailing is not only the broad range of market and development types that is available, but also the evolutionary pattern characterizing retail development trends in the past thirty years or so. Historically, and until the beginning of the 1950s, the nation's retail structure had a very distinctive downtown orientation. The 1950s then spawned the initial development of the regional shopping center in concept and application. The 1960s witnessed the increasing

sophistication of the regional shopping center as an urban form, very successfully repackaged. The 1970s will be remembered as a period of transition which started with the emergence of the superregional center, saw
the emphasis shift to smaller markets in the middle part of the period, and
finally witnessed the reemergence of downtown and selective in-town
areas for development at the end of the period. It is highly probable that
the diversity of the 1970s serves as a preview of the many directions that
new retail development will follow in the 1980s. Joining forces with these
new retail developments will be a very substantial number of older
facilities which will assume new forms and greater competitive dimensions. Older structures, such as train stations and factory buildings, will
continue to be transformed into theme centers while many of our existing
regional centers will be recycled.

Up to this point, there has been an intentional failure to discuss in
detail any single major development type or market size that will be important in the 1980s. Instead the attempt has been made to stress that
retail development opportunities will not be restricted in terms of form,
size, nor market—there will be a wide range of development opportunities. In terms of *market age*, opportunities are present in older
markets as well as new ones. In terms of *market size*, development potential exists in very large markets and in relatively small ones. In terms of
geography, both the Sunbelt and the Frostbelt have tremendous development opportunity. In terms of urbanized areas, downtown areas, in-city
areas and suburban areas, all possess considerable potential. In terms of
development types, new suburban regional centers and in-city regional
centers will still represent substantial opportunities, as does the expansion
of older centers, theme centers of all types and downtown redevelopments.

There are two areas which still require elaboration. One factor is
represented by a type of market which could represent a major area of
development in the 1980s; the other is the federal government's urban
policy. First, the type of market being referred to, for the want of a better
descriptive term, can be called the "twilight zone." The twilight zones exist principally in our ten largest metropolitan areas, which collectively
contain more than 27 percent of the nation's population. Geographically
speaking, the twilight zone encompasses those areas that lie between the
central business district and the first ring of suburban shopping centers,
many of which are comparatively obsolete. Although they contain large
blocks of low-income housing, these areas also shelter very substantial
numbers of middle and upper middle-income families. The difficulty of
land assembly in these areas is, of course, of paramount consideration.
However, the problem is not insurmountable. Examples of twilight zones

are the Queen's Center in New York and the Brickyard and Ford City in Chicago. An increasing number of these types of developments will come on board in the 1980s.

In closing, a brief comment on the President's urban policy is appropriate. Although the policy is still in draft form, it appears that the federal government will make a strong commitment to the development and redevelopment of downtown areas. Personally, I commend this objective. Professionally, however, I fear that the enforcement of this policy will in many cases adversely affect the general welfare of the American public by preventing the development of well conceived and much-needed suburban retail facilities. I am afraid that local officials, for political gain or on emotional grounds or for other illogical reasons, will use such a policy to delay or abort shopping center development. More importantly, however, many downtown retail districts—because of competitive conditions, accessbility parameters, demographic characteristics and residential settlement patterns—simply cannot effectively serve the shopping needs of the broader regional market. To resurrect or to attempt to maintain a major retailing presence in downtown areas fitting this description would be a waste of millions of dollars to the tax-paying public, and over the years would deprive consumers of decent shopping opportunities.

Regional Shopping Center Issues in the 1980s

HOWARD L. GREEN
DAVID L. HUNTOON

The issues which shape the regional shopping center industry in the 80s are probably already apparent. This paper will look at what some of them may be.

Location

In the 80s, industry experts forecast marked expansion opportunities for shopping centers in middle markets, while the federal government is urging shopping centers to be built in existing downtowns. At the risk of being contrarians, let us suggest that new shopping centers are most likely to be clustered with already existing, successful shopping centers. Here's why:

For the first time in our history, in the 80s, we will see a decreased mobility of the American population because of rising fuel costs. What this will do is cause our metropolitan areas, instead of continuing to spread outward, to *stabilize* in the area they occupy. Consequently, the area we now have settled will remain relatively fixed and become more dense.

This pattern is likely to occur for three reasons:

1. Energy costs will continue to rise, so we will choose to decrease the traveling we do. In other words, we will want to minimize the cost of traveling to work, to shopping, to entertainment, etc.

This implies that the automobile will continue to be the main means of transportation in the foreseeable future. Certainly there is no alternative form of transportation available in our low-density, suburban living pattern. Our cars will be far more fuel efficient as an energy conservation measure, but, in the low-density suburbs, even buses will not be an economic alternative to the automobile.

2. Many of the functions that we used to call downtown or central-place functions—shopping, working, meeting, entertainment, or dining—can now be performed in the suburbs. Already the number of suburban jobs is double the number of jobs in the central city. Our need to get together with other people can be done via the phone (or perhaps, in the next decade, by telephone and television combined), so that we do not need to cluster in downtowns except for very esoteric functions (the diamond district on 47th Street in Manhattan as an example)—shopping can be done at the regional center, work will increasingly continue to be suburban rather than central city, entertainment and dining are equally available in the suburbs as they are in the central city.

3. New housing, to satisfy the needs of probably 20 to 25 million more households in the 1980s, will be clustered around existing shopping centers and office complexes in order to minimize the costs of travel. In short, metropolitan areas today are multinucleated, i.e., every metropolitan area has a number of "downtowns." In fact, since 1946, as growth outward has proceeded, many downtowns have become off-centered and not as well located as the outlying centers. As an example, Northland, in Southfield, Michigan, is much more central to the Detroit market than is downtown Detroit itself. Consequently, it is the outlying shopping center, in conjunction with the office and service complexes associated with them, that will be the "other" downtown in every major metropolitan area in the United States in the 1980s.

What of the location of new shopping centers? If there is little opportunity for them to be built at the edges of existing settlements (since we do not anticipate outward growth), is there opportunity for more new centers? There will be substantial opportunity for both the expansion of existing centers (where there is space) and for new centers clustered *adjacent* to existing, well-located centers. We foresee continued opportunity for the kind of clustering that has occurred in Bergen County, New Jersey, Peabody (Boston), Massachusetts, and Warwick (Providence), Rhode Island, with a number of centers close to one another. There is, and will continue to be, more potential in our largest metropolitan areas for this kind of clustering than for the searching out of new trade areas to fill unmet needs, such as we have had in the 1970s.

What of existing downtowns: should they not be regenerated? Undoubtedly they will continue to perform certain central-place functions, such as governmental, legal and banking. Also, certain cultural activities which historically developed in the original downtown will remain there, such as museums, universities, convention centers, and teaching and research hospitals. Other activities, such as retailing, manufacturing and nongovernment-related office activities, have, in large measure, already moved to new, outlying downtowns. The original downtown retail function will continue in the 80s to serve four groups: a large population of daytime workers, those who choose to live near the central city downtown, those who have access to some form of mass transportation and, in selected cities, tourists and conventioneers.

For all of these people there should be modern, exciting shopping opportunities available. There is a ready market, and to fulfill the unmet needs of these people, we shall certainly see innovations in downtown shopping center development. But it will only be one segment—an important 15 or 20 percent of regional shopping center development—but will be far from *all* of the development in the 80s.

Energy

The impact of rising energy prices on shopping center *locations* was addressed in the previous section. What other effects will rising energy costs have on shopping center development? Probably little. Energy will represent an ever-larger portion of tenants' expenses. Developers, however, have little reason to build more energy-efficient centers. In today's leases, tenants are responsible for their HVAC costs, and also pay common-area maintenance costs. There is little incentive for shopping center owners to minimize costs that can be directly passed on to their tenants, or for tenants with short-term leases to invest in more efficient HVAC equipment (that pays off only in the long run).

Periodically, some government intervention relating to energy use will probably be witnessed in the coming years. Already regulations are in force concerning minimum and maximum temperatures which can be maintained. At selected times (i.e., during the natural gas shortages in the Middle Atlantic states during the winter of 1977), governments have restricted the number of hours that shopping centers could stay open.

As long as the cost of energy can be passed from developer to tenant to consumer, it is doubtful that substantial changes in shopping center design as a result of rising energy costs will be witnessed in this decade.

Government

Always late in reacting to the ever-evolving free market economy, government at all levels will try to introduce restrictions to solve the problems of the *last* decade:

1. In order to restore poorly functioning CBDs, government at the federal level will attempt to induce downtown redevelopment by grants and assistance. This help will occur whether or not (1) the downtown is truly performing CBD functions, (2) mass transit exists to get the market to the CBD, (3) the downtown is centrally located to the total market, or (4) "the dramatic increase in those persons who both live and work in the suburbs . . . would inhibit a return to city dwelling" (Vincent Barabba, director of the Bureau of the Census).

2. Economic impact analysis is a recent development of government, presumably to preserve the viability of existing commercial areas from incursion by new shopping centers. This argument ignores the fact that rejuvenation of older areas is as attractive to the developer as new shopping centers, *if* (1) the existing physical facilities can be modernized, (2) the trade area potential calls for preservation and upgrading and (3) existing lease terms and conditions allow changes in tenants to be made.

New and Changing Markets

At least six growing and changing markets will need to be served in the 1980s:

1. Our society will continue to remain affluent. Income itself will undoubtedly remain close to constant, in fixed dollars, because income is largely indexed to the rate of inflation. Within this income there will, however, be shifts in expenditures. The costs of housing and energy are going to rise as a percentage of the total. Expenditures for food and for apparel in the 1980s will continue to decline as a percentage of total income, as will the amount of money spent for travel and entertainment. Big ticket items, such as automobiles, home furnishings, etc., will continue to maintain their share of our total expenditures. These shifts will have substantial influence on the tenant mix in regional shopping centers.

2. The bulge in new families—the post-World War II babies—is moving into middle age, buying homes, furnishings and durables. This generation is largely white collar and well educated, and its *real* income will grow. Here is the prime market for retailers in malls in the 80s.

3. Completely overlooked is the emerging market of the fifty-five to eighty-year-old population. Thanks to private pensions, Social Security, good health and later (not earlier, *later*) retirement, this group has increasing disposable income. Next to the post-war, baby-boom generation, the growth in absolute numbers and in real purchasing puts this group second. We will consequently be seeing the return of the drugstore to the shopping center is tenant mix and a search by the owner/manager to restructure the merchandise lines carried by the retailers to serve this new market.

4. A fourth growth segment is single-person households—the majority of all new households in the 70s and continuing to the 80s. A good proportion may be the affluent elderly, but also those with delayed marriages or those divorced. One will probably see a higher proportion of centers' tenant mix devoted to eating facilities, since the single-household person tends to eat out far more than other market segments.

5. The late 70s have witnessed the slowdown in the youth markets by the closing of public schools and the continuing contraction in college and university populations. With it will come the decrease in truly youth market products: the highly successful junior apparel stores of the 70s will have to adapt to the missy markets of the 80s.

6. Another market may not seem like a consumer market at all, but will impact the centers of the 80s: the small business market. Let us explain.

As corporate tax rates increase, as government regulations becomes more and more detailed and as economics of scale don't prevail in service occupations (as they do in manufacturing), small is becoming beautiful. In 1963, there were 3 million business organizations with nine or fewer employees, in 1972 there were 4.4 million. Continued small business growth is anticipated.

Home and small-business computer/calculator/word processor stores have already started to sprout, as their products provide some of the means for achieving economies of scale in small businesses. These stores will certainly find their way into shopping centers.

New Concepts of Rent

During the next decade one can anticipate that the tenant mix of shopping centers and consumer buying habits will change significantly.

As a result, new concepts in developing rental terms and conditions will have to evolve. Three examples illustrate this point:

1. If there is a coin and stamp store in a shopping center, the operator is not only selling a great deal of collectable-type merchandise, but also purchasing as well. Yet rents are based only upon sales. There should be new concepts developed on how to charge for rent on retail purchases as well as sales.

2. Few stores in shopping centers are charged rent on mail or telephone orders, only on retail sales. Yet, starting about 1990, technology should allow sales through a combination in-home telephone/television device directly to stores. Certainly developers will have to give some thought as to how much sales are to be handled in leases.

3. For some products—especially big ticket items—the retailer may be rent insensitive. Let us explain:

In automobile dealerships, it is not uncommon to talk about rent being $150–175 per new vehicle sold. If, for example, one more car were sold, by virtue of a showroom being located in a center, the manufacturing profit on that new car might be worth more than $1 per square foot in higher rent. If several additional cars were to be sold over the course of a year because of the advantages of being located in a center, the manufacturer could afford to pay more rent because of the increased sales due to a superior location.

Is the concept farfetched? For automobiles, undoubtedly. But for other big-ticket, manufacturer retail items, we don't think so.

There are products in the marketplace for which the shopping center will be an excellent place to retail the item. The sewing machine is a case in point; the small business or home computer is another. This whole issue needs rethinking.

The Economy

There have been two recessions in the 70s and, at the opening of the 80s, we are looking at a number of unnerving economic circumstances that can affect shopping center construction, retail rents and profits.

Energy shortages of almost any kind could stunt economic growth, and we as a country have still failed to handle the most extensive inflation in our peacetime history.

One can hardly become a seer about how these issues will be resolved.

But, given North America's resources, potential and economic vigor, it will of necessity learn to manage its affairs more effectively than it has in the past decade.

To put in bluntly, economic growth and the standard of living will improve because there is no other socially or politically acceptable alternative: the large post-World War II generation will insist that it have for itself what its elders have.

Consequently, in the long run, the 80s can be viewed as a decade of continued prosperity for the shopping center industry, recognizing that, in the short run, there will be traumatic periods.

The Shopping Center is the Message

Years ago, Marshall McLuhan became famous for saying about television that the medium is the message. Of course he meant that television itself was more important than any program on it.

There is a comparison to be made for the shopping center industry. The shopping center itself is the message. This means that, with a reasonable and attractive tenant mix, the presence of the center is the important message, moreso than any single retailer within it.

If one accepts this point of view, it means that retailers will be on short-term leases and will remain within the center only if they meet the consumers' expectations, and will be eliminated or precluded from new centers if they fail to keep up with the changing desires and wants of the marketplace.

In the 80s it is the shopping center itself which is the message to the marketplace.

Community Conservation
Guidelines: A Failure

ALBERT SUSSMAN

The subject of this paper is the shopping center industry's perspective on the Community Conservative Guidelines. This is one of the developing trends which is of great concern to me, and needs to be of great concern to everyone interested in shopping centers, in retail development and in the future of this very important segment of our economic life. That trend is the federal government's shift in the focus of its attention—the focus of its assistance and grant programs to the cities of the United States to the detriment of other very important sections of the country.

I for one believe very strongly in the need to be of help to our cities. I am concerned, however, that in helping our cities we are also developing a philosophy based on the premise that the cities can be helped best by destroying what has been built up outside the cities in the last twenty to forty years.

The reality that I want to talk about is that, in the process of advancing this new theory, the federal government may at the very best only harass, delay and create problems for real estate and retail developers. Even if these problems can be surmounted, it will be at tremendous cost to the developers of the private sector. At the worst, this theory in practice can seriously damage continued suburban development and particularly shopping center development. I would like to look at this trend, this reality, from my personal view, as someone engaged in the shopping center

business. And I would like to look at it particularly from the developers'
and retailers' points of view.

We have a tendency in this country to do things in a grand and over-
powering way. We have a herd instinct. Once a herd is pointed one direction, we begin to move everybody and everything in the same direction
and trample over anything that stands in its way. We develop a theory,
and we marshall all the data we can to support it. We then frequently ignore the facts that may disprove it as we hasten to move forward to implement it.

In the sphere of urban and community planning, the current theory,
stripped down, goes something like this:

In the 1940s, right after the war, the American dream developed—
the dream of a home in the country, a fence surrounding the lawn, a car
in the garage and a family waiting at the gate for Daddy to come home at
the end of the day's work. In pursuit of this dream there was a tremendous
exodus to the suburbs. The exodus started on its own, but gained momentum with federal help. First there were the mortgage loans that were
backed by VA guarantees for the veterans, then FHA, then the interstate
highway program started under Eisenhower. There were also the federal
programs to aid education, to provide sewer and waste disposal, and all
sorts of other programs. According to this theory, these programs made it
easier for people to leave the city, and were thus responsible for the
development of the suburbs. In the process we also created urban sprawl,
we set up underutilized infrastructures, we wasted energy, and, worst of
all, we left the city stranded.

Of course, this movement was much more complicated, perhaps,
and much more involved than I have described. But I've heard it expressed now by several very eloquent and serious-minded planners, and even
some developers.

(The truth is that many people wanted to escape the city not only to
pursue their dream, but also because they were tired of being choked by
traffic and all the problems of transportation in the city, as well as over-
crowding.) Somehow we now look to those conditions, with a romantic
and nostalgic recall, as being far better than things are today. But in
many places, for example, traffic congestion was even worse than it is today.

Now there is a movement to return to the city led by young people
who are different from the young people who came out of the military service after World War II. Today's young people are looking for new
lifestyles. They want to avoid the sterility of life many of them found in
the suburbs. They want to share the excitement of city environments
where they can find museums and jogging tracks, where they have oppor-

tunities for sports and recreation—and all sorts of new things that are part of the new lifestyle of young America. They are deferring raising families, and in some cases even deferring marriage, and they are living happily in the "paradise" they want to create for themselves in the cities. To help this process along the federal government is now looked upon as the vehicle that will go "all out" to help the renaissance of cities.

One of the best ways to help cities, this view holds, is to cut off all, or virtually all, support to the suburbs. The logic seems to go this way: If you stop development in the suburbs, if you stop making the suburbs attractive to people, you will force people to go downtown where they ought to be.

Now this scenario overlooks a big part of the story. It overlooks the fact that most people in the United States today live outside of the cities; more than 54 percent live in the suburbs. Suburban and rural populations have heavy investments in where they live, in their own lifestyles, and in their own property. Their jobs, for the most part, are in the suburbs. Their plants have moved there. Their offices have moved to the suburbs. For example, in the New York metropolitan area, including Connecticut, Long Island, Westchester and New Jersey, surveys completed recently show that of the resident working population in the suburbs, four out of five work in the suburbs. Only one out of five works in New York City. Within a radius of fifty miles of the city there are millions of people who make less than two trips a year into New York City, and as many as 10 percent have not been in the city at all, for any reason, for the last five years. These people shop near their homes. Our statistics show that 50 percent of all the shopping trips made to shopping centers are made by people who live within a radius of ten miles from the center. In the Washington area some years ago a study showed that only 6 percent of total family vehicle travel was for shopping purposes.

Now these are realities that are being overlooked by the theorists, who tell us that people waste gasoline by going to nearby shopping centers, but that they should be forced to shop downtown even though they have to travel much further away from their homes to do so.

I want to call your attention to the realities that the theorists are overlooking. People, if they can, live near their jobs. They shop, first, near their homes and, secondly, near their places of work. Retailers follow their customers wherever they find they've gone. And yet we're being told that shopping centers develop ahead of the population and induce the population to go with them. We are told that shopping centers waste energy; they waste motor fuel, and they waste our facilities and our resources.

In the original policy that was drafted by HUD, called the regional

shopping center policy, there was a bill of particulars drawn up that in-
dicted shopping centers on some very, very serious counts. Some of the
things that shopping centers were blamed for in the original document
were: destroying downtown retailing, creating suburban sprawl, poison-
ing the air that we breathe, raping the land, wiping out farms, robbing
cities of jobs and businesses, stealing tax revenues from cities and adding
to the misery and oppression of minority groups. They could have gone on
and on and they might, as others have—charging shopping centers with
breeding crime and criminals, attracting dope addicts, scarring the landscape, and perpetrating other evils. They found very little good about
shopping centers. Even W. C. Fields might have found something good to
say about us. He might have at least said that it is a place to lose old people and children—possibly forever.

But, in their final guidelines, HUD and the White House didn't include all of these charges. They dropped these inflammatory, unsuppor-
table accusations, and they even dropped any references by name to shopping centers. The document that they released is now an interagency
memo. It is not a policy statement. It is not a presidential order. It is not
signed by the President. It is signed by Jack Watson, the Secretary of the
Interagency Coordinating Committee, and has been sent to eight or nine
or ten federal agencies and departments for their guidance.

The language is more restrained, the approach to the problem is
much softer and it also bears the mark of very thoughtful and considerate
changes. But many of the members of our organization, the International
Council of Shopping Centers, which is made up of developers plus major
retailers, are fearful. They are fearful that these guidelines will generate
hostile actions against shopping centers by federal bureaucrats at local
levels and even at the national level; they are fearful it will open shopping
centers to attack by thousands of cities across the country, possibly as
many as 40,000 cities, counties, state boards, and other agencies which
can now ask for urban impact analyses whenever a shopping center or a
similar development may be proposed in their area.

Our members are also concerned that these guidelines give federal
agencies and federal bureaucrats the right by edict to decide where shopping centers should not be built, even though market research and the
dynamics of retailing may have already determined that they are needed
to serve the population. Our members are worried that the next step may
be that the federal government and state agenices may come along and
dictate where shopping centers must be built—if at all. They are fearful
that this policy is substituting federal decisionmaking over land use for
local and regional planning authority.

We have tried to reassure our members by asking them to look at the total picture. We have told them that federal officials have assured us that the issue has been blown up out of proportion, that the HUD guidelines, or the White House guidelines, really are not contained in a policymaking document, only a memorandum. Federal officials assert that it is not a regulation, that it doesn't have any legal standing and that it is intended as a management tool to help federal agencies get all of the facts before making a decision whenever they receive a complaint from a mayor or a local government about a development they think will hurt them. We have been trying to point out to our members that the language is softer, and that some important concessions have been made in the final draft of this document. But we are not able to persuade many of them.

Very few developers, and even fewer retailers, are convinced that the policy does not have any real dangers for them. They are suspicious. They say the damage is already done by virtue of the fact that there has been nationwide publicity for months saying that this policy was aimed at shopping centers. They feel, with justification, that even though the words "shopping centers" no longer appear in the documents, the words "commercial establishments" clearly refer to shopping centers and that everyone will understand it that way. Our members, the developers and retailers who are responsible for the growth of retailing in the United States, are distrustful of government and distrustful of bureaucrats.

Well, we won't know the answer, of course, until we see how the program is implemented. We won't know for certain how serious these guidelines really are. Let me just tell you what I.C.S.C.'s position is at this point, and what it has been all along in the discussions that we have had with Marshall Kaplan and Bob Embry of HUD and with members of the White House staff who have been assigned to work on this document. Our position has been, as I said, that you don't have to stop suburban development in order to aid downtowns and, in fact, you will not aid urban downtowns by trying to stop suburban development. One does not necessarily follow the other. We believe that the downtowns that deserve to be saved, and need to be saved, have many alternative remedies. Many are surrounded by shopping centers now, and have produced strong, active, vital downtown retail districts, either by developing a downtown shopping center or some other type of retail development. For some areas, however, downtown shopping centers can be even more dangerous and devastating to them than centers built in the suburbs.

The information that we have from our members shows that developers are moving downtown on their own. Close to 10 percent of all the shopping centers either opening or under development, are being built within cities. Many of them, if not most of them, are being built in the heart of downtown districts. Some of them are being built with tax incremental financing or industrial revenue bonds, many more with UDAG funds and many entirely with private funds.

We had hoped back in August and September of 1979, and through the whole process of the development of the federal guidelines, that we could persuade the federal authorities that the way to go was to try to develop a program that will actually help the downtown by being an affirmative, positive, pro-urban development policy, rather than a policy that was anti-suburban shopping centers. We did not succeed in that approach. We wish that we had. We still feel that such a policy is necessary. On the basis of the experiences of our members, we have prepared and have already begun to work on the development of manuals, of programs to help cities and governments—local governments—understand what is necessary for the success of shopping centers or other retail developments in the downtowns of our country. We have the advantage of both bad and good experience. By bad, I mean the experience of unsuccessful shopping centers. We also have the experience of some excellent and successful shopping centers.

But cities need to understand that they must do more than have a desire to put a shopping center downtown. They have to understand that in the partnership that must exist between the private and public sectors, the municipality has its responsibilities and its obligation to provide all the incentives that will bring a developer downtown, incentives that will make it as attractive for him to build inside the city as it now is in the suburbs. The city must help to reduce the delays of getting the necessary approvals, to provide proper security, to make sure that the infrastructure is in place, to make sure that there is a viable market to support retail development downtown. Most important of all, the city must recognize its obligation to cover some of the costs of the project. In the Faneuil Hall development, the city of Boston had to contribute $25 million over the cost of building the shopping center, over the cost that was financeable under the mortgage, as its contribution to the completion of the center. In the city of Philadelphia, the Rouse Company had to receive from the city an additional $40 million as a direct contribution to the project in order to make that center possible.

The downtowns need all the help we can give them. And we want to move forward. When I say "we" I mean the International Council of Shopping Centers, its members and especially its developer members and its retailer members. We want to move forward on a positive program to aid downtowns. We do not think that the present government policy will help that program in any substantial way. It will not help the cities, and it will perhaps damage the development of shopping centers in the suburbs. The development of shopping centers in the suburbs is what the developers now rely on to give them the money that they need in order to develop in the downtowns. A limitation to suburban development is a serious problem for all of us. It is one of great concern to us. We hope that we will be able to work in the future—in the near future and in the long-range future—to help the federal government develop a program that will really be of aid to our cities and of aid to continued retail development. We are looking for a balanced program that will not end in the destruction of the suburbs so that in the year 2000 we will be required to have a program to aid the distressed suburbs.

Community Conservation Guidance: A Promising Initiative

MARSHALL KAPLAN

I appreciate the opportunity the editors have given me to discuss the Administration's new Community Conservation Guidelines. I realize that many readers have questions about the guidelines. I would ask you to reserve judgment until you have read the document and placed it correctly within the context of the President's urban policy. Ideological and rhetorical flourishes should not substitute for analyses. The guidelines are a modest but positive response to the Administration's commitment to help local governments and the private sector revitalize older areas and improve the quality of life in urban America.

Current Demographic Trends

Americans remain on the move. The suburbanization of our population continues simultaneously with massive regional shifts of people and jobs. Significantly, many metropolitan areas have reflected population losses, while population gains have been recorded in nonmetropolitan areas.

Aggregate data relative to decentralization trends, however, hide numerous complexities associated with demographic patterns and their often varied impact on urban areas. In the context of this conference, national figures concerning mobility and urban decline, adequately described in the paper by Dr. Berry, often mask the fact that for many distressed central cities the health of their older business districts or commercial centers relates to many varibles (e.g., transportation, density, income, shopping options, etc.) beyond total metropolitan population trends or their characteristics. At times, fringe commercial development may seriously and negatively affect promising local revitalization efforts. Similarly, options with respect to the form, shape and economic nature of the downtowns of newer, nondistressed central cities and/or central cities in still growing smaller and medium-sized metropolitan areas are related often to the number, location and structure of suburban and/or fringe commercial development.

Berry's paper, given these facts, could be construed to reflect a "head in the sand" or ostrichlike mentality. Put another way, while no one doubts that the functions of central business districts have and will continue to change, federal and local governments should expand their respective abilities to respond to revitalization needs in a strategic manner—a manner reflective to complex local conditions. Knowledge relative to probable impact of pending federal actions is crucial prior to initiating such actions. Securing such knowledge is the primary thrust of the Community Conservation Guidelines.

I would like to comment on some of the specifics concerning the response of representatives of the shopping center industry and others attending this conference to the Community Conservation Guidelines.

1. Content of Policy

A. Urban Impact Analysis
Contrary to the criticism from some in the industry, the guidelines will not vastly expand the power of the federal government to restrict the construction of planned large-scale developments outside central cities. Indeed, as you know, they contain no new statutory proposals. They will not generate any new regulations, nor will they be dependent on any significant new federal staff.

Consistent with the proposals of numerous public interest groups, local officials and private-section leaders, the guidelines (Part II), will direct federal agencies to prepare brief analyses of the urban impact of their respective actions, *if* such actions are likely to lead to a large commercial development, and *if* requested to do so by an elected local official.

The urban impact analysis process proposed in the Community Conservation Guidelines emanates out of the need to more effectively and equitably manage scarce federal resources. In the past, the federal government has been correctly criticized for initiating inconsistent actions and/or actions which inadvertently exacerbate urban problems. In response, as noted by one of the most prestigious private-sector groups, the Committee for Economic Development, "better monitoring of indirect efforts and *anticipation of future effects* of federal policy are necessary to the creation of federal sensitivity to local development issues"[1] and the successful implementation of the President's urban policy.

Urban impact analyses have now been initiated by several agencies with respect to policies and programs which relate to other-than-commercial developments. Thus, the urban impact analysis process defined in the Community Conservation Guidelines is not new. It logically extends the coverage of urban impact analyses in a manner consistent with growing agency capacity and the early experiences of agency staff. In doing so, it is consistent with the recommendations of the President's urban policy, the spirit and content of the President's Executive Order 12074, the recently amended NEPA regulations and the newly amended A-95 guidelines.[2] Further, reflecting our attempt to respond to the concerns of the shopping center industry relative to timeliness, the guidelines require that proposed urban impact analyses be completed within forty-five days (less time than current requirements governing A-95 and NEPA regulations and far less time than the planning period associated with relevant federally assisted projects). Finally, the guidelines encourage agencies to coordinate with and use the results of other on-going efforts requiring or encouraging urban impact analyses of federal actions. *The net result will likely be less paperwork, more focused information and more timely information to federal decision makers.*

B. Inducements or Restrictions

Some papers and speakers have indicated that the Community Conservation Guidelines would rely upon restrictions rather than inducements. Regrettably, none supply a definition of either term. If we apply conventional definitions, however, most of the arguments presented are factually incorrect and premised on misplaced abstractions.

First, most neglect to mention that Part I of the guidelines reaffirm the Administration's strong commitment to developing, through varied incentives, strong public/private partnerships directed at the revitalization of distressed communities. Second, while alluding rhetorically to the word "restrictions," they fail to provide any examples. This is appropriate, since while they raise the spectre of "legal restrictions," there are none in the proposed Community Conservation Guidelines.

Clearly, Congress and the American people have a right to expect this or any Administration to evaluate the impact of federal actions before they occur and to develop mitigating options, to the extent statutes permit, if the anticipated economic, social and environmental results of federal actions run contrary to public policy and/or the public interest. In this context, federal programs and/or federal actions are rarely premised on equality of geographic or household distribution or impact. For the most part, they legitimately parallel and respond to perceived national and/or local problems. *Denial of, or amendment to, a federal action, particularly involving federal aid, if premised on legitimate discretion, cannot be construed as a "legal restriction,"* if no right to the action existed in the first place.

Federal and, indeed, private actions are rarely neutral. What we, and hopefully the critics, have to insist upon are actions which lead to the greatest possible benefits and the least possible costs (economic, social and environmental). The argument of the critics, in this context, could logically result in the conclusion that a federal action likely to lead to a development in one area, which precludes or limits options in another area, is a "legal restriction on the second area." In the context of our shared concerns for appropriate use of the English language, I doubt whether we would want to generate such a conclusion.

Clearly, the question of inducements (which the industry understandably favors) versus restrictions (which it is against) is a complex one. Those who benefit from varied public actions view them sometimes correctly as inducements; those who feel negatively affected, sometimes correctly, but often incorrectly, view them as legal restrictions. I would urge you to dwell on the issues involved and not convert a needed substantive debate to a rhetorical one. Certainly, it would not be a legal restriction in the conventional use of the phrase if every landowner along a highway right-of-way were not able to secure a federally assisted interchange or off-ramp abutting his or her property. Similarly, it is not a legal restriction if water and sewer lines paid for by federal aid are not provided to every site in the metropolitan area.

C. People/Place

Most serious urban analysts would agree that there is a visible tie between place and people issues. For example, the guidelines summarized the relationship between central business districts and local employment opportunities, particularly for minorities. They also allude to the effect declining central business districts have on local tax bases and the relationship of taxes to local government's ability to provide needed public services.

The guidelines require urban impact analyses which address effects of federal actions on the central business district as well as the larger community and metropolitan area. To put it another way, they seek federal agency attention to the problems of people and places within broad urban areas prior to initiating federal action likely to affect these people and places.

D. Equilibrium

(One of the papers and several speakers) suggest that the guidelines may disrupt market equilibrium. Because of the varied and complex patterns of public and private behavior now affecting the marketplace, economic equilibrium may not, at any one point in time, reflect the most efficient or equitable response to national and/or local needs. This fact is now recognized by all but the most rigid classical economists. As numerous governors, mayors, city managers, businessmen and affected residents will relate, the pattern of land uses now reflected in most metropolitan areas does not optimize use of scarce public or private resources, nor does it merit high marks in terms of equity and/or efficiency.

E. Regional Shopping Center as Chief Culprit

Critics have indicated that the Community Conservation Guidelines explicitly or implicitly assume that regional malls are the chief culprits for a host of urban ills and that they fail to acknowledge the benefits of such malls. The guidelines should speak for themselves in this regard: Federal as well as state and local actions have sometimes reinforced or supported urban sprawl and related decentralized trends. And, while most large commercial developments on the fringe of our urban areas have responded and responded well to the needs of a growing population, some have drained economic vitality from existing central business districts in distressed small, medium and large communities and created environmental problems as well as contributed to a reduction of jobs and services available to urban populations, particularly low/moderate-income and minority households.

2. Rationale for Policy

Basically, speakers representing the industry question whether the new guidelines are premised on an adequate or supportable rationale. In doing so, they challenge the policy's implicit and explicit assumptions concerning: the costs of urban sprawl, the relationship between large-scale development and the decline of central business districts, the relationship of large-scale planned developments to inner-city employment, the link between process requirements and policy objectives, and current demographic trends. I would like to briefly respond to each point.

A. Costs of Urban Sprawl

The guidelines suggest that urban sprawl (not suburban development) has resulted in significant and often unnecessary and wasteful use of scarce public and, indeed, private action resources. While the balance sheet on sprawl (benefits and costs) is difficult to precisely determine, given the need to consider numerous often complex variables (i.e., density, land development and operating costs, level of public improvements, quality of services, etc., etc.), the preponderance of evidence suggests that it is a more costly development form.

While reputable analysts have taken issue with some of the conceptual and methodological bases of the recent publication by Real Estate Research Corporation, *The Cost of Sprawl*, their numbers remain few and their comments generally not definitive or precise. On balance, given the prototype nature of *The Cost of Sprawl*, its general findings concerning the relatively high costs of sprawl have stood up reasonably well. They have been confirmed over and over again by numerous recent state and local studies of the costs of alternate development patterns. They are consistent with the policy statements of almost every public interest group concerned with the quality of life in urban areas. They have been reflected daily by the public's experience and testing of countless numbers of governors, mayors and managers.

B. Relationship to Urban Decline and Decline of Central Cities

The Urban Institute analysis prepared for HUD last spring indicated a direct or causal link between regional shopping center development and varied urban decline indicators in many of the *studied* cities. The association illustrated in the Institute study between shopping center development in some communities and urban problems in these same communities combined with the concerns expressed to HUD by most public interest groups was sufficient to warrant federal attention and to generate the guidelines.

By and large, as indicated earlier, many regional shopping centers appear to serve their areas well and in the process provide jobs, services and taxes. But, in some instances such centers, as the Urban Institute study indicates, have reinforced, indeed, led population and job decentralization. Donald Steinnes in a recent article indicates, "These results together suggest retail trade is decentralizing independent of population and that people are following retail trade to the suburbs." The author also indicates, "First, people do not follow manufacturing and services, but retail trade." Handbooks prepared by industry-related groups suggest the "pulling" power of centers. For example, the Urban Land Institute *Shopping Center Development Handbook* indicates that while "it is very important to understand that a shopping center cannot generate new business or create new buying power, it can only attract customers from existing businesses . . . *it can cause a redistribution of business outlets and consumer patronage* . . . ."

Recent data tends to further lend credence to the argument that shopping centers may in many communities lead rather than follow population. For example, shopping goods sales in ten large northern cities declined more rapidly between 1972-1977 than would have been expected given the decline in income in these same cities and the decrease in the percent of shopping goods sales to money income. Equally relevant, the suburbs of these same ten cities increased their sales at a more rapid rate than could be explained by income growth (see Table 1). Shopping goods sales in the sampled cities decreased by $1.7 billion more than could be explained by changes in income and relationship of shopping goods sales nationally to money income. By contrast, sales in suburbs increased by $1.2 billion, or some $300 million more than should have been anticipated based on income expansion in suburban areas and changes in shopping goods expenditures.

Significantly, retail shopping goods sales declined more rapidly in the studied cities than other types of goods. Indeed, non-shopping goods sales declined by only 10 percent, or only 2 percent more than would be expected, given changes in income during the five-year interval. Ostensibly, were population and/or income the major variables determining a shift in retail sales, expected losses in nonshopping goods sales would have paralleled changes in shopping goods sales.[4]

National figures also tend to lend credence to the hypothesis that shopping center development may not always follow population and/or income growth and that mall development, particularly in a diminished aggregate market, may negatively affect some communities. Between 1967 and 1972 mall shopper goods sales absorbed 57 percent of the expanded market (see Table 2). Between 1972 and 1979, by contrast, total shopping goods sales nationally (in constant dollars) increased by only $3.9 billion, while mall sales are estimated to have grown by $17.4 billion. In northern metropolitan areas, the shopping goods sales actually declined during the five-year period. The slow increase in demand for shopper goods is attributable to only marginal growth in disposable money income during the 1970s and to an increasingly higher allocation of this income for housing and energy products such as gasoline and fuel oil. As a result of these consumption changes, the percentage of money income allocated for shopping goods was reduced by 7.4 percent between 1972 and 1977. Despite these adjustments reflecting changes in the national economy, shopping mall construction has continued at a steady rate, adding retail space at a rate about four times as great as the growth

TABLE 1

SHOPPING GOODS SALES AS SOURCE OF MONEY INCOME 1972–1977

(In Billions 1977 Dollars)

	Central City 1972	Central City 1977	Percent Change	Balance of SMSA [c] 1972	Balance of SMSA [c] 1977	Percent Change	U.S. Total 1972	(In Billions) 1977	Percent Change
Northern SMSAs [a]									
Shopping Goods Sales	$ 16.7	12.6	-24.6%	21.3	22.5	5.6%	170.1	172.9	1.7%
Money Income	$101.2	93.5	- 7.6	151.1	156.2	3.3	1140.1	1249.1	9.6
Percent S.G. of Money Income	16.5%	13.5	-18.2	14.1	14.4	2.1	14.9	13.8	-7.4
Population (In Millions)	17.6	16.4	- 6.8	22.3	22.8	2.2	208.1	216.1	3.8
Per Capita S.G. Sales	$950	769	-19.1	$955	987	3.3	$817	$800	-2.1
Southern and Western SMSAs [b]									
Shopping Goods Sales	$11.4	11.9	+ 4.4%	13.0	15.0	+ 15.4%			
Money Income	$58.7	64.9	+10.6%	91.3	105.3	+ 15.3%			
Percent S.G. of Money Income	19.4%	18.3	-5.7%	14.2%	14.2%	-0-			
Population (In Millions)	9.5	9.8	+ 3.2%	14.4	15.8	+ 9.7%			
Per Capita S.G. Sales	$1200	1214	+ 1.2%	$903	$949	+ 5.2%			

[a] Includes Boston, Chicago, Cleveland, Detroit, New York, Newark, Philadelphia, Pittsburgh, Kansas City, St. Louis

[b] Includes Denver, San Francisco, Los Angeles, Seattle, Atlanta, San Antonio, Miami, Phoenix, Houston, and Dallas

[c] Shopping goods sales are for geographic areas not strictly comparable to those used for income and population

SOURCE: Bureau of the Census

in the market for shopping goods. The combination of reduced aggregate demand and continous addition of regional mall gross leasable space has resulted in a "zero-sum" game, particularly in older northern urban areas. Thus, at a metropolitan level, regional mall sales growth in these areas typically results in reduced sales somewhere else. Based on several case studies, both the central business district and smaller, older shopping centers lose sales.

C. Relationship of Proposed Impact Analysis Process to Regional Centers

As stated earlier, urban impact analyses are primarily a means for responsible federal officials to anticipate the effect of their decisions and to avoid problems resulting from these decisions. The need to secure timely information concerning the net impact of federal actions should be obvious, and should be supported by the industry as it has been by key private-section leaders. Urban impact analyses are analogous to the studies most successful merchants initiate prior to locating in many areas.

The "trigger" mechanism criticized by Mr. Sussman was suggested by shopping center developers themselves and endorsed by representatives of several public interest groups. Reliance on chief elected officials from communities to initiate requests for community impact analyses will focus these analyses, at the outset, on areas of immediate national policy concern and will permit federal staff to more readily concentrate on priorities.

Mr. Sussman's general observations seemingly question the fairness of local officials. They are at odds with our own experience. In every instance where we have had a county or city official write us concerning shopping centers, their concerns were stated in a reasonable manner. For the most part, the letters or calls merely requested more knowledge with respect to the effect of federal decisions on their community.

Perhaps even relevant, as clearly stated in the Community Conservation Guidelines, the impact analysis requirement and process, once triggered by a local request, are, in effect, independent of that request. That is, the analysis will be initiated by agency or HUD staff. It will weigh both the benefits and costs of the pending federal action and will review impacts not only on the central business district, but the wider community including the metropolitan area. The aim of the policy is not to proscribe regional shopping centers, as suggested, but to assure that federal actions do not inadevertently hurt older existing business areas and/or generate inequitable and inefficient distribution of jobs, taxes and shopping facilities.

The guidelines obviously cannot ensure downtown revitalization.

TABLE 2

CHANGE IN TOTAL AND MALL SHOPPER GOODS SALES
1967-1979
(*In Billions 1977 Dollars*)

	1967-72	1972-1979
Change, Total Shopper Goods	$ 30.3	$ 3.9
Change, S.G. Mall Sales	17.2	17.4
% S.G. Mall Sales of Total	56.8%	336.2%

Source: 1967 and 1972 Census of Retail Trade
1972-1979 estimates by the Urban Institute (unpublished).

But, in concert with other Administration efforts to build public and private partnerships aimed at helping strengthen city economies, it can help in this regard. As relevant, because the guidelines are aimed in part as improving state and local planning efforts, they will help assure a better, more balanced and efficient mix of metropolitan land uses.

D. Relationship Between Inner-City Workers and Large-Scale Planned Developments

Aggregate job creation is vital to the general economic health of all urban areas. But, contrary to the implicit assumption of the critics of the guidelines, job markets, particularly for low-income unskilled workers, white or black, are relatively narrow and bounded by distance from place of residence. In this context, the decentralization of jobs from central business districts to fringe areas in suburbia, whether these jobs are in industrial or commercial firms, combined with the disparities between growth of jobs in suburban areas and older cities, has limited the job choices of the poor and of minorities. The reasons, as reported in the voluminous literature on the subject, should be obvious. Jobs once held by lower skilled, lower income, often minority workers in central cities, subsequent to relocation to fringe areas, are not as accessible to these same workers. Clearly, the frequent absence of an automobile,[5] combined with marginal public transit systems, makes the journey to work difficult if not impossible. Even when automobiles or transit are available, the costs are often prohibitive.

Problems for low-come *minority* households are even more difficult. Discrimination in suburban housing markets often denies minorities the choice, even if incomes permit, to follow jobs or to respond to the creation of new jobs. Further, discrimination in suburban job markets often freezes minorities out of their old jobs or reduces opportunities for them to compete for new jobs.[6]

If you are a minority, your chances of finding a job in the retail sector in the central business district or in a central city are much higher than they are in suburban areas. At the present time, 11 percent of the retail sales force in central cities is black. The comparable figure in suburban areas in only 3 per cent. In a similar vein, while retail stores represent about 50 percent of all minority-owned firms in 1969, only 1.1 percent of all minority-owned firms were in the suburbs.[7] Since 1970, minority opportunities have increased in suburban areas. Yet, the relative disparities remain significant.

Notes

1. Committee for Economic Development, *An Approach to Federal Urban Policy*, (1977), p. 28.

2. Both the NEPA guidelines and the A-95 regulations now include provisions relative to urban impact analyses.

3. Data concerning national and local shopping and nonshopping goods sales in this section emanates from an extended study of shopping centers now being carried out for HUD by the Urban Institute.

4. It should also be noted that in northern cities, apparently for the first time, the outflow of shopping goods purchases from the urban core to suburbs exceeded the inflow in purchases by commuters and shoppers to the city. This means that suburbs now enjoy a sales "surplus," while the northern cities collectively show a sales "deficit."

5. Well over 50 percent of all poor people in middle-sized and larger cities do not own an automobile.

6. For a prototype analysis of the relationship of minorities, jobs and suburban patterns of job location, refer to John F. Kain, *Housing Segregation, Negro Employment and Metropolitan Decentralization in Suburbanization Dynamics and the Future of the City* (James W. Hughes, Editor, 1974); for later relevant analyses, see John F. Kain, *Racial Discrimination in Urban Housing Markets and Goals for Public Policy* (Harvard University, 1979); *Movement of Blacks and Whites Between Central Cities and Suburbs in 11 Metropolitan Areas*, draft, (HUD, 1978); *Recent Suburbanization of Blacks: How Much, Who and Where?* (HUD, 1979); David Garrity, *Measuring Social Impact: Shopping Center as Investments*, (Columbia University, 1977).

Finally, HUD interviews with retail merchants who have left central cities for malls indicate a decline in minority employment, particularly minorities residing in central cities.

7. Albert J. Reiss, Jr., *Minority Entrepreneurship*, 1969. Conversations with minority businessmen and representatives of minority groups indicate that minority entrepreneurs find it difficult to locate in malls given high rentals and the lack of "incubation space."

Community Conservation Guidance

THE WHITE HOUSE
WASHINGTON

This Community Conservation Guidance provides implementing procedures for an important aspect of several of President Carter's policy initiatives, including his "urban" policy, energy policy, and his policy of targeting federal assistance to those areas and people that need them most. This guidance is predicated on the belief that public and private investment ought to build upon existing resources to the greatest extent possible in order to avoid unnecessary and costly duplication and waste.

It is critically important that federal policies, grants and decisions not have unintended effects of eroding existing commercial centers whether they be located in central cities or the suburbs or rural areas. Moreover, federal programs should not work at cross-purposes with each other in achieving the national goals of the President's Partnership to Conserve America's Communities. State and local leaders are virtually unanimous in recommending that there be a process through which officials can insure that federal policies and practices will be reviewed when there is a strong reason to believe that such policies and practices will erode existing community resources and investments, wherever they are located.

The Conservation Guidelines provide such a process without creating any new regulations or additional bureaucracy. There will be no excessive delays, extra staff requirements or paperwork associated with this guidance. In fact, the process outlined is characterized by rapid review, consultation, and decisionmaking without prejudgment in those instances in which (a) a private development is being significantly aided by federal actions or monies, and (b) a local community identifies in as much detail as possible how such federal actions or monies will result in damage to existing commercial areas.

The Community Conservation Guidance is not intended to delay or prevent *any* specific industry, type of development, or group from pursuing its legal and private economic purposes. Rather, it is a specific example of the implementation of the Carter Administration's policies and goals for the efficient and effective operation of federal programs.

BACKGROUND: President's Partnership to Conserve America's Communities

Guidance provided in this memorandum should be understood in the context of the many actions which have been taken to carry out the President's numerous policy commitments to reduce or eliminate federal actions which contribute to unplanned urban sprawl, to conserve energy, to target limited funds, and to encourage federal actions which help strengthen urban area economies and their downtown areas. These actions include the four Executive Orders issued by the President on August 16, 1978, and the numerous pieces of legislation proposed to the Congress during the last two and one-half years, all associated with the President's "urban policy."

Several agencies, consistent with the thrust of the President's Executive Order 12074, have agreed to subject their major programs and activities to community impact analyses prior to initiating them in order to avoid inadvertent possible negative impacts on cities and their residents. These analyses will cover the effect of federally assisted projects on central cities and surrounding communities and will result in greater consistency between federal aid and national policies.

INTRODUCTION: Initiatives to Strengthen Existing Business Districts

Healthy existing commercial areas are essential to a community's overall well-being. As commercial centers, they are vital sources of jobs, goods and services and tax revenues. Historically, Congress and the Executive Branch have made significant commitments to help localities preserve and strengthen their present commercial areas. President Carter's policy initiatives in economic and community development renew and reinforce that commitment.

Federal efforts to assist in the revitalization and growth of older commercial areas have ranged from subsidizing the development of, or improvements to, costly infrastructure to providing loan guarantees and grants for the development or rehabilitation of commercial areas and establishments. They have included activities aimed at eliminating traffic congestion and expanding transportation options, reducing environmental and safety problems, and actions to increase employment and training assistance to private-section businesses to hire the structurally unemployed.

Part I: Strengthening
Older Commercial Areas

This Administration, consistent with the President's New Partnership to Conserve America's Communities, is committed to help older distressed areas (whether city, town, or suburb) preserve and protect their investment in existing commercial areas. As relevant, it is resolved to assist all communities, in partnership with all levels of government and the private sector, enhance the economic vitality of older commercial areas and the ability of such areas to respond to the commercial, cultural, service and job needs of urban residents.

To improve this Administration's ability to encourage, through appropriate federal action, the development and/ redevelopment of healthy older commercial areas:

(1) The President's Interagency Coordinating Council (IACC) will encourage closer cooperation with respect to federal programs directed at helping revitalize older commercial areas. Agencies will be asked to work together to (a) simplify current guidelines governing economic and community development assistance programs in order to improve their responsiveness to locally defined needs, and (b) facilitate strategic use of economic and community development programs in order to build public/private partnerships directed at older commercial area revitalization.

(2) State, areawide, and local governments will be encouraged to use available federal technical and planning assistance programs to develop comprehensive policies and growth strategies responsive to the overall revitalization needs of existing older commercial areas.

(3) Federal agencies should review their present policies, procedures and regulations for the purpose of identifying which of their key policies, programs and activities now provide (and could provide with revisions) direct and/or indirect assistance to older commercial areas for revitalization needs. Agencies should change their policies and programs, if

necessary, to permit a more effective and strategic response to such revitalization needs.

(4) Each agency administering programs relevant to revitalization of older commercial areas and central business districts will be asked to consult on a continuing basis with relevant private sector and public interest groups, as well as with state and local governments in order to improve the administration of their programs.

Part II: Community Conservation

As indicated in the President's national policies, unplanned sprawl can often be wasteful of our nation's resources. It requires heavy expenditures of scarce public resources for often underutilized infrastructure, it consumes valuable land, and it leads to the wasteful use of limited energy resources. It can weaken the economic, social and environmental health of existing communities.

Federal as well as state and local actions have sometimes unintentionally reinforced or supported unplanned sprawl and related decentralizing trends. And, while most large commercial developments on the fringe of our urban areas have responded well to the needs of a growing population, some have drained economic vitality from existing business districts in small, medium, and large communities. This can create environmental problems as well as contribute to a reduction of jobs and services available to center-city populations, particularly low/moderate income and minority households.

The primary objective of the guidelines enumerated below is to encourage, through appropriate federal, state and local action, the targeting of limited resources on the redevelopment and/or development by the private sector of older commercial areas. In order to accomplish this, they are aimed at discouraging major federal actions that will directly lead to the construction of those, and only those, large commercial developments that clearly and demonstrably weaken existing communities, particularly their established business districts. Federal actions, where relevant, should help assure the location of large commercial developments in areas consistent with state, areawide and local plans and the provisions of the President's Policy to Conserve America's Communities.

To accomplish these goals, the Administration will undertake the following steps:

(1) If the chief elected official of an affected community formally requests it,[a] federal agencies will prepare a community impact analysis of pending federal actions[b] which might lead to a large commercial devel-

opment inside or outside the boundaries of the affected community. Such an analysis will be prepared within forty-five working days from receipt of the local official's request.

(2) Community impact analysis should be directed at determining the consequences (positive and negative[c] of the pending federal action on the existing business districts of the communities requesting it, as well as on the community itself. It should also indicate the general impact of the pending federal action on the surrounding metropolitan area and the area where the federal action is to take place. The community impact analysis should acknowledge, and not duplicate, relevant and available local demographic, economic and market studies. It should be considerate of the views of appropriate local public officials, community groups and private sector leadership, and, where relevant, developers of affected large commercial developments concerning, particularly: (a) the effect of the pending federal action; (b) the economic health of the business district(s) of the community requesting the analysis; and (c) the willingness and desire of the public and private sector from the community requesting the analysis to work together to strengthen development and revitalization opportunities in the existing business district(s).

(3) If the community impact analysis demonstrates that significant negative consequences will result from the pending federal action, the federal agency responsible for the action should consider modifications or mitigating options consistent with relevant statutes, the agency's mission and the President's national policies.

(4) As part of the President's program to reduce paperwork and to avoid burdening state and local officials and the private sector with unnecessary red tape, community impact analyses, when prepared, should be coordinated with the requirements of NEPA regulations.[d] Whenever possible, the information required to be compiled under 40 CFR S1502 should be utilized in preparing community impact analyses.[e] Similarly, information used to compile Clearinghouse Community Impact Analyses pursuant to Circular A-95 should be used whenever possible in preparing community impact analyses resulting from this policy.

Each federal agency will provide periodic reports to the IACC descriptive of its performance with respect to implementation of the initiatives described in this memorandum.

Notes

(a) The formal request by local officials must, at a minimum, include the following: (1) a statement indicating why local officials are concerned with the federal action; (2) evidence of city/town council or, where relevant, county supervisor of commission support; (3) a statement establishing the link between the federal action and the development of the large commercial development; (4) a statement describing the local officials' perception of the effect the commercial development will have on the business district; (5) a statement illustrating local public and private actions which have been taken, which are being taken, and which will be taken to strengthen the economic vitality of existing commercial areas; and (6) a statement indicating that local government has sought to discuss or negotiate the concerns expressed with the applicant for Federal action which is in question. Conversely, an applicant who seeks to respond to the possibility of negative community impact before beginning a project can petition the governing body of the affected jurisdictions request a community impact analysis.

(b) Action is defined in NEPA Regulations, 1508.17. "Actions" refers only to actions which will be approved and/or initiated subsequent to the effective date of the policy. It is not the intent of this policy to initiate community impact analyses on approvals which have already been granted or on actions which have already been initiated by federal agencies.

(c) Negative impact shall include, but not be limited to, the following (1) significant loss of aggregate jobs; (2) significant reduction in tax base; (3) significant loss of employment opportunities for minorities; and (4) significant impact on strengthening population decentralization trends and increasing use of energy; and (5) a significant adverse impact on future cost and availability of retail goods and services.

(d) NEPA regulations and the reference to 40 CFR S1502 refer to regulations promulgated as a result of the National Environmental Policy Act, the Environmental Quality Act of 1970, and related Executive Orders.

(e) Although much of the information utilized in community impact analyses and environmental impact statements will be the same, the community impact analysis is not technically or legally an environmental impact statement since it is prepared pursuant to this guidance, rather than pursuant to NEPA.

Section II

Legal and Land Use Issues

Section II

Legal and Policy Issues

Preface

The stresses on land use regulation in the United States have intensified in recent years. The long term near dominance of local zoning, set in place in the mid-1920s, is eroding under the complexities of assuring individual and broad public interests. While this evaluation has been most clearly defined in terms of housing development—the ensurance of appropriate provision of facilities to a variety of economic groups—there are a number of other arenas of activity. Most recently the new exigencies of energy development, for example, have brought in their wake equivalent drives for federal preemption.

The last thirty years of intensive shopping center development have provided relatively little legislative structuring of a role for communities in limiting the development of such facilities within their own boundaries, much less their capacity to alter decisions made in other jurisdictions. But this process has been under significant review in the courts.

The new interest in the field has engendered reexamination of case law with some surprising findings of precedents in a variety of locations. However, the issues of zoning as a specific limit to economic competition are most complex; their full ramifications clearly require much more in the way of conceptualization than has been brought to bear upon them. The very standing of the issue, as exemplified in the papers which follow, is far from clear-cut. Administrative mechanisms and the enthusiasms that guide them come and go with the political tides—the law provides a much more powerful (if sometimes seemingly inconstant) flywheel with which to form the future foundations of land use regulation. The objective of this section is to explore these issues, attempting to reveal their structural underpinnings, and to provide a basis for future public policy decisionmaking.

In the first paper, Professor Charles M. Haar of the Harvard University Law School examines shopping center location decisions in the context of national competitive policies and local zoning regulations:

1. Land use controls and zoning may not be used to insulate a property owner's land from free competition in the marketplace. Clearly, every time a community zones, it reduces competition to some extent. But the power to regulate without compensation—zoning—has never been held to extend to the outright protection of one use from the rigors of free competition in the marketplace.

2. There are areas in land use where regulation is justified because the market itself is not capable of forcing landowners to take into account adverse consequences visited on others, resulting from their maximization of private benefits. Zoning has been used to perfect the market by meeting the problem of externalities and by limiting uses which impair its operation.

3. Regulation on the ground of economic considerations impairs and frustrates the operation of the land market; it twists the police power to subvert the end goals a competitive market has always been understood to seek. If the proposition of insulating one property owner from competition were to be upheld, it would destroy the very market functions that land use planning attempts to improve.

4. The legal prohibition against using the zoning power to restrain economic competition is especially compelling where its violation would confer a monopoly on one property over all others. By their nature, shopping centers starkly raise the monopoly issue. To grant a monopoly license—through zoning—to build the only regional shopping center in an area would distort the market and impair the public welfare of the residents of a region.

5. A major issue stands forth: is it worth destroying the delicately balanced system of planning and zoning by using the latter to forestalling competition between existing commercial centers and new commercial developments?

In the following contribution Daniel R. Mandelker, Professor of Law, of Washington University in St. Louis, provides further commentary on the legal aspects of controlling shopping center competition:

1. Downtown areas in many major cities would not revive even if all new suburban shopping centers were eternally prohibited. In the middle-sized communities now dubbed the "mid-market," the picture is different—here downtowns remain viable and competition from new outlying shopping centers can be destructive.

2. Commercial competition, particularly competition between new and existing shopping centers, remains a problem in large metropolitan regions as well.

3. While the principle that "zoning may not be used to control competition in the use of land" appears frequently in judicial decision, time could profitably be spent pointing out that this well-accepted principle is also a cliche without meaning. Recent zoning cases avoid it by holding simply that the control of competition is permissible provided it is an "incidental" effect of zoning.

4. This change in judicial opinion may also reflect some deeper judicial perceptions of the zoning power that courts do not articulate. Zoning has traditionally had a spatial "fix"—it regulates land use conflicts in a spatially circumscribed area—allowing municipalities to control harmful "spillover" effects.

5. Shopping centers also have spillover effects which may not be spatially confined or are of a different order, e.g., a new shopping center may adversely impact a downtown several miles away, creating a blighted environment which adversely affects the entire community. Courts can properly conclude that a zoning refusal to prevent these negative spillover effects on the general public properly falls within the zoning power.

6. Similar judicial interpretation recognized that external environmental impacts on distant areas fell under the National Environmental Protection Act. The federal Community Conservation Guidelines are a step in this direction, recognizing the social waste that unnecessary suburban centers can produce. Control of competition? Isn't that what land use control is all about?

*Further exploring the legal right of a municipality to control com-
mercial competition through land use regulation, Clifford L. Weaver and
David T. Hejna, attorneys with the Chicago firm of Ross, Hardies,
O'Keefe, Babcock and Parsons, examine recent developments in land use
law in the context of one ancient principle: zoning may not be used to
regulate commercial competition:*

1. A new development is the U.S. Supreme Court's decision, in 1978,
of *City of Lafayette v. Louisiana Power and Light Co.*, which held that
municipal governments enjoy no automatic exemption from federal antitrust laws, except when their actions are pursuant to a state command
and "policy to displace competition with regulation or monopoly public
service."

2. If it is not part of the zoning power to regulate commercial competition, then attempts to do so are clearly not undertaken pursuant to
any "contemplation" of the state legislature, much less pursuant to any
state policy to displace competition in favor of monopoly.

3. While it would seem to follow that attempts at such zoning would
give rise to a sure-fire antitrust cause of action, nothing, in the law, is as
simple as it appears.

 a. In many recent decisions, the principle that zoning may not be used
 to regulate commercial competition was upheld.
 b. However, a small minority of cases held zoning regulations to be
 valid despite their assumed impact on free competition.

4. The different results depend upon the court's perception of
whether the zoning ordinance had been adopted or rejected to promote
the narrow private interests of one businessman at the expense of another
or to promote some broader public interest, i.e., where the zoning
authority has in all good faith determined that the general public interest
demands some restriction of commercial competition.

5. In cases where a municipality denies commercial zoning, the disappointed developer can plead enough facts to get a hearing on both zoning
and anti-trust issues (*Lafayette*). On both grounds the developer may
plead that the municipal action was prompted by an unlawful conspiracy
to advance private interests rather than by any proper public purpose.

Howard E. Kane and Elizabeth H. Belkin, senior partner and associate, respectively, at the Chicago law firm of Jenner and Block, focus more specifically on the methods that have been used by both city and federal governments in an effort to protect and strengthen central city shopping districts. In particular, five methods of preserving the central city are examined:

1. The power of a city to refuse zoning required for a mall siting within city boundaries,

2. The use of court orders to enjoin development of centers in outlying areas,

3. Central city annexation of the outlying area in question, thereby bringing its zoning control within the ambit of central city control,

4. Control of outlying development by use of extraterritorial police power such as extraterritorial zoning, and

5. The employment of economic incentives as a means of encouraging developers to locate within the central city.

Each of these methods is first considered in terms of the success each has achieved, and then some of the setbacks that cities have suffered in attempting to preempt mall siting and, thus, inhibit suburban centers, are examined. Realistically the greatest problem to developers, as a result of city government action, concerns the time delays and expense that the developers may incur because of such activities.

Finally, Michael Fix of the Urban Institute addresses the issue of the economic and fiscal impact of regional malls on central cities in legal proceedings.

1. As regional malls have proliferated and reached saturation in a number of major urban markets, "mid-market" locations have gained increasing attention. The latter, more so than before, may lead to interjurisdictional struggles, since the competitive injuries caused by the operation of such regional malls will be felt by merchants in jurisdictions which are some distance from the development site.

2. If zoning is ineffective in this context, strategies founded on other more legal bases will have to be relied upon. Three fields of regulation can be used to address the relevant economic issues.

3. The first is the use of restrictions or conditions attached to the use of federal funds or grants. The second is the use of state and federal environmental impact review requirement, and the third is the employment of state land use and environmental laws.

Fix concludes that regional malls are now more vulnerable to challenges made under state and federal regulations based on projected fiscal and economic impact, and that the most effective weapon in the legal arsenal of opponents of the development of regional shopping malls may be the new White House Community Guidance regulations.

Shopping Center Location Decisions: National Competitive Policies and Local Zoning Regulations

CHARLES M. HAAR

The question discussed in this paper—the relation of the national policy fostering competition to the zoning power of local communities—goes to the very heart of the police power in a constitutional democracy. When probing into that mysterious sovereign power which regulates land use and economic activities of the private sector without compensation, fine lines abound; the complexities of constitutional law intrude and the inquirer is thrown into the philosophic underpinnings of the society—always a disturbing undertaking. And it is even a more difficult task for lawyers, whose calling is to clarify, simplify (even though that may be hard for many to believe), to resolve. For the task is not only to isolate, but to present the issues in such a way that a decision can be reached. Society cannot pause and say, "well, there's a lot to be said on both sides," true as that is in this particular case of regulating the siting of shopping centers. Exploration of fundamental premises and values, within Marquess-of-Queensbury rules in which we agree to discuss rationally (even though we turn red and approach apoplexy), is a luxury rarely indulged in by the legal system. It just can't be done in an ordering geared to winner take all. That is why competition among land developers (leads to the pervasive and devisive question) of what is private property and what is the appropriate role of society in directing, guiding, curbing, "incentiving" the activities of the entrepreneur and the lender as they go about maximizing their own profits.

Since the legal and policy issues of regulation of shopping center locations will be determined by the particular facts of the case, the differing situations ought to be kept in mind at the outset of analysis. *First* is the case where a business use would be excluded from within a city or within

97

a suburb. Here the question comes up: is this locational zoning, an activity engaged in all the time by zoning authorities? Or, suspicious as we rightfully are of situations where wealth is created by political processes, is this fostering anti-competitive spirit for the benefit of the entrenched?

A *second* case—one that is to the fore of our thoughts because of its dominance of the headlines—is the CBD of a locality versus another shopping center in the same community; it may be one of the smaller kinds of shopping centers, and it would be located within that same city's legislative and territorial powers. This situation invokes competition between, as it were, different areas within the same corporate unit, hence zoning out that shopping center becomes not a possibly exclusionary zoning act, but zoning on the grounds that adequate shopping facilities exist, that demand within the corporate unit will not require another center. This becomes a conflict among planning principles, for the courts, as they formulate decisions, are going to turn to the planning and the economics of the whole operation to find the underpinning for legal validity.

Third, we can stretch the possible conflict to the municipal boundaries, thus cutting into the whole question of who has the power to decide land use conflicts in the planning system. This means a conflict among municipalities, among two or more different property tax raising and revenue-sharing communities. For example, community A has a downtown struggling to succeed with urban renewal, while community B has been chosen by developers and lenders (and perhaps even by a government entity) as the site of a shopping center. Such a conflict between the central city and the suburb is the dramatic setting for this conference— the Shakespearean mold in which urban policy is often set. The legal conflict becomes one not solely between entrepreneurs, but a conflict between public governments, municipalities versus municipalities.

Finally, a *fourth* kind of conflict, a corollary of the last dispute setting, is one between two different suburbs. Neither of these entities may have much of an established business district at the time of adjudication, but both are seeking ratables, each one claiming, "I'm the better one for location of this shopping center; I'm the most deserving; I need employment most." Or they may go into land-planning factors, "I will not congest existing freeways." Rare as this fourth type of potential conflict is currently, it helps to clarify the other fact situations: for it is not a conflict between the central city and the suburb, where emotional tugs and pulls enter, demanding on whether we believe in a society of urban cores, or whether the tilt is to affirm a newer urban form of a thin lacquer of people and investments spread out over the metropolitan area.

So these are clusters of dispute that need to be sifted and analyzed as we examine the newly emerging role in the law of zoning of the ancient social policy of competition.

At this point, I will take the prerogative of raising questions, knowing full well that the most capable lawyers in this section will sweat the issue through on the front line—the infantry has to slug it out and provide the answers, albeit economists will then prove it is, after all, the wrong model. To the many provocative questions that I would like to explore, and to which the answers can be perceived but darkly, I want to couch even tentative conclusions strongly, put them in the form of a brief, so you can have a position to move against (and also a position from which I can retreat, if necessary).

The first point is that the zoning power cannot be used to insulate property owners from competition. Second, this becomes especially sharp and poignant when the result of protecting against the competition is to confer a monopoly. The third point is the proper level of decision-making because, out of previous papers in this volume and of the four factual situations outlined earlier, all—aside from the first (the center locating within one corporate unit)—involve *who is going to decide* as between competing governments, as to what is the wisest allocation of land, what produces the greatest consumer satisfaction, what renders the greatest economic efficiency. The fourth issue I want to raise is that, again, the U.S. Supreme Court has almost absentmindedly impinged upon the land-use area, this time with the recent *Lafayette* case, which bears both directly and indirectly on the shopping center cases.

1. Land use controls may not be used to insulate one property owner's land from free competition in the marketplace.

The very first case decided by the U. S. Supreme Court on the validity of zoning regulations is my starting point. In the *Euclid* case in 1926, the Court upheld the zoning power as not in derogation of private property or in conflict with the Fourteenth Amendment. What has to be kept in mind is that the favorable outcome was a culmination of a long struggle that had gone on for over ten years in state courts, in planning boards, and in the forum of public opinion. It was a national discussion about whether the districting of land and buildings by use, height, and bulk, in accordance with a comprehensive plan, was too sharp a curtailment of property rights or whether it was an intrusion that the American constitutional system could tolerate. The opinion is an interesting construct of old nuisance doctrine and of constitutional flexibility to meet the evolving needs of society. And in the *Euclid* opinion there are several themes for the shopping center controversy, as you go back, for every generation rereads history in the light of its own needs.

One insight, for example, is the warning in the District Court opinion that zoning may lead to segregation. Since that was not the way people saw the world in the twenties, he did refer to segregation by income, but the major constitutional infirmity of exclusion by race was only dimly perceived. Of course, that has emerged as the big issue in the seventies in the state courts—the resolution that zoning is a tolerable mapping and location necessary in order to deal with incompatible land uses and for sound community development, but—and a big but—if zoning is used to exclude by race, to keep blacks out of the suburbs, or to exclude minority low-income housing, that is an abuse outlawed by more basic principles of the society. Truly, this is a thin line. But the key reminder remains: the zoning power has to take into account other social policies.

This is not an uncommon judicial warning and curb. It parallels the way HUD was sharply reminded by the federal court in the *Shannon* case that, strangely, housing production is not the be-all and end-all of national housing policy. For housing programs are also intended to foster civil rights. More important, when Congress enacted those vague yearnings in the Housing Acts of 1968,1970, and1974, they were intended to be operational. Similarly, I am suggesting that competition is not only a popular slogan, not only something to be invoked during primary elections; it is, rather, a powerful policy which should dominate many aspects of social control, cutting through efficiency and other countervailing values. Like civil rights, fostering competition is a broad national factor which has to be taken account of in local zoning.

In the same *Euclid* case, there is another dictum pertinent to this discussion. The argument was raised about the Village of Euclid isolating itself from the Cleveland metropolitan area. To this the court responded that the argument was premature, but that someday, looking at the region as a whole, the general public welfare might override the parochial interest of the locality. Regionalism is a paramount factor in the last two factual situations outlined above—the conflict between central city and the suburb, and the conflict among suburbs, competing for what they regard as attractive businesses, taxpayers, and job producers. Again, this is a policy which overrides and modifies local zoning power.

Clearly and concededly, every time a community zones, it reduces competition to some extent. Where, earlier, the landowner might have put up a business center, competing with other commercial uses, that option has been eliminated. But, standing alone, that does not necessarily render the regulation invalid. In the same fashion, zoning raises the costs of land by reducing the supply side of the market, increasing the cost of housing; such cost aspects are a necessary and accepted part of zoning, except for found discrimination against low-and-moderate-cost housing. Hence, with conflicting social policies, and, depending on the factual situations, the different intensities they bring to bear on the outcome the judges are forced back to the line-drawing process—which bores laypersons and which delights lawyers—the angels dancing on the head of the dividing line. In sum, when should the policy of free competition prevail over the policy of social control of land; when should it falter?

Out of the *Euclid* tradition, out of the zoning system as it has come down today, an answer does emerge. The zoning power extends to all land use regulations that advance the public health, safety, morals and welfare. While the scope of the "public welfare" necessarily undergoes continuous expansion to meet new societal needs, the zoning power, the power to regulate without compensation, has never been held to extend to the outright protection of one use from the rigors of free competition in the marketplace. Rather, three basic lines of land use control have emerged as the national model of what are appropriate legislative spheres of action.

One is the nuisance doctrine, on which the *Euclid* decision itself is based. The locality can exercise its police power to eliminate or forestall incompatible land uses. Thus, zoning can be regarded as an organized way of dealing with the common law kinds of nuisances. At times, adapting from the profession of economics, judges elaborate the rationale for controls in terms of externalities: if developers would cast certain costs on society, society has a right to force them to internalize those burdens. This government power evolves to the protection of the capital budget—localities can zone to prevent the social costs of premature expansions of roads, sewers and water.

Subdivision controls, another form of the police power, build on this concept: society does not have to provide the builder with the schools and parks, and other infrastructures, the need for which has arisen due to his construction and seeking for profits. Environmental impacts have come in as a subclassification here: as trustees for spaceship Earth, as social fiduciaries for future generations, governments can prescribe standards for the clarity of the air and the purity of the water.

Thus, there emerges a solid platform for the appropriate regulation of shopping centers. In planning and zoning for a shopping center, proper considerations include its compatibility with the neighborhood, that (1) it is not nuisancelike in nature—it does not create externalities harmful to surrounding uses, and, further, that (2) as part of compatibility with its setting, it does not have adverse effects either on the environment or the provision of municipal services. This is the classical statement of zoning power.

Physical externalities that threaten harm to the public, such as air or water pollution, or externalities requiring public expenditures, such as for roads and sewers, can be internalized to the property owner by application of police power regulation, thereby avoiding costs thrust upon the general public. In short, there are areas in land use where regulation is justified, because the market itself is not capable of forcing each land-owner to take into account adverse consequences visited on others, resulting from his maximization of private benefits.

When a locality chooses to regulate by excluding a shopping center on the ground that it competes with existing centers or that the community cannot support an additional business, that becomes a different breed of "zoning." Use of zoning to artificially insulate one business center from competition would extend the police power far beyond its defined historic bounds, bring it into unnecessary conflict with public and private interests underlying the American economic system—the autonomy of the marketplace, healthy competition, limited restraints on individual choice, and the benefit to the consumer resulting from different producers vying to meet societal needs as efficiently as possible.

To briefly restate the proposition, the police power, which regulates land without compensation, has traditionally been used through zoning to perfect the market, by meeting the problem of externalities and by limiting uses which impair the operation of the market, such as those imposing costs on others and therefore not taken into account by the user. Zoning can help force the producer of externalities to pay for them, thus helping set true prices for the use of land and generating efficient allocation of resources. Regulation on the ground of economic considerations impairs and frustrates the operation of the land market; it twists the police power to subvert the end a more perfect competitive market has always been understood to seek. If the proposition of insulating one property owner from competition were to be upheld, it would destroy the very market that landuse planning attempts to improve, in effect "throwing out the baby with the bath water," cutting at its essence. The would-be entrant is saying there is no market failure here; it is willing to compete, it is willing to take normal market risks, it is willing to pay whatever costs of externalities it produces. There appears to be no extenuating reason, then, to expect that the market will not operate efficiently in the allocation of resources, forcing the landowner to use the property to the property extent and therefore in the interests of the community.

This view of the inappropriateness of a police-power measure to protect a site from competition in the marketplace is so commonly accepted that it is only rarely litigated. It is taken for granted by legislatures, administrators, courts, and the general public that the competitive free market is the dominant way that scarce land resources are to be allocated, hence the relative paucity of cases in this otherwise highly litigated area of the law. Where it has arisen as a major issue in a case, and been seriously elaborated and considered, the need to preserve free and fair competition has been emphasized.

2. The legal prohibition against using the zoning power to restrain economic competition is especially compelling where its violation would confer a monopoly on one property over all others.

By their nature, shopping centers raise the monopoly issue starkly. The essence of the enterprise is the one unified owner—with leases and, always, the covenants against competition, dealt with as between the lessor and lessee, the inter sese issue. Zoning pits the two centers against each other. And the situation is more sounding in monopoly than the competition between center city and suburb. The situation is unlike the CBD where there is fragmentation of title and disparate and many owners. If zoning in the CBD limits access to a particular site, a developer can go on another. He can buy elsewhere; he can negotiate for an alternative site. With a shopping center, the locality says, "That's it, this center is the chosen instrumentality and you can't build another shopping center because of competition which will destroy you both; in order to avoid loss of taxables or the prospects of boarded-up stores and eyesores, we will prevent you from entering the market."

Hence, the conferral of monopoly makes this exercise of the zoning power more suspect—there is need for greater legislative and judicial scrutiny when dealing with excluding the shopping center.

Failure to grant a zoning for a later shopping center property not only would be an improper insulation of an existing center from competition, but would additionally result in conferring upon it a monopoly detrimental to the public interest. Where the zoning power is used to guarantee the economic viability of one private property owner as against another private property owner—not simply one use as against other potential uses—it enters the arena of long-standing common law hostility to monopoly power, and the curative framework of the federal anti-trust statutes.

The reasons for prohibiting a monopoly for one person are many and varied, relating to the very basis of our market system: parties compete with each other to provide the best goods and services at least possible costs, and this system creates incentives to provide broader or more efficient goods and services for the public. To grant a monopoly the license to build the only regional shopping center would distort this essential market function and impair the public welfare of residents of the region.

The monopoly would be a strong and coercive one—a monopoly for a regional shopping center is far more pervasive than one given to help avoid the decline of an existing central business area. Where zoning limits the location of retail stores to the downtown area, it does not go as far as to create an absolute monopoly. Anybody can choose to locate downtown—there are many sites and potential landlords. One can build more, higher, and thereby produce more space; sites are open for bidding and the air is full of competititve spirit and activity. But a single shopping center, with its unified leases, selection of types of tenants, covenants not to compete, and control over use of space, results in far more restrictions of basic commercial freedoms than those engendered by many landlords and buildings.

The question of the monopoly shield can be seen in yet another context. What if the New York City Planning Commission decided to ban all further construction of office buildings in Manhattan, not on grounds of inadequacy of subways, police or fire protection, water and sewer capacity, or environmental impact, but simply because it wanted to assist the present stock of office buildings, agreeing with existing office-building owners that there was an oversupply of office space? Such a decision would certainly be regarded as an infringement on the rights of private investors and public office-space tenants and users. Such intervention in the workings of supply and demand factors would artificially bid up the price of existing office buildings and rents, increasing the incomes of present owners at the expense of prospective ones. Patently, it would be regarded as an impermissible protective tariff, probably put in arbitrarily and under political pressures by the existing owners of office buildings. This sort of regulation would undermine the rationalilty of landuse controls.

3. If the local zoning agency is an inappropriate body to determine on a purely economic basis how many shopping centers should be built, then where should that power be lodged ?

In addition to local zoning authorities, shopping center locational decisions are increasingly determined by the federal government and by the courts. The Carter Administration has just issued its policy on review of shopping center locations when petitioned by adjoining municipalities. When dealing with federal expenditures to make the center viable, such as highway access, this seems perfectly appropriate. Indeed, the case can be made that it is but a logical corollary and sub-version of the A-95 metropolitan review function. Increasingly, especially in the power vacuum of intercommunity disputes, courts are making decisions over the most appropriate locations for shopping centers. Reluctantly they do so;

they are well aware of their suspect qualifications, especially on economically viable aspects.

It is not the best allocation of decisionmaking powers for a court, a planning board, or a development commission to determine financial viability or to conclude what are the possibilities of bankruptcy. Instead, it is for the investors to decide what the market will bear. After all, they put out the money and are at risk with their own equity contribution. It is for the banks and insurance companies, since they put up the mortgage monies and can judge most competently whether it is prudent to make the loan. It is for the judgment of each individual tenant as to the desirability of opening a store at the shopping center, based on the tenant's perception of its location, attractiveness to the ultimate consumers, rent levels, and other factors.

This established system of checks and balances in the market helps guarantee against abuses of an oversupply of shopping services. The decision on the economic wisdom of prospective development must properly be left to private investors, both mortgage lenders and equity investors, all subject to the final judgment of tenants and the consumers that there is indeed room in the market for what they offer.

One wonders, indeed, whether the zoning authorities in fact desire the role of developer. Decisionmaking as to compatibility with the neighborhood, adequacy of sewers, waters, roads, and infrastructure, and environmental impact on water and air is well within the province of planning and zoning agencies. They have always used their expertise to resolve these issues, clearly within their declared competence. But decisions about competition and the economic wisdom of the introduction of two regional shopping centers are better left for determination by the investment community, and the public welfare is furthered only by such determination.

4. Still awaiting further clarification, the recent Lafayette case decided by the U. S. Supreme Court is a reminder of the significance of the antitrust decisions in local zoning decisions based upon protecting existing businesses.

My final point is a brief reference to *Lafayette Power Company*. The implications of this case are unclear. Who would dare to tread where there are four opinions—and the majority seems, at times, to be disagreeing with itself?

The question is whether the federal antitrust laws apply to municipalities in their regulation of commerical developments. They apply to private persons; *Parker v. Brown* ruled they do not apply to the states. Now the question comes up: what about municipalities, the creatures of the state? Where do they fall? Three justices are quite clear that they are exempt, just as the states are. But this is all that can be read into the case. And there is, also, the negative corollary: the local community will not automatically enjoy immunity from the antitrust acts. A fourth justice, Blackmun, goes along with the minority, but says when there is activity between the public and the private that he's reserving for himself the right to change his opinion; so he may very well swing over that it does apply. Since local zoning power is based on *enabling* state acts—landuse controls are not usually mandateed or required—there might be enough language in the decision to expose local officials to treble damage suits.

Ambiguity runs though all the opinions. For example, Chief Justice Burger draws a further line depending on how the locality action can be classified. When government acts as an entrepreneur—again we are down to this marvelous, thin line of what decisionmaking belongs to the private sector or to the public sector—then it is not excused from the antitrust cases on the ground that it is mandated by the state. So, ultimately, his swing opinion may entrap economic zoning: if the zoning is part of an entrepreneurial package, the city will not exempt. And the interesting potential is that zoning agencies will be increasingly acting as entrepreneur in the United States of the 1980s. For urban development is more and more a joint venture. Municipalities seek to revitalize their central business districts by a joint venture with the private sector. In the process, the city gives property tax breaks. It opens up streets, confers grants, makes loans. It applies for UDAGs and provides CDBG funds. It undertakes all sorts of supportive acts; as a co-sponsor with the private developer, it is increasingly acting in an entrepreneurial capacity, hence subject to the national policy of antitrust.

Clearly, the potential of damages relief, as in the *Mason* case in the Iowa District Court, will affect zoning based (in whole or in part) on economic considerations, and the re-enumeration of potential elevance of federal antitrust laws by the Supreme Court will undoubtedly affect the decisions of the state courts. It seems a safe assumption that state courts will draw inferences; they will be on the alert to the anti-competitive effects of zoning. And for the first line of zoning authorities, the *Lafayette* decision and its progeny may chill overzealous regulations. But the outcome will be a slow, common law process of amplification.

Finally, one issue for us all: is it worth straining, perhaps breaking, the delicately wrought system of comprehensive planning, unified zoning, and police power achieved to this point by placing yet another straw (in the guise of local economic controls) to carry on its back? Inevitably, this will be raised if zoning provisions making determinations between existing commercial centers and new commercial developments have to be continuously scrutinized in order to ascertain whether forestalling competition is their primary or ancillary purpose.

Commentary on Legal Aspects of Controlling Shopping Center Competition

DANIEL R. MANDELKER

Americans for years tolerated the slow destruction of their downtown retail centers. Cheap gasoline carried urban dwellers to pretty new homes in the suburbs where they shopped in suburban shopping centers and ultimately in the air conditioned wonder of enclosed malls. Downtown, the lines on the retail sales charts fell along with the buildings and once busy shopping streets became rows of abandoned storefronts. I once walked endlessly in a Great Plains urban center through a desolate downtown interrupted only by a cluster of hotels and a convention center, the bleak product of a downtown urban renewal program.

New perceptions and priorities have changed social opinion on the acceptability of endless commercial flight to outer suburbia. The energy crisis, a growing concern with urban social and economic commitments, and a perception of the waste in commercial decentralization prompt new policy initiatives. In many metropolitan areas this social reaction comes too late. Downtown areas in many major cities would not revive even if all new suburban shopping centers were eternally prohibited.

In the middle-sized communities now dubbed the "mid-market," the picture is somewhat different. Here downtowns often remain viable and capable of salvation, shopping trips are short, and competition from new outlying shopping centers can be destructive. Commercial competition remains a problem in large metropolitan regions as well. New suburban shopping centers will compete with inner suburban shopping areas. In some cities and certainly the larger county jurisdictions and metropolitan regions, commercial competition within geographic sub-areas presents a planning and regulatory problem.

These underlying urban and retailing patterns create the setting for what has been called the "control-of-competition" problem in land use control. This problem legally is more a characterization than a taking issue. Why this is so is apparent in a hypothetical problem that raises the control-of-competition question.

Assume a limited-access highway interchange in a somewhat remote sector of a metropolitan area. Assume a developer wishes to construct a surburban shopping center on a large site in one of the quadrants of this interchange. The site is presently zoned residential. Assume next that the appropriate zoning authority refuses a rezoning for this site to allow the suburban shopping center.

The would-be developer now raises a taking issue. He argues that without the commercial rezoning he cannot put his land to any reasonable use. In the language some courts use, the refusal to rezone could be unconstitutional as a confiscatory "taking" of property. The developer is likely to lose his case. He can put his site to many other possible uses, and, indeed, a residential development at this location would be a reasonable use of the land.

The refusal to rezone does present a characterization problem. Another constitutional provision, the substantive due process clause, created this problem. Any land use control, such as zoning, must be used for an acceptable public purpose. Inquiry will tell us that the zoning authority refused the suburban shopping center rezoning to protect a downtown shopping area several miles away. The developer now argues that the zoning authority cannot characterize this reason for the shopping center denial as a proper public purpose. It is, he claims, an improper regulation of commercial competition through the zoning power. In a free market society, this use of governmental power to control land use should be unconstitutional. Alternatively, he argues, it does not meet the requirement in zoning enabling legislation that zoning be used for the "general welfare." The zoning denial protects the commercial investment of merchants in the downtown area several miles away. This is a private, not a public, purpose.

These arguments have received a sympathetic judicial reception. The principle that "zoning may not be used to control competition in the use of land" appears frequently in judicial decisions. Time could profitably be spent pointing out that this well-accepted principle is also a cliché without meaning. Recent zoning cases avoid it by holding simply that the control of competition is permissible provided it is an "incidental" effect of zoning. The "incidental" dodge is a favorite with the courts. It means that the courts close their eyes to whatever they consider incidental. In this instance they simply ignore the effect zoning has on the distribution of commercial opportunity.

This change in judicial opinion may also reflect some deeper judicial perceptions of the zoning power that courts may not articulate. Zoning has traditionally had a spatial "fix." Most zoning regulates land use conflicts in a spatially circumscribed area. The typical example is the zoning restriction that excludes industrial uses from a residential neighborhood. Courts since the Supreme Court's landmark *Euclid* opinion view the harmful effects of an industrial use in a residential area as a "spillover" the municipality can properly control through the zoning power.

The difference in the suburban shopping center example is that the shopping center has spillover effects not spatially confined and of a different order. Competition from the suburban center in our example will adversely affect the downtown area several miles away. Many of its merchants will probably move to the more attractive shopping center location. The decline of the downtown shopping area will create a blighted environment which adversely affects the entire community. Courts can properly conclude that a zoning refusal to prevent spillover effects on the general public properly falls within the zoning power. They can characterize this use of the zoning power as an acceptable public purpose.

A favorable judicial climate for the control of ruinous commercial competition does not mean that municipal policymakers will use this newfound authority. I have attended more than one hopeful meeting on downtown revitalization while hammers fell on new suburban shopping facilities not too many miles away. The initiative must often come from elsewhere.

It is noteworthy that a law presumably intended to control adverse environmental effects at individual sites has been applied to harmful spillovers that have distant impacts. The National Environmental Policy Act requires environmental impact statements on any major federal action significantly affecting the environment. When the U.S. Postal Service proposed to relocate a downtown Rochester bulk mail facility to an outlying area, litigants successfully challenged in court the refusal to consider the effect of the move on the downtown area.

A judicial recognition that external environmental impacts on distant areas fall within NEPA was inevitable. NEPA commands attention to environmental impacts without limiting their character and with no spatial limitation. Unfortunately, only a federal action triggers a federal impact statement. Private development alone is not enough. Neither is federal investment in highways and other facilities necessary to service a private suburban shopping center probably enough to trigger the environmental impact statement requirement.

Enter the federal executive. A federal Community Conservation Guidance policy issued by the White House, which is really suburban shopping center policy, provides the links NEPA may not make. When federal investment supports a suburban shopping center proposal, the chief executive of a municipality with a threatened downtown may ask for federal review. This review is coordinated with any review necessary under a federal environmental impact statement. Federal agencies may withhold funding for supportive facilities if analysis indicates that the impact of the shopping center on the downtown area is negative.

Land use policymakers may finally be serious about halting the social waste that unnecessary suburban shoppng centers can produce. The national Community Conservation policy is a step in this direction. Control of competition? Isn't that what land use control is all about?

Antitrust Liability and Commercial Zoning Litigation

CLIFFORD L. WEAVER
DAVID T. HEJNA

It is difficult to begin this discussion without first offering some reaction to what has been presented by the preceding papers at this conference. Philosphically, I find this a very difficult area. My social and political beliefs are forever running into themselves when I try to think about the problems of competition between existing commercial areas and new commercial developments.

If there is one thing that has impressed me (and raised my envy) about all the preceding papers, it is the assurance with which each has defended its position. In fact as I compare their self-assuredness with my own confusion in this area, the only thing that gives me any comfort is remembering some practical advice once given to me by one of my college professors. This man held no degree of higher education whatever, but despite that had risen to the rank of full professor of western civilization at the University of Chicago--a tribute, I thought, to his wisdom and practical understanding of our civilization. His advice was this: "If," he said, "you ever meet anyone who is sure he is right, shoot him on the spot, for such people present a clear danger to a free society."

I do not intend to do violence to my compatriots in this volume; in return, I hope they will forgive me for having no clear answers to the questions raised by competition between existing central business districts

and major new commercial developments and by the government's role in
regulating that competition.

Part of my quandry arises out of some trends presented earlier. Jack
Gould indicated that he sees no single dominant new market area for the
1980s. New development will occur in central city and suburb alike. But it
does seem clear that even where the new markets are in the city, they will
be largely *replacement* markets, not redevelopment markets. In my city,
State Street and the Loop can be killed as easily by inner-city malls like
Ford City and the Brickyard as they can by a mall in the suburbs. So the
first imponderable is whether we should be trying to preserve cities as we
now know them or whether our goal is simply to keep them economically
viable. The answer will have enormous effects on the type of regulatory
program you pursue.

As for Brian Berry, the more I believe him, the more frightened I get.
I frankly don't like his picture of a society where we never rub elbows
because we can satisfy all our needs by remote communication from our
dispersed cubicles. Technology surely does, as he suggests, dictate land
use patterns. But, at least in this society, government money and regulation dictates technology, and so it is a cop-out to suggest we should simply
go where technology leads us. I could not agree more with Berry's suggestion that we must abandon "heavy-handed negativism" in our regulatory
programs in favor of positive responses to our urban problems. But we
must also consider the need, at this stage of our development, to at least
neutralize some of the erroneously positive encouragement we have given
to dispersal, sprawl and throw-away thinking.

These are heady policy issues of the first importance. However, one
of the joys, as well as one of the sorrows of being a lawyer is that I don't
have to resolve philosophical and social issues involved. I'm just paid to
talk for people who already know the right answers.

All of which brings me to what I am supposed to be discussing, which
is the legal right of a municipality to control commercial competition
through its land use regulations. In that regard, I wish to discuss one recent development in land use law and one ancient principle of land use
law, and to explore how their interaction may affect future zoning litigation with respect to commercial land use. The law is sufficiently confused
that I can offer each of you something to be happy about and something
to worry about, no matter what your philosophical persuasion.

The ancient principle was capsulized by Edward Bassett, one of the
fathers of zoning, over forty years ago. He said, "Neither can the distribution of business be forced by zoning.... It is not a proper field for zoning."
In other words, zoning may not be used to regulate commercial competition. Chris Duerksen and I have previously addressed this ancient princi-

ple in great detail[1] and I shall return to it after discussing the new development that bears on this issue.

MUNICIPAL ANTITRUST LIABILITY

That new development is the U.S. Supreme Court's decision, in 1978, of *City of Lafayette v. Louisiana Power & Light Co.*[2] In essence, what *Lafayette* held is that municipal governments enjoy no automatic exemption from federal anti-trust laws. Beyond that it is difficult to say what *Lafayette* says. It has been widely discussed in a flurry of articles.[3] Many of these articles suggest that *City of Lafayette* may bring antitrust liability to municipalities even for a variety of planning and zoning activities. In a speech shortly after the *Lafayette* decision, Joe Sims, Deputy Assistant Attorney General of the U.S. Antitrust Division, announced that *Lafayette* raised the possibility of municipal liability for activities involving not only zoning but a host of other regulatory and proprietary endeavors.[4] To even begin to evaluate the credibility of such predications and opinions, it is necessary to understand something about the general antitrust law of this nation and to be aware of the long history that led to *Lafayette*.

Basic Antitrust Law and the Pre-Lafayette Exemptions

The basic federal antitrust laws that might apply to municipal activities involving zoning are the Sherman Antitrust Act of 1890[5] and the Clayton Antitrust Act of 1914[6]. Sections 1 and 3 of the Sherman Act prevent contracts, combinations, or conspiracies in restraint of interstate trade or commerce. Section 2 of the Sherman Act prevents monopolization, attempts to monopolize, and conspiracies to monopolize interstate trade, with a primary focus on single-firm conduct designed to achieve or maintain monopoly power in a defined product and geographical market, or to use a lawful monopoly power to unlawfully monopolize another market.[7] Violations of the Sherman Act are felonies. Sections 1 and 4 of the Clayton Act authorize private treble damage and injunctive actions for violations of both the Sherman Act and the Clayton Act.

Prior to its decision in the *Lafayette* case, the Supreme Court had created two significant exemptions to the basic fabric of the antitrust laws which seemed to give municipalities substantial protection from antitrust liability. The first of these, commonly known as the "state action" exemption, orginated in the Court's decision of *Parker v. Brown*[8] a case involving California's Agricultural Prorate Act. That Act directed state officials to take "action . . . to restrict competition among the growers [of raisins] and maintain prices in the distribution of commodities to packers."[9]

Relying on the legislative history and consideration of federalism, the Court held that the California statute was exempt from the federal antitrust laws. The Court found that "nothing in the language of the Sherman Act or in its history...suggests that its purpose was to restrain a state or its officers or agents from activities directed by its legislature,"[10] and that "the state...as sovereign, imposed the restraint as an act of government which the Sherman Act did not undertake to prohibit."[11] The Court did suggest that no immunity would be available if a state or its municipality becomes a participant in a private agreement or combination by others for restraint of trade.[12]

Between 1975 and 1978, three decisions by the Supreme Court suggested a retreat from the *Parker* exemption with respect to entities not constituting direct arms or agencies of the state, if the state as sovereign had not clearly authorized or directed those entities to act anti-competitively. Two of these decisions involved regulation of the practice of law.

In *Goldfarb v. Virginia State Bar*,[13] the question was whether a minimum fee schedule for lawyers published by the Fairfax County Bar Association and enforced by the Virginia State Bar violated the Sherman Act. By stature, the Virginia Supreme Court was authorized to regulate the practice of law, and the State Bar was assigned a role as an administrative agency of that court. However, no statute provided for or referred to minimum fees, and the Virginia Supreme Court had never taken action with respect to establishing or enforcing minimum fee schedules. The United States Supreme Court therefore found that the anti-competitive effects of the minimum fee schedules were not directly by the state acting as sovereign, and that the State Bar, though acting within its broad powers, had "voluntarily joined in what is essentially a private anticompetitive activity"[14] and was not executing a mandate of the state.

In contrast, *Bates v. State Bar of Arizona*[15] raised the question of whether a ban on attorney advertising, imposed directly by the Arizona Supreme Court, violated the antitrust laws. The Court held that the antitrust laws did not apply because the Arizona Supreme Court was the ultimate body wielding the state's power over the practice of law, and therefore the restraint was compelled by direction of the state acting as a sovereign. The Court emphasized that the state policy requiring the anticompetitive restraint was part of a comprehensive regulatory system and was clearly articulated, affirmatively expressed, and actively supervised by the State Supreme Court.

In 1976, In *Cantor v. Detroit Edison Co.*,[16] a pluarality of the Court rejected a claim by the Detroit-Edison Company that its action in supplying light-bulbs free of cost to its customers was immune from the antitrust laws. Detroit-Edison argued that, because it was a regulated utility and the light-bulb program was included in its rate structue approved the State Public Service Commission, and further because it was required by state law to follow the rate structure as long as it was in effect, the *Parker* state action exemption applied. The pluarality disagreed, finding that no Michigan statutes regulated the light bulb industry and that neither the state legislature nor the Public Service Commission had considered the desirability of such a light bulb program. The plurality concluded that the Commission's approval of the program did not "implement any statewide policy relating to light bulbs" and that "the State's policy is neutral on the question of whether a utility should, or should not, have such a program.[17]

A second exemption from the federal antitrust laws which, at least prior to *Lafayette*, seemed to have special relevance to municipal zoning activity grants antitrust immunity to private parties for lobbying and other political activities. This immunity, commonly known as "Noerr-Pennington Immunity," was established by the Supreme Court in *United Mine Workers v. Pennington*,[18] and *Eastern Railroad Presidents Conference v. Noerr Motor Freight*,Inc.[19]

Noerr was brought by trucking companies against railroads, a railroad association, and public relations firm which had been engaged by the railroads to conduct a publicity campaign designed to influence legislation injurious to long-distance competition from the trucking industry. There was no evidence of agreements with any governmental entities, although there was evidence that some governmental action had been taken in response to the publicity campaign.[20] The Supreme Court reversed the lower courts' judgments for the plaintiff truckers, holding that no Sherman Act violation could be predicated upon mere attempts to influence the passage or enforcement of legislation, even when such attempts arise from anti-competitive motives and purposes.[21]

Pennington involved an agreement between a union and coal operations intended, in part, to obtain uniform labor standards for the coal industry. There were no allegations or evidence of any anti-competitive agreement between the private parties and any public official.[22] The Court held, *inter alia*, that to the extent evidence adduced an agreement between the private parties involving a concerted effort merely to influence action by the Secretary of Labor, the agreement would not be in violation of the Sherman Act.[23]

City of Lafayette

With this background, *Lafayette* is more easily understood. In *Lafayette*[24] two cities, which owned and operated electric utilities, sued an investor-owned electric utility for violation of the antitrust laws. The investor-owned utility counterclaimed, charging that the city utilities had themselves violated the antitrust provisions. The district court dismissed the counterclaim, finding the cities exempt under the state action exemption established by *Parker v. Brown*.[25] The Fifth Circuit reversed and held that *Parker v. Brown* had been overruled by the more recent Supreme Court decisions. The United States Supreme Court affirmed the Fifth Circuit, but only after creating near-total confusion concerning the law in this area.

Four of the nine Justices of the high court thought that all local government acts should be immune from antitrust liability under the *Parker* state action exemption. However, the other five thought the exemption should not be automatically available for all municipal actions. Unfortunately, those five were not able to agree as to when the exemption should be available and when it should not be available.

Justice Brennan wrote the main opinion for the prevailing plurality. All nine Justices joined in Part I of Brennan's opinion, holding that the antitrust laws provided no direct express or implied exemption for municipalities, noting:

> In 1972, there were 62,437 different units of local government in this country. Of this number 23,885 are special districts which have a defined goal or goals for the provision of one or serveral services, which the remaining 38,552 represent the number of counties, municipalities, and townships, most of which have broad authority for general governance subject to limitations in one way or another imposed by the State. These units may, and do, participate in and affect the economic life of this nation in a great number and variety of ways. When these bodies act as owners and providers of services, they are fully capable of aggrandizing other economic units with which they interrelate, with the potential of serious distortion of the rational and efficient allocation of resources, and the efficiency of free markets which the regime of competition embodied in the antitrust laws is thought to engender. If municipalities were free to make economic choices counseled solely by their own parochial interests and without regard to their anticompetitive effects, a serious chink in the armor of antitrust protection would be introduced at odds with the comprehensive national policy Congress established.[26]

Parts II and III of the Justice Brennan's opinion, dealing with the state action exemption, were joined by Justices Stevens and Powell, and by Justice Marshall in a separate concurring opinion. In Part II, the plurality traced the history of the state action exemption, and concluded:

> These decisions require rejection of petitioners' proposition that their status as such automatically affords governmental entities the "state action" exemption. *Parker's* limitation of the exemption, as applied by *Goldfarb* and *Bates*, to "official action directed by (the) state," arises from the basis for the "state action" doctrine -- that given our "dual system of government in which, under the Constitution, the states are sovereign, save only as Congress may constitutionally

subtract from their authority," ...a congressional purpose to subject to antitrust control the State's acts of government will not lightly be inferred...

On the other hand, the fact that municipalities, simply by their status as such, are not within the *Parker* doctrine, does not necessarily mean that all of their anticompetitive activities are subject to antitrust restraints. Since "municipal corporations are instrumentalities of the State for the convenient administration of government within their limits,"...the actions of municipalities may reflect state policy. We therefore conclude that the *Parker* doctrine exempts only anticompetitive conduct engaged in as an act of government by the state as sovereign, or, by its subdivisions, pursuant to state policy to displace competition with regulation or monopoly public service.[27]

In Part III, the plurality affirmed the Fifth Circuit's holding that the case should be reversed and remanded for further inquiry to determine whether the cities' actions were taken pursuant to state policy to displace competition, noting:

In the absence of evidence that the state authorized or directed a given municipality to act as it did, the actions of a particular city hardly can be found to be pursuant to "the state('s) command," or to be restraints that "the state ... as sovereign" imposed....The most that could be said is that state policy may be neutral. To permit municipalities to be shielded from the antitrust laws in such circumstances would impair the goals Congress sought to achieve by those laws...without furthering the policy underlying the *Parker* "exemption." This does not mean, however, that a political subdivision necessarily must be able to point to a specific, detailed legislative authorization before it properly may assert a *Parker* defense to an antitrust suit. While a subordinate governmental unit's claim to *Parker* immunity is not as readily established as the same claim by a state government sued as such, we agree with the Court of Appeals that an adequate state mandate for anticompetitive activities of cities and other subordinate governmental units exists when it is found "from the authority given a governmental entity to operate in a particular area, that the legislature contemplated the kind of action complained of."[28]

In short, the *Lafayette* decision leaves us extraordinarily unclear as to the proper test for applying the state action exemption to anticompetitive activities undertaken by municipalities. On the one hand, the plurality draws from the *Goldfarb* and *Cantor* opinions, requiring that the action be taken pursuant to a state command and "policy to displace competition with regulation or monopoly public service," and that in the absence of evidence that the state has authorized or directed a given municipality to act as it did, "the actions of a particular city can hardly be found pursuant to the 'state(s) command,' or to be restraints that 'the state...as sovereign' imposed.... The most that could be said is that state policy may be neutral."[29] On the other hand, the plurality also draws from the Fifth Circuit's opinion in the case below, noting that a municipality need not be able to point to a specific, detailed legislative authorization, and that an adequate state mandate for anti-competitive activities of cities exists "when it is found 'from the authority given a governmental entity to operate in a particular area, that the legislature contemplated the kind of action complained of.' "[30]

Further confusion is created by the plurality's suggestion that the remedy of treble damages might not be "appropriate" in antitrust actions against a municipality.[31] Dissenting Justice Stewart notes that the language of Section 4 of the Clayton Act [32] is mandatory on its face, and requires that any person injured in his business or property by reason of an antitrust violation "shall" recover threefold damages.[33]

To add to the confusion Justice Marshall, one of the plurality Justices, wrote a separate opinion in which he said he concurred in the plurality opinion only because he felt it incorporated the core of the concern expressed in another opinion written by Justice Burger. Justice Burger, however, concurred only in Part I and the judgment, and declined to join Parts II and III because he favored an altogether different test for the state action exemption that would distinguish between "governmental" activities and "proprietary" activities which compete with private enterprise and make the exemption dependent on whether the municipality could demonstrate that its challenged activity was somehow essential to carrying out a state program.

Justice Stewart—joined by White, Blackmun, and Rehnquist—dissented, favoring state action exemption for virtually all municipal activities. Stewart's dissent focuses in particular on the uncertainties the plurality's opinion may create and the substantial problems arising for municipalities in making routine governmental decisions, including planning and zoning decisions:

> Each time a city grants an exclusive franchise, or chooses to provide a service itself on a monopoly basis, or refuses to grant a zoning variance to a business . . . state legislative action will be necessary to ensure that a federal court will not subsequently decide that the activity was not "contemplated" by the legislature.

*　*　*

> [T]he very vagueness and uncertainty of the new test for antitrust immunity is bound to discourage state agencies and subdivisions in their experimentation with innovative social and economic program. In the exercise of their powers local govermental entities often take actions that might violate the antitrust laws if taken by private persons, such as granting exclusive franchises, enacting

restrictive zoning ordinances and providing public services on a monopoly basis.[34]

MUNICIPAL AUTHORITY TO REGULATE
COMMERCIAL LAND USES

Thus, all we know from *Lafayette* is that a bare, and shifting, majority of the Court thinks there are some situations in which municipalities are not exempt from antitrust liability and that whether or not they are exempt depends in some way upon the extent to which they are carrying out a governmental mandate from the state.

When we try to figure out what all this means with respect to a municipality's authority to regulate land use—especially commercial land use— we are thrown quickly back to Bassett's ancient principle: If is is not part of the zoning power to regulate commercial competition, attempts to do so are clearly not undertakien pursuant to any "contemplation" of the state legislature, much less pursuant to any state policy or express state direction to displace competition in favor of monopoly. And, from that conclusion, it would seem to follow that attempts at such zoning would give rise to a sure-fire antitrust cause of action.

However, in the law, nothing is as simple as it appears. A couple of years ago —just before *Lafayette*—Chris Duerksen and I wrote the *Urban Law Annual* article cited in footnote 1 of this paper. In it, we argued that Bassett clearly didn't know what he was talking about, at least not when it came to zoning ordinances designed to prevent commercial competition for the purpose of promoting the revitalization of an existing central business district. Without restating that entire argument, it can be said that, after examining all of the zoning/competition cases we could find, Duerksen and I concluded that a rather clear pattern was discernible in the land use and zoning law pertaining to the regulation of commercial competition. We found that the great majority of cases supported Bassett's idea that zoning adopted to impede commercial competition was invalid; there were however, a small minority of cases that squarely held zoning regulations to be valid despite their assumed impact on free competition. The different results seemed to us to depend upon the court's perception of whether the zoning ordinance had been adopted or rejected to promote the narrow private interests of one businessman at the expense of another or to promote some broader public interest.

There are any number of cases in which one businessman has attempted to get a competitive advantage over another by manipulating the zoning ordinance; those cases hold almost universally that such a use of zoning is invalid. In a few cases, however, the zoning authority has in all good faith determined that the general public interest demands some restriction of commercial competition. In most of those cases, the zoning action has been sustained despite the alleged impact on competition. As set out in the article, we found several other current trends in land use law which seemed to support our general hypothesis that the zoning commercial competition is whether it serves a purely private purpose or whether it serves some broader legitimate public purpose.

WHAT DOES IT ALL MEAN?

If our hypothesis on the zoning law is right, we seem to find ourselves running in circles on the antitrust issue. Under the zoning law, if you have valid public purpose, you have valid zoning. If you have valid zoning, you have zoning that is authorized by the state zoning enabling act and, under the antitrust law, if you have municipal action taken pursuant to state statute, you have (at least according to some parts of some of the Justices' opinions in *Lafayette*) an exemption from antitrust liability. On the other hand, of course, if your zoning action is not supported by a valid public purpose, then it is invalid zoning. If it's invalid zoning, it's not authorized by state statute and if it's not authorized by state statute, it's not immune from antitrust claims.

This logic suggests that cases involving challenges to commercial zoning decisions may, in many respects, be not much different after *Lafayette* than before. They will have to decided on a case-by-case review of the facts, and a central issue will be the extent to which the action was prompted by a legitimate public purpose rather than by a desire to single out one owner or one parcel for special benefits or burdens unrelated to the purposes for which state enabling acts authorize municipalities to exercise their zoning powers. As in other zoning cases, the outcome may be significantly influenced by the extent to which a particular court is sympathetic to a particular land use policy. And, as in other zoning cases, the particular facts will be of critical importance—making dismissal of complaints prior to a full trial on the merits unlikely in most cases.

While *Lafayette* has produced a veritable parade of municipal antitrust litigation, only a few post-*Lafayette* cases involving competition between existing and proposed commercial facilities have reached even the most preliminary stages. Those few, however, seems to follow the pattern outlined in the preceding paragraph.

In *Miracle Mile Associates v. City of Rochester*,[35] the city had been engaged in a massive urban revitalization effort. State and federal funds had been expended in excess of one-quarter billion dollars, more than seventy-eight million of which had been spent on renewal of the CBD alone. Nevertheless, the city continued "to face the national urban experience of waging an uphill battle merely to maintain the status quo against flight to the suburbs."[36] In 1974, the plaintiff developer obtained zoning and site plan approval for a regional shopping mall in the neighboring town of Henrietta: in 1977 the plaintiff made known his intent to proceed with construction. In late 1977 or early 1978, according to the plaintiff, the defendant City of Rochester and other developers formed a conspiracy to exclude or delay development of the shopping center, by engaging in various activities, primarily instituting numerous proceedings before a variety of state and federal environmental agencies.

After finding that all of the actions taken by the city were prompted by a concern for the possible adverse effects the proposed shopping center might have on the city's downtown revitalization projects, the Court dismissed the antitrust action in a summary judgment proceeding, relying primarily on a statement of facts contained in an affidavit filed by the city's corporation counsel. The Court held that the city was entitled to the *Lafayette* state action exemption, and the private co-defendant developers were entitled to *Noerr-Pennington* immunity.[37]

While recognizing that the New York Urban Renewal Law did not specifically authorize or direct these actions, the court nevertheless found a general authorization and policy to protect the downtown and displace competition, and on that basis applied the state action exemption:

No state or federal law previously ordered the City of Rochester to take the specific steps it took in this case. The legislature understood that unique urban environment and redevelopment problems require flexible solutions and did not circumscribe the power of municipalities to deal with problems as they deemed necessary. The legislature contemplated that action of this sort—that is, action to protect downtown renewal in the face of a suburban threat—would be taken by municipalities. The activity challenged by the plaintiffs was "clearly within the legislative intent" and more than meets the requirement of state authorization or mandate.

As to the second inquiry to establish state action immunity, the state policy to displace competition in the context of urban-versus-suburban commercial development is clear. State and federal urban renewal and environmental policy reflect dissatisfaction with the effects of unplanned, unregulated commercial development. The Urban Renewal Law was designed especially to give urban developers a competitive boost vis-a-vis suburban entrepeneurs, not only in the manner in which developement property can be disposed of to low bidders who will build in accordance with the renewal plan, but also directly through subsidies. Federal policy follows a similar pattern. The environmental laws, both state and federal, are intended to supplement purely economic considerations as well. The City defendants dispute the plaintiff's claims that in seeking to have determined the effects of plaintiffs' project on the City's revitalization programs, the City engaged in antitrust laws, or even that the City is engaged in competition with the plaintiffs as that term is contemplated by the application of such laws. Even assuming that it were otherwise, the state and federal policies to displace competition with regulation are plainly expressed in the laws that gave the city the authority and a mandate to act as it did in this case and immunize it and its agents from antitrust liability.[38]

The court's willingness to take this strongly pro-municipal exemption view of *Lafayette* may be explainable in terms of a rather obvious sympathy for the public policy and program at stake:

> For City officials to have ignored the proposed construction of the Marketplace Mall and its potential impact on the downtown environment would have been a gross derelication of their lawful duty. Because the City acted pursuant to clearly articulate, inherently anti-competitive state and federal mandates, *Parker v. Brown* and *City of Lafayette v. Lousisana Power and Light Co.*, require that the antitrust causes of action be dismissed.[39]

On the other hand, two cases from Iowa demonstrate that it is not very difficult for a plaintiff, given any degree of receptiveness on the part of the court, to allege facts that will get him by the preliminary motion stage and force the city to a full trial. In *Mason City Center Associates v. City of Mason City*,[40] the plaintiff, a private developer, wished to construct an outlying regional shopping center, but the city refused to grant the necessary rezoning. The plaintiff developer then brought suit against the city, each member of the city council, and two other private developers engaged in planning a downtown regional shopping center. The plaintiff developer claimed that the city council had agreed with the defendant developers not to permit the construction of any regional shopping center that would compete with the one proposed by the defendant developers for the downtown area. The defendants moved to dismiss, claiming the state action exemption.

The court denied the motion to dismiss, finding that, under the *Lafayette* tests, the state legislature had not clearly mandated a policy favoring anti-competitive agreements by municipalities with private developers:

> Nor can the court find as a further matter that in enacting its zoning statute the Iowa legislature even contemplated, much less mandated, that its municipalities would enter into anticompetitive agreements with private developers in connection with exercise of their zoning powers . . . At best, the Iowa zoning law is

totally neutral on the question whether the municipalities should or should not enter into such agreements, and then use their zoning powers in furtherance thereof, so as to exclude competitive elements from the relevant market. Indeed, the more probable view is that the State would intend its municipalities to exercise their zoning powers in the manner consistent with the bounds imposed by the federal antitrust laws and the strong national policy favoring competition those laws embody . . .

Even if it could fairly be concluded that the Iowa zoning statute and its underlying policy conflict with the Sherman Act because they compelled or possibly contemplated defendants' anticompetitive activities alleged here, the Court would further have to find that the grant of a Parker "state action" exemption in favor of these defendants *is necessary in order to make the state's zoning statute work, and even then only to the minimum extent necessary.* [Citations omitted, emphasis by the Court] The court cannot so find upon the allegations set forth here. Clearly, the City of Mason City could adequately and effectively exercise its legislatively delegated zoning powers without entering beforehand into anticompetitive agreements with private entities. Denying the defendants any "state action" exemption to the Sherman Act under the circumstances alleged in this case will not extirpate the Iowa zoning statute . . .

The point is not that Mason City is subject to the Sherman Act simply because its zoning decisions have some anticompetitive effect, Rather, it is that the city is not necessariiy and automatically exempt simply because it is exercising its state delegated zoning powers,especially when it is alleged that those zoning powers were exercised in furtherance of an unlawful anticompetitive agreement with private developers.[41]

A month after *Mason City*, the same court was presented with a remarkably similar set of allegations in *Scott v. City of Sioux City*.[42] In *Scott*, the plaintiff land developers alleged that the city and certain other private developers had conspired together to eliminate competition with a downtown urban renewal program. They claimed that the defendants had imposed new restrictive zoning classifications on the plaintiffs' land to prevent them from developing a competing regional shopping center. The defendants moved to dismiss, claiming the *Noerr-Pennington* political activity exemption. However, the Court denied the motion because of the allegation of an actual agreement between the city and the private developers. The *Court* reasoned that *Noerr-Pennington* immunity was derivative from, and dependent on, a valid *Parker* or *Lafayette* state action exemption for the city's action. The court noted that, under *Parker* and *Lafayette*, there is no exemption where the state or municipality enters an anti-competitive agreement with private parties, and that therefore there could also be no *Noerr-Pennington* immunity.

Thus, it can be expected that in many cases in which a municipality denies commercial zoning, the disappointed developer will be able to plead enough facts to get a hearing on both the zoning and the antitrust issues. On both grounds the developer will plead that the municipal action was prompted by an unlawful conspiracy to advance private interests rather than by any proper public purpose.

At first blush, then, it seems that *Lafayette* should be hailed by commercial developers and bemoaned by municipal officials—especially those desirous of using their zoning power to preserve or promote an ailing central business district. On closer reflection, however, there may be reason to suspect an ironical turn of events in the wake of *Lafayette*. Getting by a motion to dismiss an antitrust claim is one thing; proving the claim is another. Purely on the technical merits one can imagine some interesting municipal defenses—and discoveries—concerning just who is trying to eliminate competition with whom when, as is so often the case, a major retailer proposes to develop a major shopping center in the midst of an existing market. Beyond that, however, a more subtle psychological factor may come into play as judges begin to face the talk of deciding the merits of these cases.

Invoking the antitrust law in a zoning dispute may be akin to providing the death penalty for stealing bread. Traditionally, if a court found that a zoning action was unlawful, it simply enjoined the action. The developer got, at most, the right to go ahead with the development. However, in the post-*Lafayette* age, finding that the denial of commercial zoning was unlawful leads directly to a finding that it was also an antitrust violation. That finding, in turn, carries some rather grave consequences.

Violations of Sections 1 and 2 of the Sherman Act are felonies. Corporations can be fined up to $1 million. Individuals can go to prison for three years and pay fines up to $100,000. Private parties who prove such violations are entitled to recover triple their actual damages, plus their attorney's fees and costs, from those found guilty of the antitrust violation. One can imagine that, when faced with those consequences, a judge is going to demand very clear proof before he rules in favor of a disgruntled developer.

If finding the zoning action invalid means finding antitrust liability, one must expect to find judges more reluctant to side with the developers on the underlying zoning issues. The end result may be that developers who try to win their zoning cases by rolling out the antitrust artillery may find the big gun backfiring.

Notes

1. Weaver and Duerksen, Central Business District Planning and the Control of Outlying Shopping Centers, 14 Urban L. Annual 57 (1977).

2. 435 U.S. 389 (1978). Another significant decision is *Monell v. Department of Social Services of the City of New York*, 435 U.S. 658 (1978), which held that municipalities are "persons" within the meaning of the federal Civil Rights Act of 1871, 42 U.S.C. §1983, and can therefore be sued directly for damages and injunctive relief against deprivations of federal constitutional rights. While municipalities may now be subject to both antitrust and §1983 claims, individual municipal officials may have qualified, for good-faith, or even absolute, immunity from damages, either provided by state statute or at common law.

See generally, *Lake County Estates, Inc. v. Tahoe Reg. Plan. Agency*, 440 U.S. 391, 99 S. Ct. 1171 (1979); *Fralin & Waldron, Inc. v. County of Henrico*, 474 F. Supp. 1315 (E.D. Va. 1979); *Martin v. Wray*, 473 F. Supp. 1131 (E.D. Wis. 1979).

3. Smith, "The Applicability of *City of Lafayette v. Louisiana Power & Light* to Municipal Land Use Regulations," 423 NIMLO Law Rev. 179 (1979); The Availability of the *Parker* State Action Exemption to Municipalities Under the City of Lafayette Legislative Intent Test, *Ibid.* at 192; Municipal Antitrust Liability After City of Lafayette, *Id.*, at 203; Bosselman, Does the Lafayette Case Bring Zoning Under the Antitrust Laws? _____ Commentary 4 (19___); The Supreme Court, 1977 Term, 92 Harv. L. Rev. 1, 277 (1978); Note, United States Supreme Court Defines Scope of Immunity Under the Federal Antitrust Laws, 24 Loyola L. Rev. 804 (1978); Note, The Erosion of State Action Immunity From the Antitrust Laws: City of Lafayette v. Louisiana Power & Light Co., 45 Brooklyn L. Rev. 165 (1978); Note, Antitrust-Whether Municipal Antitrust Liability After Lafayette? 15 Wake For. L. Rev. 89 (1979); Note, the Airport Car Rental Concessions: The Role of City of Lafayette v. Louisiana Power and Light Co. in Restricting Threats to Free Competition, 14 Cal. W. L. Rev. 325 (1978); Comment, Recent Cases, 47 (Cinc. L. Rev. 469 (1978).

4. Remarks by Joe Sims, Dept. Ass't Att. Gen., Antitrust Div., "Antitrust Comes To Main Street," 72nd Annual Conference of the Municipal Finance Officers Association, Houston Civic Center, Houston Texas, May 15, 1978.

5. 15 U.S.C. §§1-7 (1976).

6. 15 U.S.C. §§12-27 (1976).

7. *United States v. Grinnell Corp.*, 384 U.S. 563 (1966); *United States v. Griffith*, 334 U.S. 100 (1948).

8. 317 U.S. 341 (1943).

9. *Ibid.* at 346.

10. *Ibid.* at 350-51.

11. *Ibid.* at 352.

12. *Ibid.* at 351-52.

13. 421 U.S. 773 (1975).

14. *Ibid*. at 792.
15. 433 U.S. 350 (1977).
16. 428 U.S. 579 (1976).
17. *Ibid*. at 585.
18. 381 U.S. 657 (1965).
19. 365 U.S. 127 (1961).
20. *Ibid*. at 129-35.
21. *Ibid*. at 138.
22. 381 U.S., at 671.

23. *Ibid*. at 669-72.
24. *City of Lafayette v. Louisiana Power & Light Co.*, 435 U.S. 389 (1978).
25. 317 U.S. 341 (1943).
26. 435 U.S. at 407-408, footnotes deleted.
27. *Ibid*. at 411-12, emphasis added, footnotes deleted.
28. *Ibid*. at 414-15, footnote deleted.
29. *Ibid*. at 414.
30. *Ibid*. at 415-16.
31. *Ibid*. at 401-402, and n.22.
32. 15 U.S.C. §15 (1976 ed.).
33. 435 U.S. at 440-41, Stewart, J., dissenting.
34. *Ibid*. at 438-39.
35. 1979-2 CCH Trade Case. ¶62,735 (W.D. N.Y. May 19, 1979). For a related case involving claims only against other private developers, in which the court applied the *Noerr-Pennington* Doctrine, see *Wilmoute, Inc. v. Eagan Real Estate, Inc.*, 454 F. Supp. 1124 (N.D. N.Y. 1977) *aff'd*, 578 F.2d 1372 (2d Cir. 1978), *cert. denied*, 439 U.S. 983 (1978).

For other *Noerr-Pennington* decisions in the zoning and land use area, see *Miller & Son Paving, Inc. v. Wrightstown Township Civic Assn.*, 443 F. Supp. 1268 (E.D. Pa. 1978) *aff'd mem.* 595 F.2d 1213 (3d Cir. 1979), *cert. denied*, 100 S. Ct. 96 (1979); *Ernest W. Hahn, Inc. v. Codding*, 423 F. Supp. 913 (N.D. Cal. 1976); *Bob Layne Contractor, Inc. v. Barlet*, 504 F.2d 1293 (7th Cir. 1973).

An interesting decision in which antitrust claims were dismissed on the basis of lack of standing rather than state action exemption is *City of Rohnert Park v. Harris*, 601 F. 2d 1040 (9th Cir. 1979). The city of Rohnert Park sought to enjoin the City of Santa Rosa, the Santa Rosa Urban Renewal Agency, the U.S. Department of Housing and Urban Development, and a private developer from constructing a regional shopping center as part of an urban renewal project. Rohnert Park claimed that the proposed shopping center would restrain trade and monpolize retail merchandise space, and would prevent development of a regional shopping center in Rohnert Park, for which Rohnert Park had already made a special assessment. The court held that Rohnert Park had no standing to assert the antitrust claims. No proprietary interest of the city was threatened, and the city was not entitled to assert the state's "parents patriae" basis for standing.

36. *Ibid*. at 78,147.
37. *Ibid*.
38. *Miracle Mile Associates v. City of Rochester*. See note 35 at 78,149.
39. *Ibid*.
40. 468 F.Supp. 737 (N.D. Iowa 1979).
41. 468 F.Supp. at 742-44.
42. No. C79-4990, Civil (N.D. Iowa, May 18, 1979).

Legal and Land Use Issues: Suburb Versus Central City

HOWARD E. KANE
AND
ELIZABETH H. BELKIN

Much has been written about the decline of the central city as the hub of commercial activity. Commonly the decline of the central city business district has been accompanied by a general deterioration in living conditions, particularly an increased incidence of crime. This circumstance has been accompanied by an exodus of families from the cities and the rise in importance of the suburban shopping center.

Recently, however, it appears that the trend is being reversed; people are returning to the city. One of the factors contributing to a renewed interest in the city is the diversity of people and broad range of cultural opportunities that a city has to offer. Although the magnitude of this factor is not yet determinable, clearly some people have assumed a city residence because of the wide variety of experiences available there.

In addition, our politicians, both locally and nationally, have become increasingly committed to a rejuvenation of the central city. This renewed interest in the central city as a commercial hub probably is, at least in part, the result of the widespread publicity being given to the nation's energy shortage. Nonetheless, it should be recognized that this commitment to resurrect the importance of the central city is predicated on more than a desire to solve these energy problems. This commitment also reflects financial pressure felt by city governments due to the loss of tax revenues as businesses flee the central city and a governmental desire to solve some of the problems of urbanization. Consequently, a solution to the nation's energy problems will not necessarily portend a change in governmental priorities.

Governmental attempts to protect and revitalize central city shopping districts pose a potential, and, in some cases a present, threat to developers of suburban malls. The central cities have, in many instances, resorted to both legal and economic pressures to retard development of outlying centers. Further, the local governments are not alone in their endeavors to revitalize the central city. Federal monies have been made available to those willing to locate within the inner city.[1]

The purpose of this article is to examine methods that have been used by both city and federal governments in an effort to protect and strenghten the central city shopping district.[2] Specifically, this article will identify, and discuss from a legal perspective, various tools that can be employed by a central city to preempt mall siting.

Five methods of preserving the central city will be examined: (1) the power of a city to refuse zoning required for mall siting within city boundaries, (2) the use of court orders to enjoin development of centers in outlying areas, (3) central city annexation of the outlying area in question, thereby bringing its zoning within the ambit of central city control, (4) control of outlying development by use of extraterritorial police power such as extraterritorial zoning, and (5) the employment of economic incentives as a means of encouraging developers to locate within the central city. Each of these five methods will be considered first in terms of the success each has achieved. Then some of the setbacks that cities have suffered in attempting to preempt mall siting and thus retard development of suburban centers will be examined.

Methods by Which Development of Centers in Outlying Areas May Be Stopped

The primary tool whereby a central city government may retard the development of shopping centers is the city's zoning power. Since 1926 and the United States Supreme Court decision in *Village of Euclid v. Ambler Realty Co.*[3] the ability of a municipality to control the use of land within its boundaries has been firmly established, and courts have been loath to overrule local zoning decisions.[4] They will defer to local authorities as long as the approach taken by these officials is not arbitrary, capricious or discriminatory.[5] This attitude of judicial restraint is predicated, at least in part, on a belief that local officials are in a better position to evaluate local needs than the courts and are thus entitled to wide discretion.[6] As an example, the Missouri Supreme Court[7] upheld the refusal of a city council to rezone land on the outskirts of a city so as to permit development of a shopping center.[8] In so doing the Court stated, "Zoning is an exercise of the police power and 'the rule is that, if the question as to whether or not the legislation is unreasonable or arbitrary or an equal exercise of power is fairly debatable, the legislation must be upheld as valid.' "[9] Cases such as this indicate that if a government refuses to zone for a shopping center and if it is at least debatable whether such zoning is reasonable, the denial of requisite zoning generally will be upheld on the presumption that government acts objectively and is in the best position to determine the requirements of the citizenry.[10]

The second method whereby central city governments have attempted to prevent development of shopping centers involves proposed centers located outside of the municipality, territory out of the normal reach of its legislative powers. In situations where the city government is unable to control zoning, it sometimes seeks to enjoin construction in the outlying area by appealing to the judiciary. In order for a municipality to successfully enjoin such development, however, the court to which it brings the case must decide that the municipal government has standing to challenge the zoning in question. Courts have not been consistent in ruling as to whether a nonresident may challenge a zoning ordinance, but authority does exist to the effect that a nonresident, under certain circumstances, may have standing.[11]

Once a local government is able to establish the standing necessary to challenge the zoning of a neighboring area, to defeat that zoning it then must show that the zoning was unreasonable.[12] A line of cases from the Illinois courts have held that in order for a party not owning property to establish its zoning is unreasonable he must show the existence of special damages, a higher burden than that required where the zoning of the challenger's own property is in question.[13]

In one such Illinois case,[14] a group of individuals, firms and corporations owning property and operating businesses in the central business district of Peoria, Illinois, attacked the validity of a Peoria ordinance that rezoned thirty acres of land some three to four miles from their property to permit the erection of a new shopping center. In their complaint this group alleged that the rezoning would have " 'a destructive effect . . . [on their] . . . . businesses;' "[15] that their business and property would " 'be greatly depreciated in value;' "[16] that they " 'have been deprived of their property without due process of law;' "[17] and that they " 'invested large sums of money in their respective businesses and properties in reliance upon the classification of lands (existing prior to the rezoning)' "[18] The lower court hearing the case granted summary judgment for the defendants, but the appellate court reversed stating, it knew "of no law, and none has been cited to us, to support the legal conclusion that the distance which separates the properties here involved, standing alone, 'precludes any damage to any plaintiff.' "[19]

In another Illinois case,[20] nonresidents sought to invalidate the rezoning of land to permit development of a multiple family and regional shopping center district. The plaintiffs in that case owned property immediately adjacent to the rezoned area. In ruling the court dealt with the question of plaintiffs' standing by stating, "We believe that the controlling criteria on the question of whether one has standing in a court to challenge the zoning or use to which another's property may be put, is that the party has the burden of proving that he suffered a special damage by reason of the change in the use or zoning—different from that suffered by the general public."[21]

The court went on to state, "We believe that fundamental fairness requires that a property owner is entitled to more security in his property rights than that urged by the defendant municipality."[22]

A line of cases also exists to the effect that when determining whether the zoning granted by a municipality is reasonable, it is proper, and indeed necessary, for the courts to look both within and without the territory so zoned.[23] For example, in an Illinois case,[24] where the plaintiffs challenged the rezoning of land immediately adjacent to their property, but not within the same village, so as to allow multiple family dwellings and a regional shopping center, the court stated:

Generally, it is conceded that the Village of Woodridge may independently exercise its governmental functions with reference to other adjacent corporate bodies and individual property owners not within its corporate limits. However, in amending a zoning ordinance and carrying out these functions, property rights of adjacent owners may be adversely affected, and this effect should be weighted and considered in determining whether the legislative act bears a proper relation to the public safety, health and welfare. Our courts have long held that consideration of the uses made of abutting property is proper in determing the validity of a given zoning ordinance, regardless of whether or not the adjoining property is within the corporate limits of the entity enacting the ordinance.[25]

Similarly, in a case involving the question of whether the effect on property outside of the zoning entity should be considered when zoning for a shopping center,[26] the New Jersey Supreme Court stated:

Knickbocker Road and Massachusetts Avenue are not Chinese walls separating Dumont from the adjoining boroughs. At the very least Dumont owes a duty to hear any residents and taxpayers of adjoining municipalities who may be adversely affected by proposed zoning changes and to give as much consideration to their rights as they would to those of residents and taxpayers of Dumont.

To do less would be to make a fetish out of invisible municipal boundary lines and a mockery of the principles of zoning.[27]

A third method that a municipality may attempt to use in controlling the development of an outlying shopping center is to annex the territory upon which this center is to be built. Once annexed by the neighboring polity, the land is under its jurisdiction and, at least in some cases,[28] the annexing municipality may zone the property so that the center cannot be built. Obviously, this method will be most successful where the land has not yet been sold to a shopping center developer. Once a developer has purchased the land and has submitted plans, the annexing municipality will have more difficulty preventing the development of the center by rezoning the area after it is annexed.

Whether the municipality will be successful in controlling zoning through annexation depends, in part, on how easy it is for that municipality to annex the property in question. Missouri, Nebraska, Oklahoma and Texas apparently have the broadest unilateral annexation powers, with Indiana close behind.[29] Nebraska and Indiana appear to be becoming even more liberal in granting more unilateral power in this regard.[30]

The fourth way in which a central city might control the development of an outlying area is by employing a concept called extraterritorial zoning, i.e., using municipal powers to impose zoning restrictions beyond its own borders.[31] In some states, statutes explicitly grant municipalities the right to control zoning in outlying territories.[32] Usually such statutes are explicit in terms of how far such authority goes.[33] Some make the size the municipality determinative of whether any, or how much, extraterritorial zoning power exists.[34]

Whether a municipality's power to zone extraterritorially is constitutional is not absolutely clear.[35] Nonetheless, cases do exist affirming its constitutionality[36] and, consequently, at present the use of this tool does not appear to be seriously threatened from a constitutional perspective.

Finally, a city can attempt to control development of shopping centers in outlying areas by influencing whether public monies will be appropriated on behalf of the development. Since shopping centers often rely on both federal and local cooperation and funds, the possibility that this aid will be denied may severely dampen development plans.

As "saving the central city" increases in popularity, state and local officials will be encouraged to use their influence to direct funds to those developers opting to locate in the cities. A recent situation in Massachusetts illustrates what may become a trend. In that state, public funding was offered to build a parking garage for an urban renewal site in downtown Pittsfield but the state refused to provide funds to build an access road to a state highway for a mall in Lenox.[37]

Potentially even more significant than denial of local and state funds is the approach that has been adopted by the Carter Administration, which threatens to sharply reduce federal assistance available to shopping centers in outlying areas. The Carter Administration has committed itself to reducing or eliminating federal assistance to projects which contribute to urban sprawl.[38] Instead, federal funds are to be directed toward strengthening downtown centers.

Under the Community Conservation Guidance program adopted by the President, local officials can ask the federal government to study a project proposed for a neighboring community to determine if the project will have an adverse effect on the city seeking the review.[39] Such a study can be requested for projects with any federal involvement, including one that contemplates use of federal monies to provide such things as highways, sewers or dredging. If an adverse effect on the neighboring city can be established, federal funding may be jeopardized.

Although the Community Conservation Guidance program is relatively new, a number of cities have already sought to take advantage of it.[40] Since withholding of federal funding is a possible outcome of a negative finding, the use of Community Conservation Guidance studies is potentially an extremely potent weapon available to a city seeking to preempt outlying mall citing.

Situations Where Efforts to Stop Development of Centers in Outlying Areas Have Failed

Even though the central government has a variety of methods whereby it can discourage or even prevent development of shopping centers in outlying areas, to conclude that such efforts are always successful would be erroneous. Many cases have been decided in which the attempt to prevent the development in outlying areas has failed.[41] In addition, even though federal funding and incentives are available for businesses willing to either stay or relocate in the city, such inducements do not, in many cases, control decisions.

Although a number of cases have been cited in which a government has been successful in having a zoning ordinance that prohibits development of a shopping center upheld,[42] government is not always successful in checking development of unwanted malls. For example, in a recent New York case[43] the court held that where the main use as set forth in the applicable ordinance was for a regional shopping center, it was improper for the town board to reject a site plan on the ground that the proposed center might weaken existing retail shopping areas and burden neighboring roads.[44]

Further, even though in some cases courts have enjoined development of shopping centers in outlying areas, the central city has not always been successful.[45] In a number of instances, the city seeking to stop the building of a center was unable to even reach the first threshold—establishing standing to bring the suit.[46] For example, in a New York case[47] the court dismissed a proceeding brought by a town to prevent the development of a shopping center in an adjoining area by finding that the town was not an "aggrieved party" as required under the appropriate statute.[48] Similarly, in an Illinois case[49] the court held that the plaintiffs did not sufficiently allege special damage[50] as a result of the rezoning to permit development of a regional center and thus concluded that the plaintiffs lacked standing.[51] In the Illinois case, defendant's property consisted of unimproved land located a substantial distance from the downtown area and outside city limits.[52] Furthermore, in addition to these cases, a number of other decisions exist in which the courts have been explicit in stating that the fact that the new center poses an economic threat to established businesses does not give these businesses standing to challenge the zoning.[53]

A city's use of extraterritorial zoning powers to stop construction of a center not located within that city also may not be successful. For example, in a recent case[54] the city of Appleton, Wisconsin sought to prevent construction of a mall in a town located three miles from downtown Appleton[55] by invoking extraterritorial zoning powers provided under a Wisconsin statute.[56] The lower court invalidated the city's attempt, and this result was affirmed on appeal.[57]

Finally, although federal and local governments may offer economic perks to developers who select central city sites, on balance choosing an outlying location may, nonetheless, remain more attractive. Nighttime shoppers tend to prefer suburban malls, and nighttime shopping has become increasingly important with the emergence of the two-income family. Indeed, more than a one-time grant is needed to entice retailers into voluntarily abandoning plans to construct a mall in an outlying area in favor of relocating or choosing to remain in the inner city.

Conclusion

On balance, shopping center developers should take note of the potential threat to development of new suburban malls that a city government might construe as a challenge to or further weakening of the central city shopping area. Such developers should be cognizant that a variety of methods exist whereby the city government may attempt to preempt development of a shopping center in an outlying area, and the developer should be aware that in some cases such efforts have been successful. On the other hand, they should also realize that governmental powers in this respect are in no way absolute, that mere fear of competition generally will not be deemed to be, in itself, a sufficient reason to prevent development in an outlying area, and that, in general, governmental powers are indeed rather limited. Probably the greatest problem to developers as a result of city governments endeavoring to preempt mall siting concerns the time delays and expense that the developers may incur because of such governmental activities.

Notes

1. *See* notes 37-40 *infra* and accompanying text.
2. This article will not discuss antitrust implications of central city preemption on mall siting. For a consideration of antitrust implications *see Mason City Center Associates v. Mason City*, 468 F. Supp. 737 (N.D. Iowa 1979); see also Weaver & Hejna, Antitrust Liability and the Regulation of Commercial Land Uses, Shopping Centers U.S.A., Center for Urban Policy Research Conference (1979).
3. 272 U.S. 365 (1926).
4. Numerous cases exist affirming governmental refusal to zone an area so as to allow construction of a shopping center. See, e.g., *Elmhurst Nat'l Bank v. City of Chicago*, 22 Ill. 2d 396, 176 N.E.2d 771 (1961); *Paka Corp. v. City of Jackson*, 364 Mich. 122, 110 N.W.2d 620 (1961); *Schilling v. City of Midland*, 38 Mich. App. 568, 196 N.W.2d 846 (1972); *Wrigley Properties, Inc. v. City of Ladue*, 369 S.W.2d 397 (Mo. Sup. Ct. 1963); State *ex rel. Beerman v. City of Kettering*, 120 Ohio App. 309, 29 Ohio Ops. 2d 126, 201 N.E.2d 887 (1963).
5. See, e.g., *Elmhurst Nat'l Bank v. City of Chicago*, 22 Ill. 2d 396, 176 N.E. 2d 771 (1961); *Hardesty v. Board of Zoning Appeals*, 211 Md. 172, 126 A.2d 621 (1956); *Bowman v. City of Southfield*, 377 Mich. 237, 140 N.W.2d 504 (1966); *Brooklyn Plaza, Inc. v. City of Brooklyn*, 83 Ohio L. Abs. 89; 162 N.E.2d 342 (1959); *Price v. Cohen*, 213 Md. 457, 132 A.2d 125 (1957); *Wrigley Properties, Inc. v. City of Ladue*, 369 S.W.2d 397 (Mo. Sup. Cit. 1963).
6. See *Hardesty v. Board of Zoning Appeals, 211 Md. 172, 126 A.2d 621 (1956)*.
7. *Wrigley Properties, Inc. v. City of Ladue*, 369 S.W.2d 397 (Mo. Sup. Ct. 1963).
8. *Ibid.* at 402.
9. *Ibid.* at 400.
10. See also *Bolger v. Village of Mt. Prospect*, 10 Ill. N.E.2d 22 (1957); *LaSalle Nat'l Bank v. City of Chicago*, 4 Ill. 2d 253, 122 N.E.2d 519 (1954); *West Ridge, Inc. v. McNarmara*, 222 Md. 448, 160 A.2d 907 (1960).

11. See, e.g., *Scott v. City of Indian Wells*, 6 Cal. 3d 541, 492 P.2d 1137, 99 Cal. Rptr. 745 (1972) ("We are satisfied that the City of Indian Wells owes adjoining landowners who are not city residents a duty of notice to the extent given similarly situated city residents, a duty to hear their views, and a duty to consider the proposed development with respect to its effect on all neighboring property owners. We are also satisfied that adjoining landowners who are not city residents may enforce these duties by appropriate legal proceedings and have standing to challenge zoning decisions of the city which affect their property."
Id. at 549, 492 P.2d at 1142, 99 Cal. Rptr. at 750).

Koppel v. City of Fairway, 189 Kan. 710, 371 P.2d 113 (1962) ("It is true that even though two of the plaintiffs are located in an area just beyond the boundaries of the defendant city of Fairway they have, as abutting and frontage owners to the city, benefited from the past zoning ordinance and are now directly and harmfully affected by the rezoning ordinance. As property owners they are entitled to the enjoyment of their property." *Id.* at 713, 371 P.2d at 116).

Allen v., Coffel, 488 S.W.2d 671 (Mo. Ct. App. 1972) ("We understand the allegations in plaintiffs' count for declaratory relief as assertions that as owners of property outside the limits of the City of Peculiar, but contiguous to property within the boundaries of the city—which property has been rezoned by ordinances—they have a legally protectable interest, and therefore standing, to contest the validity of the ordinances by declaratory judgment. We conclude that the petition sufficiently pleads an interest which will qualify plaintiffs for relief by declaratory judgment." *Ibid.* at 674).

12. *Construction Indus. Ass'n v. City of Petaluma*, 522 F.2d 897, 906 (9th Cir. 1975), *cert. denied*, 424 U.S. 934 (1976); *Township of River Vale v. Town of Orangetown*, F.2d 684, 687 (2d Cir. 1968); *Allen v. Coffel*, 488 S.W. 2d 671 (Mo. Ct. App. 1972).

13. See, e.g., *Garner v. County of DuPage*, 8 Ill. 2d 155, 133 N.E. 2d 303 (1956).

> "This case is not the normal one where an owner of land is complaining of restrictions placed upon its use, but is the comparatively rare case in which it is claimed that corporate authorities have wrongfully permitted a use on the property of someone else. Under such circumstances we have held that for a party to have standing in a court of equity to complain about the use of another's property, he has the burden of proving that he has suffered a special damage by reason of such use which differs from that suffered by the general public."
> *Ibid.* at 158-59, 133 N.E. 2d at 304.)

14. *Hughes v. City of Peoria*, 80 Ill. App. 2d 392, 225 N.E. 2d 109 (1967).

15. *Ibid.* at 394, 225 N.E. 2d at 110.

16. *Ibid.*, 225 N.E. 2d at 110.

17. *Ibid.*, 225 N.E. 2d at 110.

18. *Ibid.*, 225 N.E. 2d at 110.

19. *Ibid.* at 936, 225 N.E. 2d at 111.

20. *Whittingham v. Village of Woodridge*, 111 Ill. App. 2d 147, 249 N.E. 2d 332 (1969).

21. *Ibid.* at 150, 249 N.E. 2d at 333.

22. *Ibid.* at 151, 249 N.E. 2d at 334.

23. See, e.g., *Whittingham v. Village of Woodbridge*, 111 Ill. App. 2d 147,

249 N.E. 2d 332 (1969); *Borough of Cresskill v. Borough of Dumont*, 15 N.J. 238, 104 A.2d 441 (1954).

24. *Whittingham v. Village of Woodbridge*, 111 Ill. App. 2d 147, 249 N.E. 2d 332 (1969).

25. *Ibid.* at 151, 249 N.E. 2d at 334.

26. *Borough of Cresskill v. Borough of Dumont*, 15 N.J. 238, 104 A.2d 441 (1954).

27. *Ibid.* at 243, 104 A.2d 445-46.

28. See, e.g., *Boise City v. Better Homes, Inc.*, 72 Idaho 441, 243 P.2d 303 (1952); *City of Highland Park v. Calder*, 269 Ill. App. 255 (1932); *City of Louisville v. Bryan S. McCoy, Inc.*, 286 S.W.2d 546 (Ky. Ct. App. 1956); *White v. City of Dallas*, 517 S.W.2d 344 (Tex. Ct. App. 1974).

29. *The Constitutionality of Local Zoning*, 79 Yale L.J. 896, 915 n.75 (1970).

30. *Ibid.*

31. See *Extraterritorial Zoning: Reflection on its Validity*, 32 Notre Dame Lawyer 367 (1957). Generally, when authorized, these powers do not extend to land located within another incorporated community.

Becker, *Municipal Boundaries and Zoning: Controlling Regional Land Development*, 1966 Wash. U.L.Q. 1, 25.

32. See, e.g., Ala. Code § 11-52-30 (1975); Ill. Rev. Stat. ch. 24, § 11-13-1 (1977); Ky. Rev. Stat. § 100.131 (1971); N.C. Gen. Stat. § 160A-360 (1977 Supp.); Okla. Stat. Ann. tit. 19, § 863.19 (West 1962). Tenn. Code Ann. § 13-711 (1973); Wis. Stat. Ann. § 62.23(7a) (West Supp. 1979-1980).

See also Ga. Code Ann. § 69-1207 (1976) (granting a county power over unincorporated areas).

33. See, e.g., Ala. Code § 11-52-30 (1975) (five miles); Ill. Rev. Stat. ch. 24, § 11-13-1 (1977) (one and one-half miles); Ky. Rev. Stat. § 100.131 (1971) (five miles); Wis. Stat. Ann. 8 62.23(7a) (a) (West Supp. 1979-1980) (three miles of a first-, second-, or third-class city; one and one-half miles of a fourth-class city or a village).

34. See, e.g., N.C. Gen. Stat. § 160A-360 (1977 Supp.) (power of city determined by its size); Wis. Stat. Ann. § 62.23(7a) (a) (West Supp. 1979) (power of city determined by its classification).

35. For an excellent discussion of the constitutionality of extraterritorial zoning, see 1966 Wash. U.L.Q. 1, 32-40.

36. See, e.g., *City of Raleigh v. Morand*, 247 N.C. 363, 100 S.E.2d 870 (1957), appeal dismissed, 357 U.S. 343 (1958).

37. See McManus, "Subsidizing Suburban Malls Hurts Our Cities," Chicago Sun-Times, (November 26, 1979), p. 26, col.1.

38. See, e.g., Exec. Order No. 12074, 43 C.F.R. 36875 (1978).

39. The formal request by local officials must include a statement indicating why local officials are concerned; evidence of city/town council or, where relevant, county supervisor of commission support; a statement establishing the link between the federal action and the development of the large commercial development; a statement describing the local officials' perception of the effect the commercial development will have on the business district; a statement illustrating local public and private actions which have been taken, which are being taken, and which will be taken to strengthen the economic vitality of existing commercial areas; and a statement indicating that local government has sought to discuss or negotiate the

concerns expressed with the developer for federal action which is in question.

40. Such studies have been requested by such cities as Duluth, Minnesota; West New York, New Jersey; New London, Connecticut; and Indio, California. See "*Behind the First Four Community Guidance Filings,*" *Today* (International Council of Shopping Centers), (March 1980), p. 1, col. 1.

41. See, e.g., *Swain v. County of Winnebago*, 111 Ill. App. 2d 458, 250 N.E.2d 439 (1969); *In re Darswan, Inc. v. Capellini*, 58 A.D.2d 892, 397 N.Y.S.2d 4 (1977); *Town of Huntington v. Town Board*, 57 Misc. 2d 821, 293 N.Y.S.2d 558 (1968); *Town of Grand Chute v. City of Appleton*, 282 N.W.2d 629 (Wis. App. 1979).

42. See, e.g., the cases cited in note 4.

43. *In re Darswan, Inc. v. Capellini*, 58 A.D.2d 892, 397 N.Y.S.2d 4 (1977).

44. Id. at 893, 397 N.Y.S.2d at 5.

45. See, e.g., *London v. Planning & Zoning Comm'm*, 149 Conn. 282, 179 A.2d 614 (1962); *Swain v. County of Winnebago* 111 Ill. A.2d 458, 250 N.E.2d 439 (1969); *Kreatchman v. Ramsburg*, 224 Md. 209, 167 A.2d 345 (1961); *Circle Lounge & Grille, Inc. v. Board of Appeal*, 324 Mass. 427, 86 N.E.2d 920 (1949); *Lehrer v. Board of Adjustment*, 137 N.J.L. 100, 58 A.2d 265, (1948); *Paolangeli v. Stevens*, 19 A.D.2d 763, 241 N.Y.S.2d 518 (1963); *In re* Lieb, 179 Pa. Super. 318, 116 A.2d 860 (1955).

46. See, e.g., *Swain v. County of Winnebago*, 111 Ill. Appl. 2d 458, 250 N.E.2d 439 (1969); *Town of Huntington v. Town Board*, 57 Misc. 2d 821, 293 N.Y.S.2d 558 (1968).

47. *Ibid.*

48. *Ibid.*

49. *Swain v. County of Winnebago*, 111 Ill. App. 2d 458, 250 N.E.2d 439 (1969).

50. *Ibid.* at 464, 250 N.E.2d at 444.

51. *Ibid.*, 250 N.E.2d at 444.

52. *Ibid.* at 460, 250 N.E.2d at 440.

53. See, e.g., *London v. Planning & Zoning Comm'n.* 149 Conn. 282, 179 A.2d 614 (1962); *Swain v. County of Winnebago*, 111 Ill. Appl. 2d 458, 250 N.E.2d 439 (1969); *Exchange Nat'l Bank v. Village of Skokie*, 86 Ill. App. 2d 12, 229 N.E.2d 552 (1967); *Kreatchman v. Ramsburg*, 224 Md. 209, 167 A.2d 345 (1961); *Cord Meyer Development Co. v. Bell Bay Drugs, Inc.*, 20 N.Y.2d 211, 282 N.Y.S.2d 259, 229 N.E.2d 44 (1967).

54. *Town of Grand Chute v. City of Appleton*, 282 N.W.2d 629 (Wis. App. 1969).

55. An 800,000 square foot mall was proposed for the town of Grand Chute, which is located approximately three miles from downtown Appleton. Under Wisconsin law cities and surrounding suburbs are to form boards to decide how an area is to be developed. Such boards have two years to render a decision. Appleton took the position that it could prevent construction of the proposed mall until the board had an opportunity to act. Although downtown Appleton is still quite strong as a shopping center, Appleton officials feared that construction of the new mall would weaken the downtown stores. *Shopping Centers Today*, March 1979.

56. 282 N.W.2d at 630.

57. *Ibid.* at 631.

Addressing the Issue of the Economic Impact of Regional Malls in Legal Proceedings[1]

MICHAEL FIX

The advent of the surburban shopping center and, later, the regional shopping mall, has transformed the location and scale of American retailing enterprises. Over the past two decades sales of shopper goods have been made with increasing frequency in surburban and exurban centers. And, until recently, the size of these commercial clusters grew consistently larger as the strip shopping center evolved into the regional mall, which in turn evolved into the superregional mall.[2]

However, as suburban shopping centers and malls began to proliferate a parallel decline in retail sales in central cities and central business districts began to take place.

These changes produced a number of identifiable effects on central cities—reduced taxes and retail employment, a more limited selection of consumer goods, and the surburban flight of professional services. It has been asserted that each can be partially explained by the intensive new economic competition between stores in the central city and the suburbs.

Before 1958, malls captured less than 5 percent of shopper goods sales. By the early 1980s one out of every three dollars spent on department store type merchandise will be spent in a mall. However, while malls and the share of sales garnered by them have increased, overall sales of shopper goods have declined during the last decade. The proportion of disposable income spent on shopper goods dropped from 14.8 percent in

1972 to 13 percent in 1979. Moreover, disposable personal income which grew in real terms by 5 percent annually prior to 1972, has grown only 2 percent in the past seven years.[3]

While overall sales have been declining gradually, sales in central business districts have been plummeting. In thirteen large SMSAs, sales in CBDs declined 47 percent between 1970 and 1979 when adjusted for inflation. Sales in CBDs located in smaller SMSAs suffered comparable and frequently larger losses.[4]

As construction of regional malls has surged in the past decade a number of major urban markets may have been overbuilt or built up to capacity. As a result, shopping mall analysts and developers today believe that the regions surrounding smaller cities—"mid markets" serving a population of around 150,000—may hold the greatest potential for the further development of regional malls.[5] This shift from more saturated markets within larger conurbations may have significant legal implications. Perhaps to an even greater extent than before, struggles surrounding the development of malls will prove to be interjurisdictional in nature, as the competitive injuries caused by the operation of regional malls will be felt most strongly by merchants in jurisdictions which are some distance from the development site. As a result, zoning—the legal instrument most commonly applied in the regulation of large-scale development—may not be available to jurisdictions which are forced to bear the economic brunt of new development.[6]

With zoning unavailable, strategies founded on other legal bases will have to be relied upon. Three fields of regulation can be used to address the relevant regional economic issues: compliance with federal grant conditions, state and federal environmental impact review requirements, and state land use and environmental laws.

The regional retail competition brought about by the proliferation of suburban malls has forced lawyers and policymakers to confront a range of questions previously unaddressed: should an economic impact rationale be used to safeguard the fiscal well-being of urban areas from competition by regional malls? When would the adoption of such a rationale constitute an unprecedented preference for the economic vitality of one geographic area over another, and when would it advance the welfare of the larger population?

This paper will describe the ways in which state and federal regulations have been relied upon to protect older urban areas from the fiscal damage purportedly inflicted by the development of regional shopping malls. It will also explore the current Administration's policies regarding the extension of federal aid to assist in the development of malls—focusing on the regulatory precedents for that policy.

Thus, the three sections of the paper will explore, in order, the use of conditions imposed on federal grants, state and federal environmental review requirements, and state land use and environmental laws as instruments for impeding or halting the development of regional shopping malls.

I. A. Restrictions on the Use of Federal Funds: Federal Economic Development Acts

Congress and agency rulemakers have placed a number of constraints on the use of federal funds which could restrict their use in the development of regional shopping malls. Among the federal programs carrying the restrictions, which apply to both private and public recipients, are: the Economic Development Act,[7] the Appalachian Regional Development Act,[8] and legislatively authorized loan and grant programs of the Farmer's Home Administration[9] and the Department of Housing and Urban Development.[10] While the motivation for the restrictions was originally to control interregional industrial and commercial movement—a policy product of Sunbelt-Frostbelt political struggles—they are also applicable to the intraregional relocation of major retail outlets.

The restrictions on the use of federal monies under the economic development acts can be grouped into two primary categories: (1) a prohibition on the use of grant funds to support proposals which would lead "to the transfer of any employment or business activity from one area to another";[11] and (2) a prohibition on the use of federal support for projects which would lead to an increase in "the availability of services or facilities in the area when there is not sufficient demand for such goods, materials, commodities, services, or facilities to employ the efficient capacity of existing competitive, commercial or industrial enterprises."[12]

There are, thus, two principal rationales for the invocation of these constraints. The first is employment related. Federal funds are to be withheld from projects which might lead to increased unemployment arising from the relocation of firms from one area to another. The second is market-related as government policy is aimed at keeping excess supply in check. Accordingly, federal support is not to be provided to projects which would lead to an oversupply of manufactured or sales goods within a market area.

Regarding employment, the development of regional shopping malls on the urban fringe in competitive market conditions leads to the transfer of sales from city stores to mall stores which can, in turn, result in a reduction in retail sales employment in the urban center. Moreover, as malls are claimed to be more labor-efficient than retail stores in downtown districts, retail employment within the regional labor market may drop as well.[13]

It has frequently been postulated that a significant proportion of the retail workers affected by relocation of central city stores to regional malls are low-wage minority employees. It is further argued that, as wages for retail workers are close to the minimum wage and that the distances to suburban malls from central cities are substantial, there will be little incentive for prior employees to commute to new, suburban locations.[14]

Federal aid may also be withheld from proposed projects when it is determined that the resulting relocation of firms might produce an excess of supplied goods, thus preventing existing commercial enterprises from operating at an efficient capacity. The regulations, then, tie the denial of federal aid to market conditions—an excess of supply over existing demand.

These two types of restrictions on the use of federal funds were recently raised in litigation over the development of a regional mall in Cumberland, Maryland. The City of Cumberland filed suit in federal court in Delaware to enforce the restrictions found in FMHA's grant program for Community Water and Waste Disposal Facilities, claiming that the primary user of the completed water main network would be a regional shopping mall and not rural residents.[15] Asserting that the mall would compete for retail sales with merchants in downtown Cumberland, the city's attorney argued that the federally financed project would result in a transfer of both employment and business activity from one area to another—namely, from the City of Cumberland to the planned regional shopping mall in outlying Lavale, Maryland. The city further maintained that the construction of the mall would lead to an increase in the availability of shopper goods where there was not sufficient demand. However, the merits of the case were not reached and the city's claims were dismissed as construction of the water main network was complete by the time the case came to trial.[16]

The thrust of the conditions on the use of federal economic development monies is consistent with recent Administration initiatives which would require the preparation of urban impact analyses when either a "significant loss of aggregate jobs" or a "significant loss of employment opportunities for minorities" is likely to result from the construction of a regional mall.[17]

Like the grant restrictions here discussed, the impact analysis authorized by the White House's Community Conservation Guidance Memorandum can also be triggered by market conditions. It authorizes the preparation of an impact analysis whenever the development of a regional mall would have "a significant adverse impact on future cost and availability of retail goods and services" within the central city.[18] The construction of regional and superregional malls leads to large increases in the quantity of shopper goods available in a consumer market area—increases which frequently are not accompanied by a concomitant rise in the demand for those goods. Intensive competition between the newer malls, which are often more accessible and provide more amenities, and older central city stores results. This competition leads, in turn, to the failure or relocation of downtown stores and a reduction in the availability of consumer goods within the central city.

Another similarity between the President's Community Conservation Policy and the restrictions imposed on federal assistance under the economic development acts discussed herein is the type of complex economic questions which are posed by each. Determining market size, the efficient capacity of existing commercial enterprises, and the economic and employment impacts of relocating enterprises, all require difficult, speculative and expensive analyses—analyses which can be beyond the ability of some lawyers and judges.[19]

Indeed, the problems raised by these regulations apply to each of the rapidly proliferating number of laws which mandate impact assessment—how accurately can we forecast the future effects of development in dynamic market and environmental conditions? What level of resources should private and public agencies devote to knowing the future, and how certain can we be of those results?[20]

It would be misleading to imply that conditions attaching to the receipt of federal economic development aid will prove very fruitful for city administrators or attorneys opposing the development of regional shopping malls. While the use of economic development loans and grants to aid the construction of malls may be increasing—particularly in the rehabilitation of central business districts—federal economic development funds are rarely employed in supporting suburban regional shopping malls. However, as of January 1, 1980, the implementing regulations for the two sources of federal aid which are most relevant to the development of malls—the Department of Transportation's Federal Highway Administration Aid Program[21] and the Environmental Protection Agency's Construction Grants Program[22]—contained no comparable funding restrictions.

The absence of such constraints in these acts is not surprising as the construction of highways, highway exchanges, wastewater treatment plants and water and sewer lines, can by its very nature, lead to the transfer of population and development from one area to another. Imposing such constraints could impede the operations of both programs as few grants would be immune from long and expensive legal challenges.

However, a number of the components of the President's urban policy, among them the White House Community Conservation guidelines, have been designed to place all federally funded projects under scrutiny to determine their economic impact on central cities. It is to the current Administration's urban policy that I now turn.

B. Restrictions on the Use of Federal Funds:
The President's Urban Policy

In December, 1979, the Administration issued its Community Conservation policy as a White House Memorandum to all Agencies.[23] The policy creates a number of new obligations for federal agencies. They arise when agency officials consider actions leading directly to the construction of large developments which would "clearly and demonstrably weaken existing communities, particularly their established business districts."[24]

The Community Conservation policy requires that federal agencies prepare urban analyses whenever:

(1) a formal request has been submitted by the chief elected official of a central city or suburb with an existing and commercial district,

(2) a federal action as defined by NEPA regulations is pending,[25] and

(3) the federal action is likely to lead to "a large commercial development inside or outside the boundaries of the affected community."[26]

The Urban Impact Analyses are to determine "the consequences (positive and negative) of the pending federal action on the existing business districts of the communities requesting it, as well as on the community itself. They should also indicate the general impact of the pending federal action on the surrounding metropolitan area and the area where the federal action is to take place."[27] Thus the analysis would explore the long-term effects of federal actions on two areas: (1) the region in which proposed development is to be located, and (2) the community which asked for the analysis—presumably an aging, neighboring city which feels economically threatened.

Should the analysis reveal "significant negative impacts"—a reduction in aggregate and/or minority employment opportunities, a reduction in the fiscal tax base, or a reduction in the availability of retail goods or services—then the federal agency is to "consider appropriate modifications or mitigating options consistent with relevant statutes, the Agencys mission and the President's national policies."[28]

The Community Conservation program represents a logical extention of the Administration's urban policy. One of the objectives of that policy has been to assure that federal programs do not adopt conflicting strategies toward reviving the nation's declining urban areas. To insure that diverse grant programs are pursuing a coherent approach toward the economic development of older commercial districts, the policy requires that federal agencies analyze the urban and community impact of all major federal initiatives. Of course, one of the most profound impacts to be evaluated is the economic effect that projects subsidized with federal funds have on local governments.

To date, the policy has been implemented primarily by executive action through four Executive Orders issued on August 16, 1978.[29] Those mandated, among other things, that:

(1) a process be developed for analyzing the urban and community impact of all major federal initiatives,[30]

(2) central business districts be given first consideration in the location of new federal facilities,[31] and

(3) an Interagency Coordinating Council be created comprised of heads of major federal agencies involved in the implementation of federal urban and regional policy. The mission of the Council is to work to conserve and strengthen America's communities.[32]

At the time they were issued, opponents of the Community Conservation Guidelines claimed that they represented a vast expansion of government power. These claims were inaccurate, as the policy did not represent an unparalleled extension of government economic authority by either state or federal standards. As I have shown, a number of federal economic development acts require that federal support be withheld from developments which would lead to an interregional or intraregional transfer of large-scale commercial enterprises where that shift would result in a decline in economic or employment conditions in older urbanized areas.

One important way in which the constraints found in the economic development acts resemble those proposed by the Community Conservation policy is that neither proposes to create a federal veto over planned regional shopping malls. Rather, the Urban Conservation guidelines only limit federal subsidization of malls which would "clearly weaken established business districts."[33] The restraints found in the regulations of the economic development acts also limit federal subsidization of private investment rather than restrict private initiative—regardless of the interregional or intraregional impact.

However, some minor distinctions between the restrictions imposed by the economic development regulations and the Community Conservation Guidelines should be noted. Federal Economic Development funds can be withheld, it appears, on the basis of an *a priori* prediction of their economic effects. However, the Urban Conservation Policy requires that an impact analysis be prepared before funds are withheld and that the review only be *considered* before a grant is made.[34]

The stringency of federal policies in the regulation of malls pales in comparison to the regulatory authority exercised by a number of states. Recognizing the serious social, economic, and environmental consequences of large-scale developments, these states have enacted laws which provide for much more stringent regulation of regional and superregional malls[35] than any current or pending federal law or policy. For example, Vermont's Act 250 authorizes regional review and permitting of proposed developments of over ten acres.[36]

The extension of state and federal environmental impact review requirements to include economic impacts—among them those imposed on central cities by large-scale commercial developments—is further evidence of the consistency of the Administration's Urban Conservation policy with other regulations presently in force. Indeed, one potential problem posed by the Community Conservation Guidelines may be in the extent to which they duplicate current impact evaluation requirements rather than the degree to which they depart from them.

A number of administrative actions taken in advance of the promulgation of the Community Conservation program were already anticipating the policies embodied in the forthcoming guidelines. For example, in November 1979 the Secretary of Transportation announced that federal funding had been disapproved for a 13.5-mile stretch of interstate highway intended for suburban Dayton, Ohio, because the proposed highway would conflict with the President's urban policy by taking jobs and business away from the city.[37]

While the Community Conservation program advanced by the President may not represent a significant expansion of federal authority, the fact that it has been promulgated by Executive Order and by interagency memoranda distinguishes it from other, legislatively enacted, forecasting requirements—the National Environmental Policy Act, for example.[38] Without undertaking a major study of the constitutionality of the President's power to implement his urban policy through executive actions, a few observations should be made on the use of this political strategy.

During a period of strong antiregulatory sentiment, even rules aimed only at federal agencies could fail to clear legislative hurdles and require summary action on the part of the Executive. Thus, the promulgation of the urban policy by Executive Order and the Community Conservation Guidelines by interagency memoranda fits neatly within a political tradition of relying on executive action to enact programs which would be likely to meet with substantial Congressional opposition. In this case, that opposition would most likely derive from a collective antipathy to new federal regulations *per se*, rather than to strong opposition to the goal of increasing the degree of consistency among federal aid programs.

The selection of Executive Orders as mechanisms for implementing the President's Urban Policy may be explained in another manner. The approach adopted by the policy consists of mandates "which are directed to, and govern actions of, government officials and agencies" rather than orders directed at private citizens.[39] In addition, the objectives of the President's urban policy can be seen as an extension of prior legislative enactments. Thus, that policy appears consistent with clearly stated legislative action in two areas: (1) the importance of determining in advance primary and secondary impacts of federal actions, and (2) the importance of strengthening urban economies. The latter has been the objective of a wide range of economic and social programs which have been enacted over the past several decades, among them the Urban Development Action Grant Program,[40] the Economic Development Administration Act of 1965[41] and the like. In this sense, the President's urban conservation policy can be viewed as an attempt to preserve the Congress's past financial investment in the nation's central cities.

II. A. Analyzing the Impact of Regional Malls on Central Cities— The Use of State and Federal EIS Laws

A. NEPA and Economic Impact

The importance of anticipating the wide range of primary and secondary impacts which flow from governmental action received Congressional acknowledgement with the enactment of the National Environmental Policy Act of 1969.[42] Among other things, the act required that responsible federal agencies prepare a detailed statement of projected environmental effects for major federal actions significantly affecting the quality of the human environment. In the wake of the federal act, fifteen states have passed their own "little NEPAs" requiring the preparation of environmental impact statements for developments of varying types and sizes.[43] These laws have imposed demands on states similar to those imposed on the federal government by NEPA.

The history, purpose, effect and problems of the federal act and the various state acts have been fully and frequently documented over the past several years.[44] Those efforts will not be duplicated here. Rather, I intend to explore the narrower question: to what extent have federal and state EIS requirements been interpreted to require fiscal and economic impact analyses for developments likely to have a regional economic effect? And, in particular, when must a federal EIS include data on the potential effect of a regional mall on a central business district within the same consumer market area?

The EIS requirement is raised in two principal ways in administrative and legal controversies—either the need for an EIS is contested or the adequacy of a prepared EIS is challenged. The issue of extra-jurisdictional fiscal impact of development typically falls within the latter category.

An application for a federal permit, license or grant can trigger federal environmental review requirements. It should be noted that the scope of the resulting review may extend beyond the element of the project for which federal permits or funds are being requested. Thus, an applicant for a Section 404 wetlands permit[45] may find that the regional fiscal impact of his proposed commercial development must be taken up in an environmental impact statement in order to obtain the necessary permit. While the need for an EIS may be commonly accepted when the potential physical consequences of development could be significant, the need to submit data on the regional fiscal effects of large-scale projects remains less clear cut and less widely acknowledged.

At first blush it appears that the drafters of the federal EIS regulations considered them to be a necessary supplement to a kind of economic and fiscal impact analysis which was already being satisfactorily accomplished.[46] And, since the enactment of NEPA in 1969, there has been forceful opposition from some legal quarters to the introduction of economic issues into the environmental review process. For example, a number of courts have ruled that injuries to a petitioner's economic interest do not fall within the purview of NEPA. Thus a claimant who pleads only economic injury will not be found to have any injury "within the zone of interests protected by NEPA."[47] Moreover, claims of environmental harm which are subordinate to, or which cloak underlying economic motives, will be either dismissed by courts or weighted accordingly.[48]

However, economic injury which can be linked to physical environmental impacts or to the secondary effects of growth can trigger the EIS requirement. Guidelines for EIS preparation issued to federal agencies by the Council on Environmental Quality raise expressly the fiscal issues triggered by growth:

Secondary or indirect as well as primary or direct consequences for the environment should be included in the analysis. Many major federal actions, in particular those that involve the construction or licensing of infrastructure investments, (e.g. highways, airports, sewer systems, water resource projects, etc.), stimulate or induce secondary effects in the form of associated investments and *changed patterns of social and economic activities*. Such secondary effects, through their impacts on existing community facilities and activities, through inducing new facilities and activities, or through changes in natural conditions, may often be even more substantive than the primary effects of the original action itself. (author's italics)[49]

It appears then, that growth, which is a secondary impact, can compel the drafting of an EIS even in cases where the primary impact of proposed development would not.[50] In most instances the physical aspects of growth cannot be disassociated from its fiscal aspects—the "associated investments" and "changed patterns of economic activities" referred to in the CEQ quidelines. Shifts in the character of communities are accompanied by outlays for the construction of new infrastructure which in turn result in the commitment of scarce local resources over extended periods of time. Additionally growth in one area can lead to economic decline in others, resulting in reduced tax revenues and steady or increasing costs.

Accordingly, most courts and commentators recognize that the fiscal impacts of population growth—in particular the effect of proposed development on the cost and provision of utilities and services—are necessary components of many environmental impact statements.[51]

However, it is interesting to find that most of the decisions dealing with the secondary impact of growth reach the issue of the adequacy or necessity of an EIS by using a somewhat indirect path. They hold that the growth-induced effects on public services are to be considered one of several physical consequences of development.[52] They focus, then, on the results of sudden growth—the congested secondary road or the overcrowded classroom—and not on the cause: an inadequate local revenue base.

This reliance on linking fiscal effects to the physical consequences of development can be found elsewhere in NEPA litigation. In *City of Rochester v. U.S. Postal Services*,[53] the U.S. Court of Appeals for the Second Circuit found that the transfer of a regional postal facility from downtown Rochester, New York, to a neighboring suburb could lead to the suburban migration of up to 1,400 postal employees and/or a loss of job opportunities for inner-city residents. In each instance, the Court held that the consequences of the transfer could be ". . .economic and physical deterioration in the (downtown Rochester) community."[54] In addition, the Court found that the abandonment of the main post office could contribute to an "atmosphere of urban decay and blight."[55]

Perhaps the most significant holding in *Rochester* is its finding that the Post Office's preliminary assessment of the need for an EIS addressed only the impact of the transfer on the suburban jurisdiction and failed to consider its effect on the City of Rochester. Thus, the Court holds that the economic impact of transferred development on the abandoned jurisdiction must be considered along with the environmental impact on the site surrounding future development. The application of the holding in *Rochester* to the economic issues raised in the siting of regional shopping malls is clear. The competitive injuries which malls inflict are felt by merchants in political jurisdictions beyond the range of immediate environmental harm and outside the area of analysis typically covered by an EIS. *Rochester* extends the coverage of the EIS to geographically remote jurisdictions in which environmental damage in the form of urban blight arises as a result of economic injury.

In another federal case from New York, *Dalsis v. Hills*,[56] a group of downtown merchants were granted standing to bring an action under NEPA to petition for the drafting of an EIS for a downtown mall. Despite the fact that they would be in direct competition with the new mall, their claimed injury was found to be within the zone of interests protected by the Act as they also alleged that they were seeking to "avert blight and deterioration" of the central business district of the town. Thus, a well-grounded claim of physical/environmental degradation was found sufficient to grant standing to plaintiffs whose financial interests would have otherwise placed them outside the scope of NEPA's protection.

Dalsis is interesting for another reason. Unlike the bulk of the cases which address the issue of the secondary impact of development which have been referred to herein, the development in *Dalsis* was a privately financed commercial venture. In each of the other cases the development in question was being built by and for the federal government. In *Dalsis*, two "major federal actions" were involved: (1) HUD's approval of an urban renewal project—granted with the knowledge that a private developer would build a shopping mall, and (2) federal funding for the demolition of substandard buildings on the proposed site. Plainly, the "major federal action" designation in *Dalsis* is readily applicable to the development of shopping malls which are privately financed if there is a significant nexus between the project and prior federal efforts.

It appears, then, that the economic impact of the development of a regional shopping mall could trigger the drafting of an EIS under federal law. However, the conditions under which a petition for an EIS could succeed are many. First, there must be a "major federal action" which will foreseeably lead to growth. The creation of federally funded interchanges off a highway built wholly or partially with federal funds, a federally assisted extension of water and sewer lines, any direct federal grant or state grant made up of federal funds, or even the grant of water quality or wetlands permits could be seen as "major federal actions."

Second, there should be some tie between claims of economic injury and potential physical effect upon the environment. Thus, congested streets, unmaintained public buildings, overcrowded classrooms, and decaying infrastructure—the tangible products of insufficient services or inadequate funding to provide for services—should be amply illustrated. As a result of the decision in the *Rochester* case, the area of physical deterioration need not be restricted to the area immediately adjacent to the development site. It could include a separate geographical jurisdiction within the same consumer market area which might decay as a result of the planned action. And, according to *Dalsis*, the competitive posture of opponents of the mall need not prevent them from obtaining standing as long as they can make a credible claim of physical deterioration.

Other problems remain for opponents of the development of malls who hope to use NEPA. Some courts have found that developments which do not, per se, lead to growth—dams, for example—are immune from claims that their construction will lead to increased population pressures.[57] Thus, the foreseeability of population growth brought about by the construction of malls may have to be demonstrated.

The conduct of third parties—state, local and regional officials who have review power over the development—may influence the extent to which courts acknowledge the foreseeability of growth. The greater the number of intervening parties—local zoning boards, regional planning commissions and the like—the more speculative is the potential for growth, and the less likely are courts to call for the preparation of an EIS.

In summary, the effort to obtain an order calling for a federal EIS evaluating the economic impact of regional shopping malls on central cities can require that a maze of conditions be met. However, the path through that maze has recently been substantially simplified by a number of legal decisions, among them *Dalsis* and *Rochester*.

B. Economic Impact and State Environmental Impact Requirements

While many state environmental impact review statutes simply restate federal objectives, a number depart from the federal formula and derive independent standards for evaluating the effects of large-scale developments. This section of the paper will focus on the use of New York's Environmental Conservation Law[58] and the regulations promulgated under it[59] to prompt an analysis of the economic need for regional shopping malls within a designated consumer market area.

In 1975, the New York State legislature passed a broad environmental conservation act which required an environmental impact statement for every state and local agency action which might have a significant effect on the environment. "Action" was defined by the statute to include: (1) projects or activities directly undertaken by an agency or those involving the issuance of a law, permit, license, or certificate and (2) policy, regulations and procedure making.[60]

On June 22, 1979, the Commissioner of the State Department of Environmental Conservation approved the application of the Pyramid Company to build an 850,000 square foot mall in the Town of New Hartford outside of Utica, New York. Permits for the mall were approved for three reasons—each adequately documented in a state EIS and each critical to the agency's holding. They were: (1) the economic need for the mall counter-balanced and mitigated its competitive impact on other surrounding shopping areas, including downtown Utica; (2) the success of efforts undertaken to avert environmental harm, and (3) the absence of any feasible alternative site.[61]

When it was initially considered in 1978, the proposed Utica Mall was rejected and the necessary permits denied by the Commissioner of the Department of Environmental Conservation who wrote that:

> . . . the record in this case reflects a conjectural estimation of a business opportunity, and risk calculation, which falls far short of demonstrating a convincing public need, or necessity, for this project.[62]

The Commissioner's decision was consistent with the New York State law elaborating the required elements of an environmental impact statement. That law mandates that the first factor to be addressed in any environmental statement is "A concise description of the proposed action, its purpose and *need*."[63]

Thus, after the decisions in the Utica Mall case it appeared that New York law required that an EIS address the question: does sufficient demand exist in the consumer market area to support a regional shopping mall? According to state law, then, the issue of unsatisfied market demand could be interpreted as being preeminently important. The meaning and implications of the Utica holding can be illustrated by administrative interpretations or state regulations in Vermont which found regional fiscal impacts to be of paramount importance.

Economic need as advanced in the Utica decision focuses on an unmet demand—leakage from the market brought about by the unavailability of goods. Unsatisfied demand can be used to justify the development of a regional mall regardless of the resulting fiscal impact felt by central city merchants and by the city economy. However, evidence of substantial unmet demand—typically demonstrated by market leakage—is usually an indication that competitive injury will be mitigated.

The analysis undertaken in demonstrating fiscal impact under Vermont's Act 250 is somewhat different from this test of market need. Under the Vermont statute, if sufficient evidence were introduced to demonstrate: (1) that the mall would make existing stores noncompetitive; (2) that a migration of city retailers to outlying suburban malls and a closing of stores in the CBD would be likely to ensue; (3) that there would be a resulting drop in property taxes in the city; and (4) that a significant reduction in the provision of public services would result; then a proposed development would probably be disapproved regardless of the level of unsatisfied consumer demand that would result. However, it should again be noted that there is probably a positive correlation between mitigation of competitive impact and leakage from the market.

The Hearing Officer's Report, which was appended to the Commissioner's decision, found that the Utica-Rome area did not have a "full-line conventional department store," and that 14 percent of the total sales dollars available for the purchase of department store type merchandise was either flowing out of the consumer market, not being spent, or diverted to other purposes.[64]

In arriving at his decision, the Commissioner concluded that there was no correlation between vacancies found in strip commercial developments and the market demand calculated to exist for the proposed mall. He also concluded that the development of the mall would have the positive outcome of spurring competition between existing merchants.[65]

In August of 1979 the Department of Environmental Conservation held hearings on the development of another proposed regional shopping mall—this one to be located in the town of Henrietta, on the outskirts of Rochester, New York.

Before its withdrawal from the controversy, the City of Rochester submitted a memorandum of law to the Department of Environmental Conservation claiming that the applicant's EIS was "legally deficient" and "substantively defective."[66] The city argued that the EIS failed to adequately discuss the need for the proposed mall and the social and economic impact of the mall upon the City of Rochester and the region.[67]

The City's memorandum relied on two economic studies which concluded:

> The sales and resulting taxes generated by the proposed Marketplace Mall would not be new sales to the Rochester region, but, rather, would be sales merely transferred from existing locations in the Rochester area, primarily the Rochester Central Business District.[68]

The studies found that the mall would not generate any substantial increase in sales revenues within the region, that the proposed mall would create a surplus of department store space in the area and, thus, that no market need for the project could be demonstrated.[69] Accordingly, the city claimed that permission to develop the proposed mall should be withheld under the rationale of the Utica decision.

The decision on the Marketplace Mall was handed down on December 6, 1979 by the Commissioner of the Department of Environmental Conservation.[70] All relevant state permits as well as the project's environmental impact statement were approved. Three relevant findings of fact and law can be found in the decision which illuminate the outcome of the case:

1. The Commissioner's decision states that the degree to which social and economic impacts of a proposed development are to be taken into account in reviewing an application for permits and an EIS under the State Environmental Quality Review Law "varies directly with the significance of the purely environmental considerations. Thus the greater the potential adverse economic effect, or the more valuable the affected resources, the greater is the scrutiny which must be brought to bear upon social and economic factors."[71] As the Commissioner found that the construction and operation of the mall would have minimal adverse environmental effects, economic considerations were not to be afforded much weight in the final analysis.[72]

2. The conclusion of the accompanying Hearing Report stated that marketing surveys conducted by the applicant had determined that the mall "would be successful, that is, economically viable." In addition the report found that the public had expressed a desire for a regional shopping center "both directly and indirectly through government."[73]

3. The Commissioner found the degree of economic hardship suffered by the merchants in the City of Rochester and the region to be irrelevant to the outcome of the decision as loss of sales from one area to another was the result of market competition, and "the Department will not intrude its judgment in matters which involve open competition in the operation of the free market system of our economy."[74]

It appears that the manner in which the Commissioner's decision and the Hearing Report sidestep the question of the relevance of market need as a criterion for approval of regional commercial enterprises effectively eliminates it as a relevant consideration in future cases.

The Hearing Report equated need with the potential economic viability of the mall (the probability that it will turn a profit) not with the existence of a market void as evidenced by widespread leakage from the consumer market area as was the case in Utica. Accordingly, the relative impact of the proposed mall on the retail sales of existing commercial outlets in the region and surrounding metropolitan areas can easily be discounted—whether the extent of the loss is 3 percent or 20 percent. It seems that the scale of these competitive effects has now been ruled to be largely irrelevant, even as an indicator of the existence of leakage from the market. In the future it appears that a demonstration of the potential economic viability of the mall itself, not the regional network of commercial outlets as a whole, will be sufficient to demonstrate market need.

III. State Land Use and Environmental Laws and Economic Impact

Within the past decade a number of states have enacted land use and environmental laws which provide state and local governments with a tool for regulating the siting of regional shopping malls. Two principal rationales can and have been invoked under these acts for questioning the proposed development of individual malls.

The first is "environmental"—focusing on site- or pollution-related effects of the construction and operation of the project. Site-related impacts include, for example, the creation of highway access points for road systems leading to the mall, or the disturbance of critical environmental areas. The pollution-related effects would encompass direct and indirect pollution sources, which could include individual stores within the center—dry cleaning stores, for example—or the center itself when viewed as a generator of traffic congestion and increased auto emissions.

The second rationale for government regulation of the siting of large-scale commercial development is economic and is associated with the social and political objective of mitigating the negative fiscal impacts of sprawl. Regional competitive effects are projected by market analysis, and the resulting impacts on the capacity of local governments within the region to adequately fund public services is assessed. Permitting decisions are these based in whole or in part on the outcome of that analysis.

One state law which has been interpreted and applied in this manner is Vermont's Land Use and Environmental Law—Act 250.[75] Enacted in 1970, the Act was initially considered to be primarily an environmental law. However, when it was later amended in 1973 it was given a stronger growth management emphasis to make it more effective in limiting sprawl.

The Act vests the state and nine district environmental commissions, which are charged with its implementation, with a measure of power which is rare if not unique by national standards, as each of the commissions has been granted the power of substantive review leading to approval or disapproval of proposed projects.[76]

The applicability of Act 250 to interjurisdictional controversies involving the fiscal impact of outlying shopping malls on central cities was demonstrated in a recent decision announced by District Environmental Commission Number 4, denying a development permit for a proposed mall in Chittenden County.

In 1977, the Pyramid Company of Burlington filed an application to build an enclosed shopping mall in the Town of Williston in Chittenden County, Vermont, on a site located about six miles from the central business district of Burlington. The mall was to include two department stores, eighty smaller shops and twenty restaurants, and was to provide a total of 440,000 square feet of commercial space.

As the overall project involved more than ten acres, a land use permit had to be obtained under the strictures of Act 250. After lengthy hearings the District Environmental Commission found that the project failed to conform with four of the ten statutory criteria which are used to assess the appropriateness of proposed developments. Seven separate objections to the mall were listed in the Environmental Commission's report. They included:

(1) its creation of excessive highway congestion,
(2) the imposition of an unreasonable burden on Burlington's fiscal ability to provide municipal services,
(3) the noncompliance of the mall with any duly adopted capability and development plans under Act 250,
(4) the reliance of the mall on central sewage facilities, coupled with the fact that Williston had no capital program or plan,
(5) the added cost of public services occasioned by the mall,
(6) the creation of an excessive and uneconomic demand on the region's highways by the mall, and
(7) the nonconformance of the project with a duly adopted local or regional plan.[77]

To a large degree, the decision rested on the issue of the economic impact of the mall on the surrounding region and on the City of Burlington. The Commission takes a philosophical tack in explaining its use of an economic rationale for denying a development permit to a project which met all physical environmental standards. They state:

The applicant has made a substantial effort with the proposed project to see that it would satisfy those criteria which people frequently refer to as "environmental." Considerable thought has been given to the elimination of water pollution, to landscaping, and to energy conservation. There are, however, broader environmental concerns which we are charged to consider under Act 250. Webster defines environment as "the aggregate of the social and cultural conditions that influence the life of an individual or community." It is in this sense that the economic impact of the proposed Pyramid development is so central to the matter before us.[78]

The Commission projected little future growth in either population or per capita income in Chittenden County, and found that the construction of a 440,000 square foot mall would result in an oversupply of space in 1978 which would remain unabsorbed five years later in 1983. It also found that 40.1 percent of the total sales potential of Burlington merchants, or $25 million, would be transferred to the mall if it were completed by 1978.[79] As the assessed value of property is a function of its income or rental value, and as the rental value of shopper space is a function of sales, then a resulting reduction in sales would result in a decline in the assessed value of rental space. The Commission projected that the transfer of retail sales would lead to a 10 to 14 percent reduction in Burlington's property tax base in 1978.[80]

In holding that the Pyramid Mall would impose an unreasonable burden on Burlington's ability to provide municipal services, the Commission noted that projected tax losses would not be accompanied by any significant reduction in the demand for services funded by those revenues. The Commission further noted that the city was already operating at a staffing level which was approximately 15 percent below that of other no-growth cities of similar size in the Northeast.[81]

The Commission advances as a test of the reasonableness of the burden imposed on a political jurisdiction, "whether a municipality may expect to receive back benefits from the development, either immediate or deferred, which approach its costs."[82] The "unreasonable burden" test is not only to be applied to the jurisdiction which has attracted the mall but to each jurisdiction in the consumer market area which may lose a significant percentage of retail sales to it.

Again, the Act can only be used to deny or condition construction of a mall when losses in retail areas are so great as to shift tax revenues to areas with relatively low service demand and away from areas with high service demand. The decision states:

> . . .the impact on competing private entities is irrelevant to our analysis under Act 250 unless it also can be shown that there is a resultant adverse economic impact on the ability or capacity of a municipality or other governmental entity to provide public services.[83]

The decision is also significant because it holds that permits may not only be denied when development imposes economic service costs, but also when it erodes the fiscal base of a municipality. Thus, the parochial decisions of local legislatures which stand to accrue the windfall tax benefits generated by the construction and operation of a mall cannot

determine the fiscal future of other local governments which could be
"wiped out" by that decision.

One important fiscal issue was not resolved by the Environmental
Commission's decision. Can an unreasonable burden be found when lost
local revenues are replaced by state assistance—when increased state
assistance is not offset by increased state revenues provided by the proposed project? In the case of the Pyramid Mall, Burlington's impaired ability
to meet local education expenses would be largely offset by increased state
aid. As the operation of the mall would not provide significant state
revenues to offset the increased level of subsidization due Burlington
under state education formulas, reduced aid would have to be provided to
other municipalities across the state. The decision states:

> Assuming that the legislature maintains the same relative level of funding as in
> 1977, the difference between the increased aid to Burlington and the decreased
> aid to Williston would result in reduced aid to all other municipalities in Ver-
> mont other than those receiving the minimum level of state aid to education.[84]

However, as no municipalities came forward to argue that such
reduced aid did constitute an unreasonable burden on their ability to provide educational services, no finding could be made on the matter. Thus
the issue of the existence of an unreasonable burden when lost local
revenues are replaced with state aid—making all or many jurisdictions
worse off—has yet to be fully resolved under Act 250.

Conclusion

The logical concluding question is: Are regional malls which are
welcomed by tax-hungry local officials now more vulnerable to challenges
made under the state and federal regulations based on projected fiscal impact? The answer, I believe, is yes.

The most effective weapon in the legal arsenal of opponents of the
development of regional shopping malls may be the new White House
Community Guidance regulations. Assuming that the requisite political
will existed within a given Administration, the Community Conservation
directive could easily be put to use to delay or halt any mall which requires a significant federal action. Moreover, the reach of federal
highway and water and sewer construction grants programs is wide, and
the control that can be exercised through them of large-scale commercial
developments is substantial. Thus, the economic impact reviews prepared
by federal officials within the Department of Housing and Urban
Development could prove politically as well as analytically persuasive.

It appears that the Community Conservation Guidance review will be available to all existing retail districts, not just those in central cities and not just those that are financially distressed. The only type of commercial location which will not fall within its prophylactic coverage will be the undeveloped suburban or exurban community which is proposing to build a shopping mall. Thus, it could be the case that a suburban area with a thriving commercial district could trigger an impact assessment for a mall to be built with federal aids in a distressed central city.

One result of the issuance of the White House directive may be a limiting of the usefulness of the funding conditions which attach to the economic development acts that have been discussed. It should be reiterated, however, that where these conditions come into play, they may be interpreted to *mandate* that federal categorical grant funds not be used to support developments that lead to a decline in employment or a surplus in the availability of retail goods within a given consumer market. This should be contrasted with the White House memorandum, which only requires that an impact review be performed in response to a properly prepared request but does not require that the results influence federal action.

The environmental and land use acts taken up in this paper will provide less certain aid to the opponent of regional shopping malls. The use of Federal Environmental Impact Statement requirements to raise the fiscal issues of regional mall development remains largely unexplored legal terrain, despite the fact that a number of recent decisions appear to be taking the law into the area of economic impact. At the state level, we noted, state officials in New York recently made far less effective use of that state's environmental review law in assessing the regional economic impact of shopping malls than they had in prior cases. The recent decisions departed in subtle but important ways from earlier rulings which implied that regional demand analyses could be heavily weighted in the approval process for proposed malls.

Although District Environmental Commission Number 4's decision in the *Pyramid vs. Burlington* decision has been appealed by the applicant to state district court, it appears at this time that the strongest regulatory mechanism available for raising and deciding mall-siting questions on economic issues has been Vermont's Act 250. While the fiscal orientation of the act may make it *sui generis* from a national perspective, Vermont is not alone in having strong statutory authority for regulating regional shopping malls. Other resource-oriented states, principally Hawaii, Florida, Maine and Oregon, have all enacted state laws which regulate the location of large scale commercial enterprises with differing levels of precision and stringency.

Notes

1. Prepared under a contract between the Urban Institute and the U.S. Department of Housing and Urban Development, this paper was given at a conference, Shopping Centers USA, jointly sponsored by the Center for Urban Policy Research of Rutgers University and the U.S. Department of Housing and Urban Development.

The author would like to thank Thomas Muller of the Urban Institute for his guidance and assistance in the research and writing of this paper.

2. The Urban Land Institute, *Dollars And Cents of Shopping Centers*, eds., Washington, DC, (1968, 1974, 1977).

3. cf., T. Muller, "Regional Malls and Central City Retail Sales—An Overview," The Urban Institute, (1979) pps. 7-11. (Prepared for Shopping Centers USA Conference).

4. *Ibid*. pps. 20-23.

5. F. Spink, Jr. "Downtown Malls: Prospects, Design, Constraints." The Urban Land Institute, (1979), p. 5. (Prepared for Shopping Centers USA Conference).

6. For a detailed treatment of the use of zoning to regulate competition, cf. C. Weaver and C. Duerksen, "Central District Planning and the Control of Outlying Shopping Centers." 14 Urb. L. Ann. 57 (1977).

7. The Economic Development Act, 42 USC 3211 (1970); the Act's implementing regulations, found at 13 F.R. Section 309.3 state:

EDA will not extend financial assistance which will assist establishments relocating from one area to another. . .

"Relocation" means the transferring of jobs from one area to another with EDA assistance.

"From one area to another" means from one labor area of the country to another labor area of the country. However, projects relocating within a labor area and resulting in the loss of existing jobs are not eligible to receive EDA financial assistance. . .

. . .Jobs may be transferred by

(1) Closing an establishment in one area and opening a new establishment in another area, or

(2) Expanding an existing establishment in a new area and reducing the number of jobs in the original location or in any area where the expanded establishment conducts operations. . .

(3) EDA financial assistance is not prohibited for the expansion of an existing business entity through the establishment of a new branch, affiliate, or subsidiary which will not result in an increase in unemployment in the area of original location or in any other area where such entity conducts business operations. However, EDA will not extend financial assistance if the Secretary has reason to believe that such branch, affiliate, or subsidiary is being established

with the intention of closing down the operations of the existing business entity in the area of its original location or in any other area where it conducts such operations.

8. The Appalachian Regional Development Act of 1965, 40 USC Ap. Section 224 (b) states:

. . .No financial assistance shall be authorized under this Act to be used (1) to assist establishments relocating from one area to another; (2) to finance the cost of industrial plants, commercial facilities, machinery, working capital, or other industrial facilities or to enable plant subcontractors to undertake work theretofore performed in another area by other subcontractors or contractors. . .

9. 7 F.R. Section 1823.453 implementing the Community Water and Wastewater Facilities Grant Program of the Farmer's House Administration states that grant funds will not be used:

. . .For any proposal which is calculated to or likely to result in an increase in the production goods, materials, or commodities, services, or facilities, to employ the efficient capacity of existing competitive commercial or industrial enterprises, unless such financial or other assistance will not have an adverse effect upon existing competitive enterprises in the area.

10. The Community Development Act of 1977, PL 95-128 Section 119 (1) states:

. . .No assistance may be provided under this section for projects intended to facilitate the relocation of industrial or commercial plants or facilities from one area to another, unless the Secretary finds that such relocation does not significantly and adversely affect the unemployment or economic base of the area from which such industrial or commercial plant or facility is to be relocated. . .

11. See note 7, e.g.
12. See note 7, e.g. The federal regulations implementing the Economic Development Act state:

EDA will not extend financial assistance which will assist establishments relocating from one area to another." (13.F.R. Section 309.3).

A critical definitional clause declares that:

From one area to another means from one labor area of the country to another labor area of the country. However projects relocating within a labor area and resulting in the loss of existing jobs are not eligible to receive EDA financial assistance. (13.F.R. Section 309.3).

The language of the regulations neatly fits intraregional as well as interregional shifts. Thus, they would be applied to the relocation of a national chain department store from the central business district of an aging central city to a mall in the surrounding suburbs.

13. See note 3, pps. 18-20.

14. *Ibid.*

15. *Mayor and City Council of Cumberland v. John D. Daniello*, No. (D. Del., 1979).

16. *Ibid.*

17. The White House, Community Conservation Guidance, Memorandum to All Agencies, (December, 1979), pps. 5-7.

18. *Ibid.*

19. cf. R. Posner, "The Economic Approach to Law," 53 Tx. L. Rev. 757 (1975).

20. cf. F. Anderson, *NEPA In The Courts*, John Hopkins University Press, (1973).

21. 23 USC Section—*et seq*.

22. 42 USC Section 1857 *et. seq.*; 33 USC 1251 *et. seq.*; and E. O. 11738 of September 10, 1973.

23. See note 17.

24. *Ibid.* at 6.

25. 40 F.R. Section 1500.5 states:

   (a) "Actions include but are not limited to:
       . . . .

(2) New and continuing projects and program activities: Directly undertaken by Federal agencies; or supported in whole or in part through Federal contracts, grants, subsidies, loans, or other forms of funding assistance (except where such assistance is solely in the form of general revenue sharing funds, distributed under the State and Local Fiscal Assistance Act of 1972, 31 U.S.C. 1221 et seq. with no Federal agency control over the subsequent use of such funds); or involving a Federal lease, permit, license certificate or other entitlement for use.

(3) The making, modification, or establishment of regulations, rules, procedures, and policy.

26. Supra, Note 17 at 6.

27. *Ibid.* at 7.

28. *Ibid.* at 8.

29. E. O. No. 12072, 43 F. R. 36869 (1978);
    E. O. No. 12073, 43 F. R. 36873 (1978);
    E. O. No. 12074, 43 F. R. 36875 (1978);
    E. O. No. 12075, 43 F. R. 36877 (1978).

30. E. O. No. 12074, 43 F. R. 36875 (1978).

31. E. O. No. 12072, 43 F. R. 36869 (1978).

32. E. O. No. 12075, 43 F. R. 36877 (1978).

33. Supra, Note 17 at 6.

34. *Ibid.* at 8.

35. cf. eg. Vermont's Land Use and Development Law, 10 U.S.A., Section 6001 et. seq. 1970 (amended 1973); Florida Coastal Management Act of 1978. Fla. Stat. Ann. Section 380.20 et. seq.

36. *Ibid.*

37. "Urban Policy to Guide Highway Decisions," Press Release, The U. S. Department of Transportation, (Nov. 29, 1979).

38. 42. USC Section 4332 (20) (c), (1969).

39. cf. J. Fleishman, A. Aufses, "Law and Order: The Problem of Presidential Legislation," 40 Journal of Law and Contemporary Problems, 38, (1976); and Cash, "Presidential Power: Use and Enforcement of Executive Orders," 39 Notre Dame L. Rev. 44 (1963-64).

40. Supra, Note 8.

41. See note 7.

42. 42 USC Section 4332 (2) (c), (1969).

43. As of December 1977, fifteen states had enacted comprehensive statutory EIS requirements. The 8th Annual Papers of the Council on Environmental Quality, U.S. Government Printing Office, (1977), pps. 130-133.

44. See note 20, e.g.

45. The Clean Water Act Amendments of 1977, 33 USC Section 1344.

46. 40 FR, Section 1500.2, (August 1, 1973).

"Initial assessments of the environmental impacts of proposed action should be undertaken concurrently with initial technical and economic studies. . ."

"Agencies should consider the results of their environmental assessments along with their assessments of the net economic, technical and other benefits of proposed actions. . ."

47. *Clinton Community Hospital Corp. v. Southern Maryland Medical Center*, 374 F. Supp. 450 (D. Md. 1974) aff'd, 510 F. 2d. 1037 (4th Cir. 1975), Cert. denied 442 U.S. 1048 (1975).

48. *First National Bank of Homestead v. Watson*, 363 F. Supp. 466 (D.D.C. 1973).

49. 40 F.R. 1500 8 (a)(3)(ii), (August 1, 1973).

50. cf. e.g., *City of Davis v. Coleman*, 521 F. 2d 661 (9th Cir. 1975).

51. cf. R. Caprio, "The Role of Secondary Impacts Under NEPA," 6 Env. Aff. 127, (1977); *Beckenridge v. Rumsfeld*, 537 F. 2d 864 (6th Cir. 1976).

52. cf. e.g. *Fort Story v. Schlesinger*, 7 Env'l Rep. Cases 141 (E.D. Va. 1974); *Chelsea Neighborhood Associations v. United States Postal Services*, 516 F. 2d 378 (2d Cir. 1975).

53. *City of Rochester v. United States Postal Service*, 541 F. 2d 967, (1976).

54. *Ibid.* at 974.

55. *Ibid.*

56. *424 F. Supp. 784 (1976).*

57. cf. *Trout Unlimited v. Morton*. 609 F. 2d 1276 (9th Cir. 1974).

58. New York Environmental Conservation, Section 8-0113 (1975).

59. 6 NYCCR 621.7.

60. See note 58.

61. *In the Matter of Pyramid Co. of Utica*, Decision of the Commissioner, Dept. of Env'l Cons. No. 633-19-S-002, (June 22, 1979).

62. *In the Matter of Pyramid Co. of Utica*, Decision of the Commissioner Dept. of Env'l Cons. No. 633-19-0073 FWW, (March 17, 1978).

63. 6 NYCCR 617.14 (f)(i).

64. *In the Matter of Pyramid Co. of Utica*, Hearing Officer's Report and Final EIS, Dept. of Env'l Cons. No. 633-19-S-002, (June 22, 1979), pps. 46-49.

65. *Ibid*.

66. Memorandum of Law of the City of Rochester, Submitted to the Dept. of Env'l Cons., N.Y. DEC. No. 828-09-0002.

67. *Ibid*. at 1-10.

68. *Ibid*. at 5.

69. T. Muller, "A Critique of the Economic Impacts of the Marketplace Mall," (July 25, 1979).

Real Estate Research Corporation, "Statement on the Impact On Rochester CBD Retailing of the Proposed Marketplace Mall," (July 1979).

The studies were, at least implicitly, validated by the fact that shortly after the hearing, a major discount department store in the city of Rochester, a subsidiary of Montgomery Ward, closed its doors due to excessive competition.

70. *In the Matter of Miracle Mile Associates*, Decision of the Commissioner, Dept. of Env'l. Cons. No. UPA 828-09-0002, (December 6, 1979).

71. *Ibid*. at 2.

72. *Ibid*.

73. *In the Matter of Miracle Mile Associates*, Hearing Officer's Report. Dept. of Env'l. Cons. No. UPA 828-09-0002, (Dec. 6, 1979), pps. 56, 57.

74. Se note 69 at 3.

75. 10 VSA. Chap. 151. Section 6001 et. seq. 1970 (amended 1 1973).

76. *Ibid*., at 6086.

77. *In re: Pyramid Co. of Burlington*, Application No. 4C0281, Decision of the District Environmental Commission, October 12, 1978.

78. *Ibid*. at 8.

79. *Ibid*. at 4, 5.

80. *Ibid*.

81. Cf. G. Sternlieb, et.al., "Impact of Pyramid Mall on Burlington's Municipal Fisc.," Center for Urban Policy Research, Rutgers University, (Jan. 12, 1978).

82. See note 77 at 26.

83. *Ibid*. at 8.

84. *Ibid*. at 24.

SECTION III

Appraising the Central City Option

Preface

From the inception of the suburban mall, the possibilities of a transfer of all or part of its technology to the central city has been under consideration. It is only within the last several years, however, that significant efforts have come to fruition. The increasing saturation of prime suburban locations, as well as the potential of general central-city reinvigoration, has led to a much more rigorous appraisal of urban shopping center feasibility. The path however, is hazardous; the rules of the game are still to be established. The decline of central-city retailing continues apace—the issue of critical mass—of local shopper buying power which can serve as a base for supporting new facilities—is particularly troubling.

In the first section of this volume, presentation has been made of the new federal initiative which may provide some limitation on the growth of future suburban and exurban competition. The full implications of increases in real energy costs as well have yet to be fully manifested in the market. Clearly, there is a very real potential of basic shifts in the centrifugal settlement patterns that have dominated American development since World War II. The mortgage crunch of 1980 brought a near cessation of exurban development. Is this merely a momentary aberrant or the beginning of a major shift?

The dynamics that are at work are still unpredictable—the prizes, however, are substantial. The objective of this section is to explore the full range of issues attached to the central city shopping option, exploring not only the positive prospects, but also the inherent pitfalls.

In the first paper, Dr. Thomas Muller, Principle Research Associate of the Urban Institute, provides a basic overview of central-city retail sales in the context of broader national trends and shopping central growth:

1. Shopper goods sales (department store type merchandise) nationally increased rapidly from the early 1950s to 1972. Since then, however, sales increased only nominally as consumers allocated more of their income for other goods, primarily housing and energy-related products.

While outlays for shopper goods stagnated, the number of regional malls increased during the 1970s at about the same rate as during the 1960s. Therefore, especially in northern states, new malls are competing more directly than previously with existing shopping areas, including Central Business Districts (CBDs) and other older retail centers.

2. The regional mall share of the total shopper goods market increased steadily during the 1960s and 1970s in all regions of the nation. It is estimated that by 1980 large malls will capture about one-third of all shopper goods sales and over 35 percent of all *metropolitan* shopper goods sales.

3. Central cities in northern states, particularly those not undertaking annexation, lost sales to their suburbs, with city declines in shopper goods (and growth in the suburbs) substantially greater than could be explained by changes in population or income. In smaller Pennsylvania SMSAs, for example, most central city losses could not be explained by changes in the residence of shoppers.

4. Most CBDs registered severe losses between 1972 and 1977. Among the exceptions are cities without suburban malls, including Burlington, Vermont, and Pittsfield, Massachusetts.

5. Since the early 1970s, most regional mall growth has taken place in the suburbs of smaller metropolitan areas as well as in nonmetropolitan mall sites.

6. Shopping centers built since the late 1960s are typically enclosed, air-conditioned malls with an average size of close to 700,000 square feet. In recent years, several central cities have also had malls built in or near the urban core. It appears that these malls slow down, at least temporarily, shopper goods sales losses.

In the following paper, Frank H. Spink, Jr., Director of Publications for the Urban Land Institute, appraises the prospects, design and constraints of downtown shopping centers:

1. While proponents of the "back-to-the-city" movement have rejected suburban values and lifestyles, one of the few suburban design concepts that has been identified by the new urbanites as a transferable technology has been the shopping center.

2. To isolate the potential of the central city option, the general market parameters of the regional center as it has evolved in the suburbs proves instructive.

> a. The primary trade area (the source of 60 to 70 percent of ultimate sales) should be within ten-minutes travel time of the center.
> b. The secondary trade area (15 to 20 percent of sales) should be within fifteen to twenty minutes travel time.
> c. And the tertiary or fringe trade area (10 to 15 percent of sales) would be roughly twenty five to thirty minutes away from the center.

3. Applying this concept of time/distance to the existing and/or planned regional centers of any metropolitan area will probably identify the downtown as a logical location for a regional center in a network. However, the potential of the downtown depends upon the adequacy of the market encompassed within the preceding trade area thresholds.

4. Since the resident central-city population is probably a poor market—i.e., an overall low per capita disposable income—a successful central-city shopping center must rely on what would be the tertiary market for suburban centers as a primary source of clientele.

5. Thus, downtown malls must be capable of attracting the more affluent customers from its market fringe. However, in a metropolitan area well served by regional malls, this clientele already is probably located in the secondary or primary trade area of existing suburban regional malls.

6. The latter—older shopping centers in first tier suburbs—are the real competition for downtown retail revitalization, not future malls in the outer suburbs. In turn, the latter present a major threat to older inlying shopping centers, which must renovate and expand to maintain their

markets and competitive position. As this process ensues in the coming decade the downtown must move quickly or be passed by.

7. Downtown market potential is not, however, solely limited to resident populations. Downtowns have unique characteristics—daytime workforces—that give them a competitive edge in attracting customers for at least those portions of the day that are not available to the typical suburban mall. This market sector is generally affluent but has limited availability, particularly at night. This is both a problem and an opportunity.

8. In conjunction with residential populations and daytime workforces, several new markets offer excellent opportunities for downtown mall packages.

> a. *Tourist*: A renewed interest in our historical past has rendered cities a potential magnet for tourists. A new phenomenon has evolved recently—cultural tourism. It establishes a tourist-based industry tied to cultural facilities and cultural heritage. Tourism generates hotel business and overnight accommodation downtown means shoppers downtown—at night.

> b. *Conventions*: The United States has become the country of people going to meetings. New or upgraded convention facilities present another new market for downtown retailing. This can be during the day but, like tourism, it also generates nighttime demand.

> c. *Specialty*: As mass-produced goods and services in our affluent society have become the necessities of our good life, the demand for unique, not available elsewhere goods and services have escalated. The centrality of downtown, given the large market area required to support specialty facilities, may place it in an advantageous position.

> d. *Entertainment*: This has become a major form of recreation expenditure in our society. Most major entertainment and cultural facilities are downtown. Their evening orientation and linkage to "eating out" thus offers a potential market to downtown centers.

9. Separately or in combination, the preceding opportunities appear to represent a unique foundation upon which a viable market for a downtown mall might be constructed.

10. The design issues of downtown shopping centers are legion. While it must achieve the same objectives that made the suburban counterpart successful and pleasant, it also must be made to fit into the fabric of the community as it is or will be. Four integral parts of the design process for downtown malls are: adaptive use, mixed use development, joint development and public/private development.

Subsequently, Peter D. Leibowits, President of Cadillac Fairview Shopping Centers, Ltd., explores the preliminary track record of the urban shopping mall:

1. The increasing attention of the shopping center industry on downtown areas will proceed concurrently and compete with two other alternative loci throughout the 1980s.
   a. The first is the revitalization of existing shopping centers—some of which are a generation old—renovating and remerchandising them in order to maintain their competitive postures in their respective markets.
   b. The second is the concentration on middle markets—trade areas as small as 150,000 people—which can support appropriately scaled, enclosed shopping centers.

2. Despite this competition, as downtowns attract more housing and employment, the primary central-city market may grow faster than the remaining marginal sites in the suburbs, creating more viable opportunities downtown. The potential may also exist to draw from the broader market.

3. The properly designed and merchandised retail complex in carefully selected downtowns will be successful and will become an increasingly important trend for the shopping center industry.

4. Four basic types of retail-mall developments have occurred in CBDs.
   a. Pedestrian malls have been created by closing major retailing streets and improving the pedestrian environment.
   b. Substantial retailing complexes have been established

within the spines of major office and hotel complexes.

c. Enclosed regional malls have been built between existing major department stores or by adding major department stores within the CBD.

d. The final and most difficult type of downtown facility has been the anchorless retail development of theme center.

5. Each downtown is composed of distinct and different environments and functions. The unique characteristics of each specialized setting must serve as the design parameters in developing downtown retailing complexes. There is no common format analogous to the standardized suburban mall package.

6. Nevertheless, a common element that appears significant in all successful downtown projects has been the emphasis on providing an important food and entertainment complex within an architecturally unique environment.

7. The urban large-scale enclosed regional mall may require another key ingredient for success: the presence and maintenance of flagship units of department stores (defined as significantly larger and better merchandised stores than their suburban counterparts) in downtown areas. If those stores have maintained a significant market share the central-city option for an enclosed mall anchored by flagship units is significantly enhanced.

8. While a number of negative elements persist in central cities—some downtowns have lost their economic rationale, a reality that retailing alone cannot alter significantly—other factors, such as the complexity of the approval process and basic cost structures, are approaching parity with suburban areas, as these elements escalate in the outer areas.

9. Moreover, the downtown development project is now able to call upon a new and very significant resource, public financial assistance, to enhance economic feasibility. A relationship and partnership must be established between the public and private sectors to bring downtown shopping centers to fruition.

10. Not every city should try to build a mall in its core but rather that retailing which is suited for its downtown. Cities must build on their existing strengths and be prepared to be flexible.

Finally, Margaret S. Wirtenberg, a New York City urban analyst, provides a comprehensive overview of downtown pedestrian malls; via direct empirical analyses, the impact on the structure of downtown retailing, both positive and negative, is isolated. In general, the ramifications of creating downtown pedestrian malls is far more complex than the casual observer would envision.

Regional Malls and Central
City Retail Sales: An Overview

THOMAS MULLER

SUMMARY OF FINDINGS

Shopper goods sales (department store type merchandise) nationally increased rapidly from the early 1950s to 1972. Since then, however, sales increased only nominally as consumers allocated more of their income for other goods, primarily housing and energy-related products.

While outlays for shopper goods stagnated, the number of regional malls increased during the 1970s at about the same rate as during the 1960s. Therefore, especially in northern states, new malls are competing more directly than previously with existing shopping areas, including Central Business Districts (CBDs).

The regional mall share of the total shopper goods market increased steadily during the 1960s and 1970s in all regions of the nation. It is estimated that by 1980 large malls will capture about one-third of all shopper goods sales and over 35 percent of all *metropolitan* shopper goods sales.

Central cities in northern states, particularly those not undertaking annexation, lost sales to their suburbs, with city declines in shopper goods (and growth in the suburbs) substantially greater than could be explained by changes in population or income. In smaller Pennsylvania SMSAs, for example, most central-city sales losses could not be explained by changes in the residence of shoppers.

Most CBDs registered severe losses between 1972 and 1977. Among

177

the exceptions are cities without suburban malls, including Burlington, Vermont, and Pittsfield, Massachusetts.

Since the early 1970s, most regional mall growth has taken place in the suburbs of smaller metropolitan areas as well as in nonmetropolitan jurisdictions. Frequently, sales in a new nonmetropolitan mall are close to or exceed the shopper goods volume of the CBD.

Shopping centers built since the late 1960s are typically enclosed, air-conditioned malls with an average size of close to 700,000 square feet. In recent years, several central cities have also built malls in or near the urban core. It appears that these malls slow down, at least temporarily, shopper goods sales losses.

The opening of a regional shopping center was, in the past, welcomed by supporters and endured by opponents. A proposal now to develop a regional mall at the periphery of the urbanized area can inspire vociferous dissent by city officials and vigorous defense by developers. Most impartial observers familiar with the issues agree, however, that empirical data to support contentions on shopping mall effects are lacking. It is the aim of this paper to contribute some empirical evidence.

This position reflects the general anti-regulatory mood of both the public and Congress. The legal challenges include antitrust violations that allege the constraint of the encouragement of retail market monopolies. Finally, there are economic arguments. This paper will deal with neither the appropriate government role in mall location nor the legal challenges, but will concentrate instead on economic issues, mall characteristics, and retail shopping patterns in general. A forthcoming report will deal with both general effects of shopping malls and specific case studies[1] within a conceptual framework.

1. There is a need for malls, as demonstrated by the fact that they are generally profitable.

2. Shopping malls in suburbs help central-city businesses by attracting sales from a larger market, some of which would "spill over" into the central city. Thus the central city and its CBD can actually benefit from new malls.

3. Shopping malls (and other large-scale developments) follow rather than precede population movement. Losses in central-city retail sales can thus be explained by population dispersal rather than by the construction of regional malls in the suburbs.

The first argument is based on a presumed definition of need which is demonstrated behaviorally by the act of buying. This argument is conceptually interesting, but, strictly speaking, belongs to the theoretical realm of economics. By definition, it is not empirically demonstrable. The second contention, that shopping amenities in the suburbs will induce either firms or shoppers to do business in the city, rests upon a rather tenuous linkage whose net effects appear insignificant when viewed as part of the larger question. The third argument will be taken up in this paper as the discussion concerns sales changes in central cities and CBDs and the opening of regional malls.

The author has reviewed numerous reports submitted to local authorities by developers which estimate the effects of suburban malls on central cities. Most of these studies take the position that effects will be minimal and/or temporary. Thus, the single most notable response of shopping mall proponents is to deny that a serious fiscal or economic problem can result from the shift of retail activity. Typically, the argument goes, there is enough business for everyone. The following sections explore this proposition based on recent trends.

Growth in Sales and Income National Trends

As a first step, an analysis of shopping mall growth in relation to CBD and central city sales requires an examination of historical trends in personal income, retail activity, and the demand for shopper goods.[2]

Changes in the national economy, the preference for goods, and the rising cost of housing have influenced the level of shopper goods sales in recent years, and current trends are likely to continue. Between 1967 and 1972, shopper goods sales (as defined by the Bureau of the Census) increased by 28 percent in *constant* dollars; between 1972 and the third quarter of 1979, the increase was only 2 percent, despite the fact that personal consumption increased by 18 percent (See Table 1 and Chart 1). Between mid-1977 and mid-1978, for example, the Consumer Price Index increased by 11.5 percent and retail sales by 9.2 percent, but shopper goods by only 8.5 percent.

What accounts for the dramatic shift in shopper goods sales?

Personal consumption increased *per annum* by only 2.5 percent between 1972 and 1977 compared to 4.4 percent in the previous five-year period. Outlays for housing, however, have risen by 4.1 percent in real terms between 1972 and 1977 and gasoline and fuel by 6.5 percent annually for the same period. *Thus, shopper goods sales as a percent of personal consumption were reduced by 13.2 percent, while housing outlays increased by 8 percent between 1972 and 1979.*

Given current projections of energy and energy-related costs, both housing operation and transportation costs will continue to rise, although personal income will increase by only 2 percent to 3 percent annually, a rise insufficiently large to permit the allocation of a higher share of personal income for shopper goods in the early 1980s.

Intrametropolitan Trends

Retail sales in Central Business Districts (CBDs) declined between 1967 and 1972, and their decline accelerated between 1972 and 1977. Recent losses appear unaffected by size or region. As shown in Table 2, CBD sales in *nominal* terms declined by 2 percent in large SMSAs, or about 46 percent when adjusted for inflation.[3]

An examination of thirty-five smaller cities in seventeen states shows that the CBDs of only three cities had real sales growth: Great Falls, Montana; Des Moines, Iowa; and Pittsfield, Massachusetts. The CBDs of several other cities, including Worcester, Massachusetts, had only small loses. The largest CBD sales declines in eight cities of the thirty-five jurisdictions are shown in Table 3; on average they lost about 16.5 percent in nominal dollars. This means that over half of real CBD retail sales were lost during the 1972-1977 period, since the CPI increased by 45 percent. On average, cities (as opposed to CBDs) also performed poorly, with only *two* showing *real* sales growth. Two of the cities—Springfield, Missouri, and Peoria, Illinois—annexed land between 1970 and 1977. By contrast, cities with retail growth are shown in Table 4. Two characteristics stand out: all but one annexed territory, and only one (Madison) has a regional mall in its suburbs. Further, sales in CBDs of these cities show modest declines in real terms (with the exception of Springfield). Not surprisingly, there is a strong correlation between changes in CBD and balance of central city sales: strong sales outside the CBD typically result in stronger CBD activity.[4]

REGIONAL MALL GROWTH

Market Share

Regional malls captured less than 5 percent of shopper goods sales before 1958, increasing their share to 13 percent in 1967 and about 31 percent in 1979.[5] If current trends continue, by the beginning of the 1980s one out of every three dollars in shopper goods purchases will be spent at a mall (See Table 5). National estimates, which include data from sixteen representative states, are derived as shown in Table 6. Regional malls, during the 1967-1977 time period, increased their share of all shopper goods sales from 10.5 percent to 30 percent.[6]

Between 1967 and 1972, mall shopper goods sales nationally absorbed 57 percent of the expanded market for these products (See Table 7). Between 1972 and 1979, by contrast, total shopper goods sales nationally (in constant dollars) increased by only $2.4 billion, while mall sales are estimated to have grown by almost $19 billion. In many northern metropolitan areas, shopper goods sales actually declined between 1972 and 1977, reflecting economic stagnation in a number of industrial states. The slow increase in demand for shopper goods, as noted earlier, is attributable to the marginal growth in disposal money income during the 1970s and to an increasingly higher allocation of this income for housing and energy products.[7] As a result of these consumption changes, the percentage of personal income allocated for shopper goods nationally, which had remained stable between 1967 and 1972, was reduced by 7.3 percent between 1972 and 1977.

Despite the adjustments attributable to changes in the national economy, shopping mall construction has continued at a steady rate, adding retail space about four times as rapidly as the growth in the market for shopper goods. The combination of reduced aggregate demand and continuous addition of regional mall gross leasable space has frequently resulted in a "zero-sum" game, particularly in older northern urban areas in which family income has not increased at all in real terms since 1970. As a result, regional mall sales growth in one area typically reduced sales elsewhere. Based on several case studies of cities in the 30,000 to 110,000 population range, older shopping centers as well as CBDs lose sales when a regional mall opens. In addition, an expanding market area attracts some sales from beyond traditional market area boundaries and reduces sales in semirural areas.[8]

Mall Size

The average mall increased in gross square footage from 652,000 in 1967 to 729,000 in 1978. As shown in Table 8, the growth is totally attributable to additional so-called superregional malls, defined in this paper as malls with 850,000 or more square feet. The increase in the average size of malls is traceable to several factors, including improvements in the interstate highway system, public acceptance of malls, and higher sales per square foot in large as compared to small malls. As banks, insurance companies, and foreign investors found shopping malls to be good investments, additional capital became available to construct so called superregional malls, with construction costs in the $50 million to $100 million range and above not uncommon.

Regional and State Patterns

The percentage of the shopper goods market captured by regional malls reveals little variation across regions. Considerable differences do, however, exist within each of the regions owing to different levels of urbanization. Among the large states, both Pennsylvania and California have above average capture rates; New York, probably because of New York City's dominance, a below-average rate.

States with highest mall activity (over 40 percent of the market) include Delaware and Maryland, both with high urban concentrations. By contrast, three rural states—Alaska, Vermont, and Wyoming—had no regional malls as of 1978 (although they were proposed or under construction during 1979 in two of those states), while malls in such states as Maine and Idaho captured only a small percentage of total sales. Nevertheless, highest mall construction rates in recent years have been outside the large, highly urbanized states. Thus, the percentage of square feet of mall space added since 1967 increased by a factor of over five in Iowa, close to four in Alabama, three in Missouri, but less than two in Ohio and Illinois.

One regional difference has been observed: in most western states, superregional malls dominate sales, while the majority of sales in other regions take place in smaller (350 to 849 thousand square feet) regional malls. The gap among regions is, however, closing as the average size of malls constructed in recent years exceeds that of malls built during the 1960s.

Intrastate Activity

During the past two decades, a number of central cities have constructed downtown malls which are basically replicas of those built in the suburbs—Rochester in 1961, Worcester, Massachusetts in 1971, and several others since then.[9] Earlier malls were typically built with federal assistance as part of urban renewal projects. More recently, several urban malls have been constructed exclusively with private funds—The Atrium Shopping Mall in the Water Tower Building in Chicago (1975) and smaller, specialized malls in Renaissance Center, Detroit (1977), Seattle (1979), and Washington, D.C. (1971). The urban malls cater primarily to an above-average income clientele. At the national level, however, these malls collectively comprise only a very small percentage of malls in metropolitan areas.

In a number of larger cities, some large uncovered shopping centers built in the 1950s with full-line department stores still remain active.

TABLE I

Shopper Goods and Housing as Percent of Personal Consumption 1963-1979
(In Billions of 1979 Dollars)

Outlay	1963	1967	1972	1977	1978	1979	% Change 1969-1979	% Change 1972-1979	% Change 1967-1972
Total Personal Consumption	$875	1055	1287	1465	1534	1519	44.0	18.0	22.0
Retail Sales	$510	590	769	856	884	873	48.0	13.5	30.3
Shopper Goods*		160	205	208	214	209	30.6	2.0	28.1
Gasoline, Fuel	$ 40	44	53	71	72	77	75.0	45.2	20.4
Housing, Operation of Housing	$190	210	270	316	335	336	60.0	45.2	28.6
% Shopper Goods of Personal Consumption	N/A	15.2%	15.9	14.2	14.0	13.8	-9.2	-13.2	4.6
% Housing, Fuel and Gasoline of Personal Consumption	26.3%	24.1	25.1	26.4	26.5	27.2	12.9	8.4	4.1

*GAF only
SOURCE: Department of Commerce, *Survey of Current Business*, Census of Retail Trade.

CHART 1
Retail Sales, Housing, and Shopper Goods
Expenditures: 1963 to 1990
(*In Billions of 1979 Dollars*)

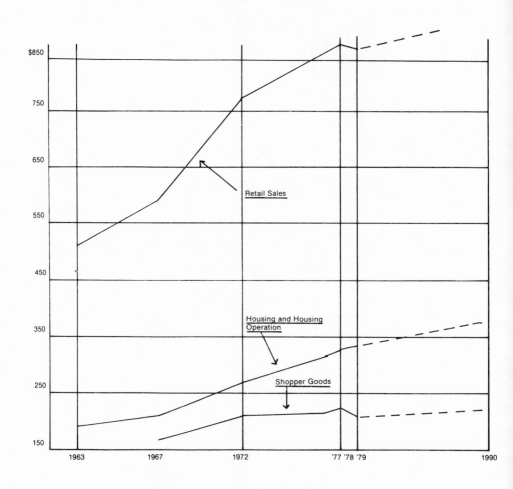

TABLE 2
Change in CBD, Central City
and SMSA Retail Sales 1972-1977
(*In Millions Current Dollars*)

	Central City		CBD		SMSA
	1977 Sales	% Change from 1972	1977 Sales	% Change from 1972	% Increase, 1972-1977
Northern Cities					
Boston	$1,832	12.8%	$463	7.3%	35.8%
Chicago	8,179	23.6	932	9.1	48.0 [a]
Minneapolis	1,265	26.2	324	14.0	62.2 [a]
St. Paul	905	35.2	91	-12.9	62.2 [a]
Kansas City	1,703	37.2	91	-22.3	58.5 [a]
St. Louis	1,373	18.1	209	14.2	55.0 [a]
Omaha	1,357	43.9	69	-15.7	57.1 [a]
Milwaukee	1,926	39.2	176	7.9	55.4 [a]
Western Cities					
Albuquerque [c]	1,434	77.3 [a]	140	-39.1	77.4 [a]
Salt Lake City	884	47.6 [a]	171	19.1	71.0 [a]
Phoenix [c]	2,524	57.3 [a]	N/A	N/A	75.3 [a]
Denver	1,860	42.2	N/A	N/A	67.2 [a]
Tuscon [c]	1,381	58.3 [a]	26.1	- 2.8	68.1 [a]
Mean, Northern Cities [b]		29.5%		0.2%	54.3
Mean, Western Cities [b]		56.5%		- 7.6	71.8

[a] Increase in sales exceeds inflation based on COL index
[b] Unweighted
[c] Annexation between 1972 and 1977

Source: *1977 Census of Retail Trade Major Retail Centers in SMSAs* (preliminary). The sample shown excludes southern, Middle Atlantic and Pacific states.

TABLE 3

Percent Change in Retail Sales 1972-1977
(*Current Dollars*)

City/State	Central City	CBD
Hartford, Connecticut	10.9%	-11.4%
Waterbury, Connecticut	40.0	-33.6
Bloomington, Illinois	N/A	-40.3
Rockford, Illinois	30.3	-40.8
New Bedford, Massachusetts	21.2	-19.0
Springfield, Missouri	62.8	-16.5
Peoria, Illinois	53.5	-16.7
Providence, Rhode Island	32.0	-13.9
MEAN	35.8	-16.5

Source: *1977 Census of Retail Trade.*

TABLE 4

Percent Retail Sales Change 1972-1977 in
Cities with Growing Sales
(*In Current Dollars*)

City/State	Central City	CBD
Reno, Nevada	86.6%**	38.5%
Springfield, Illinois	80.2**	- 7.5
Cedar Rapids, Iowa	71.5*	22.6
Green Bay, Wisconsin	70.0	21.3
Waterloo, Iowa	68.7	13.1
Wichita, Kansas	66.7	28.4
Burlington, Vermont	66.2	N/A
Madison, Wisconsin	62.5*	38.5
Lincoln, Nebraska	61.8**	19.0

** Moderate annexation
* Minor annexation
Source: *1977 Census of Retail Trade.*

TABLE 5

Change in Shopper Goods Sales, U.S. Total and Regional Mall Shares 1967-1979

(In Billions Dollars)

Year	Total Shopper Goods Sales Current	Total Shopper Goods Sales 1977 $ [b]	Mall Sales [a] Current	Mall Sales [a] 1977 $	Mall S.G. [c] Sales 1977 $	Mall Sales as % Total S.G. Sales	S.G. Mall Sales as % Total S.G. Sales
1962	$ 61.7	$123.6	N/A	N/A	N/A	--	--
1967	79.2	143.7	11.9	21.6	19.4	15.0	13.5
1972	118.4	171.5	27.9	40.4	36.4	23.6	21.2
1977	175.1	175.1	--	--	--	--	--
1978	192.2	178.6	64.5	59.9	53.9	33.5	30.2
1979	206.9[d]	173.9	73	61.4[e]	55.2	35.3	32

a/ Includes only shopping centers with 350 thousand or more square feet. *Preliminary estimates.*

b/ Deflated based on CPI index.

c/ Derived from mall S.G. sales = .90 × mall sales. (S.G. = Shopper Goods)

d/ Based on national sales, first eight months of 1979 compared to first 8 months 1978 (10.1% increase) and estimated 10.5% inflation.

e/ Estimated $1.6 billion 1978 dollars increase from malls identified as opening in 1979, which is a conservative estimate.

Data Sources: Urban Land Institute, *Dollars and Cents of Shopping Centers*, various issues

National Research Bureau, *Directory of Shopping Centers in the United States*, various issues

Bureau of the Census, *Monthly and Annual Trade Reports*, various issues.

TABLE 6

Estimated Mall and Total Shopper Goods Sales in 16 States [a] 1967-1977
(In Millions 1977 Dollars)

Year	Mall Square Feet (in millions)	Sales Per Gross Sq. Ft. ULI [b]	Sales Per Gross Sq. Ft. MRC	Total Mall Sales (in Millions) ULI [b]	Total Mall Sales (in Millions) MRC [c]	Total S.G. Sales (in Millions)	% Mall Sales of Total S.G. ULI	% Mall Sales of Total S.G. MRC
1967	63.2	$85	83	$ 5,372	5,309	$45,618	11.8%	11.6%
1972	125.3	86	82	10,776	10,425	54,442	19.8	19.1
1978	235.8	82	87	19,335	20,515	59,310	32.6	34.6
Percent Change 1967-1978	273.1			268.6	286.3	27.7		

[a] States included are Connecticut, Maine, Massachusetts, New Hampshire, Pennsylvania, Rhode Island, Alabama, North Carolina, Tennessee, Illinois, Missouri, Texas, Colorado, Montana, Nevada, and Washington. Sales in these states comprise 33 percent of the U.S. total.

[b] Based on calculating sales from values shown in *Dollars and Cents of Shopping Centers*, Urban Land Institute.

[c] Based on estimating sales from estimates derived by the use of the 1967 and 1972 *Census of Retail Trade*, Major Retail Centers, adjusting for sales outside the core center or centers (excluding CBDs). The 1977 estimates are based on sales derived from large shopping malls shown in the *1977 Census of Retail Trade* where the major retail centers are limited to one shopping mall. Sales in these centers could be slightly above the average of all malls, since they are somewhat large.

TABLE 7

Change in Total and Mall Shopper Goods Sales 1967-1979
(*In Billions 1977 Dollars*)

	1967-72	1972-1979
Change,, Total Shopper Goods	$30.3	$ 2.4
Change, S.G. Mall Sales	17.0	18.8
% S.G. Mall Sales of Total	56.1%	683.3%

Source: 1967 and 1972 *Census of Retail Trade*
Current Business Reports

TABLE 8

NUMBER AND SIZE OF REGIONAL MALLS[a]

	Regional Malls (350-849,000 sq. ft.)		Super Regional Malls (850,000 sq. ft. and over)	
	No.	Average Size	No.	Average Size
1967	82	542	23	1043
1972	152	545	47	1096
1978	230	549	103	1130

[a] Based on sample of 16 states. Preliminary analysis is subject to further verification. Based on definitions applied in the study, there were about 950 to 1,000 malls in 1977. This compares to 1450 major retail centers based on the 1977 Census definition which includes shopping centers with 25 or more stores, one or more department stores with 100,000 or more sq. feet.

Since the 1960s, almost all new malls have been covered and air-conditioned, and new malls constructed during the last decade in northern states have been concentrated outside central cities.[10] Several southern and western cities, including Dallas and Houston, annexed land areas in which malls are situated.

As one would expect, regional malls remain concentrated in metropolitan areas, with sales in these areas accounting for about 95 percent of all mall sales. Thus, regional malls capture about 36 percent of the shopper goods market at the metropolitan level. During the 1970s, however, mall development was concentrated outside metropolitan boundaries. Of twenty malls located in nonmetropolitan areas of the South, fifteen were constructed since 1970. In Pennsylvania and New York, there were sixteen such malls in 1978—all but one constructed after 1968 and all but two covered and air-conditioned. Their average size, as would be expected, is smaller than their metropolitan counterparts.

Sales in nonmetropolitan malls currently equal only about 5 percent of the state total. If the current trend continues, however, their share of the total will increase. Nevertheless, there is a practical limit to the number of regional malls the nonmetropolitan market can absorb. Therefore, it is unlikely that these malls will ever exceed 10 percent of total mall sales.

CENTRAL CITY SALES LOSSES AND
POPULATION MOVEMENT

Changes in Shopper
Goods Sales Location

The extent to which large-scale planned developments—residential, commercial, or industrial—lead or follow population is currently an unresolved issue, as is the more general question, "Do people follow jobs, or jobs follow people?" Most likely, a combination of residential, commercial, and industrial development, once in place, attracts additional households as additional jobs are created and amenities introduced. Thus, large commercial development creates a "pull" at the same time that city population losses exert a "push" outward from the urban core.

A parallel issue is whether the loss of shopper goods sales and the subsequent reduction in retail trade employment in older central cities can be explained by the shift in population, and thus income, from the city to its suburbs. One can respond, albeit tentatively, to this question.

Based on the population movement hypothesis, one would expect shopper goods sales to shift from the central city to the suburbs in rough proportion to changes in population, or more specifically, in response to changes in money income. For example, a shift of $50 million in income resulting from household relocation to the suburbs would mean that a proportionate level of shopper goods sales would be lost to the city but offset by a similar gain outside the central city. This hypothesis can be tested by examining the changes between money income and shopper goods sales between 1972 and 1977, two periods for which the data are relatively complete. As show in Table 9, shopper goods sales in ten large northern central cities declined by $4.1 billion, or by 24.6 percent during this five-year period, while personal income declined by $7.7 billion or 7.6 percent.[11] Shopper goods sales in the suburbs of these same cities exceeded the national average, which itself showed only a marginal increase between 1972 and 1977.

The hypothesis which attributes shopper goods shifts to malls on the basis of population (that is, personal income) changes appears weak, since predicted sales differ considerably from actual sales. Thus, the anticipated loss of $2.4 billion is actually shown to be a loss of $4.1 billion in northern cities. By contrast, sales in the suburbs of these cities increased by $1.2 billion while, based on changes in income, they should have been $0.9 billion. In this instance the error is not only in magnitude but also in direction.

In 1972, northern cities had a net inflow (relative to income) of shoppers from suburban areas as illustrated by higher than expected sales of shopper goods. Within a five-year period, however, conditions reversed, with the level of suburban sales in northern cities indicating net inflows from the urban core.

The data indicates that southern and western cities functioned as the metropolitan centers for shopper goods during 1972. Although suburbs gained sales more rapidly than could be explained by changes in population and income, central cities (but not necessarily CBDs) retained a strong marketing position. In part, this reflects annexation undertaken by about half the cities studied.

The analysis completed so far indicates that neither sales losses in the northern central cities nor gains in the suburbs can be fully explained by the movement of population and income. This phenomenon can be further illustrated by the fact that most losses in northern city sales were among shopper goods. Nonshopper goods sales declined by only 10 percent, or only 2 percent more than would be expected, given changes in income during the five year interval. Had population/income changes been

TABLE 9

Shopping Goods Sales as Source of Money Income 1972-1977
(In Billions 1977 Dollars)

	Central City 1972	Central City 1977	Percent Change	Balance of SMSA[c] 1972	Balance of SMSA[c] 1977	Percent Change	U.S. Total 1972	U.S. Total (In Billions) 1977	Percent Change
Northern SMSAs[a]									
Shopping Goods Sales	$ 16.7	12.6	-24.6%	21.3	22.5	5.6%	171.5	174.0	2.1%
Money Income	$101.2	93.5	- 7.6	151.1	156.2	3.3	1140.1	1249.1	9.6
Percent S.G. of Money Income	16.5%	13.5	-18.2	14.1	14.4	2.1	15.0	13.9	-7.3
Population (In Millions)	17.6	16.4	- 6.8	22.3	22.8	2.2	208.1	216.1	3.8
Per Capita S.G. Sales	$950	769	-19.1	$955	$987	3.3	$824	$805	-2.3
Southern and Western SMSAs[b]									
Shopping Goods Sales	$ 11.4	11.9	+ 4.4%	13.0	15.0	+15.4%			
Money Income	$ 58.7	64.9	+10.6	91.3	105.3	+15.3%			
Percent S.G. of Money Income	19.4%	18.3	- 5.7%	14.2%	14.2%	-0-			
Population (In Millions)	9.5	9.8	+ 3.2%	14.4	15.8	+ 9.7%			
Per Capita S.G. Sales	$1200	1214	+ 1.2%	$903	$949	+ 5.2%			

[a] Includes Boston, Chicago, Cleveland, Detroit, New York, Newark, Philadelphia, Pittsburgh, Kansas City, St. Louis
[b] Includes Denver, San Francisco, Los Angeles, Seattle, Atlanta, San Diego, San Antonio, Miami, Phoenix, Houston, and Dallas
[c] Shopping goods sales are for geographic areas not strictly comparable to those used for income and population
SOURCE: Bureau of the Census

the major factor for shifts in retail sales, one could have expected losses in nonshopper goods sales to be more closely related to changes in shopper goods.

Retail Employment and
Sales in Large SMSAs

An examination of employment trends in twenty-one metropolitan areas which include 39 percént of all employees in shopper goods stores nationally (during 1972) indicates both significant central city/suburban shifts and regional differentials (See Table 10).

The number of shopper goods-related employees in central cities declined by only 3.1 percent in ten northern central cities between 1967 and 1972, but decreased by *17.5* percent between 1972 and 1977. While these central cities lost 60,000 workers between 1972 and 1977, their suburbs gained 44,000 employees. Owing in part to annexation, shopper goods employment in the central cities of southern and western metropolitan areas has been rising slowly (with two exceptions), with suburban employment gaining rapidly.

Job losses in the city would have been more severe except for the fact that the number of employees per each $1 million in constant dollar sales increased in both cities and suburbs, meaning that sales per employee declined.[12] However, real wages and total payroll were reduced. Thus, while there were more employees per each sales dollar in 1977 than in 1972, their effective wages decreased considerably.

To what extent job losses in ten of the twenty-one cities with high minority populations were offset by relocation to suburbs is not known. However, persons typically earning low wages do not commute because of transportation costs. Given that the average earning wage for retail workers is close to the minimum wage, commuting would be discouraged, particularly since new malls are frequently ten or more miles from the CBD.

SMALLER METROPOLITAN AREAS—PENNSYLVANIA

Changes in Shopper Goods
Sales Location and Employment

Pennsylvania has been selected as a case study for several reasons, including the following:

(a) There are two large SMSAs, Philadelphia and Pittsburgh, as well as ten smaller SMSAs.

TABLE 10
Employees in Shopper[a] Good Establishments
(*In Thousands*)

| | | NORTH[b] | | | SOUTH & WEST[b] | |
	N	Central City	Balance of SMSA	N	Central City	Balance of SMSA
1967	10	354	293	11	190	152
1972	10	343	402	11	213	233
1977	10	283	446	11	228	284

[a] Employees in these 21 metropolitan areas comprise 39 percent of all employed workers in shopper goods retail enterprises nationally in 1972.
[b] For list of cities included, see Table 9.

Source: U.S. Department of Commerce, *Census of Retail Trade*, 1967, 1972, and 1977.

(b) Annexation is infrequent.[13] Therefore, boundaries have been stable over the time period for which retail sales data are examined.

(c) The state includes both declining and growing urban areas. The latter include York and Lancaster.

In 1967, Pennsylvania's smaller central cities and their CBDs functioned as metropolitan centers for shopper goods sales. Between 1967 and 1977, however, the population of the central cities declined by 10 percent, while the surrounding surburban population increased by more than one-third (See Table 11). Growth in money income closely paralleled population change. At the same time, though, shopper goods sales in the central cities declined by 27 percent, more than could be explained by changes in population and income. The declining importance of the central cities suggests that the 1980s will see a net outflow of shopper goods dollars from cities to their suburbs.

As shown in Table 12, only 38 percent of the loss in Pennsylvania central cities could be explained by changes in consumption and income, with reduced income accounting for an even smaller share. Concurrently, income changes in suburbs also account for only a small percentage of actual sales shifts. As in other areas of the nation, the shopper goods sales declined in Pennsylvania cities exceeds lower sales of other retail goods, as illustrated in Table 13.

Between 1967 and 1972, the number of employees in shopper goods stores in smaller central cities increased slightly; however, Table 14 shows that there was a sharp drop during the next five years, reflecting reduced sales.

Mall Expansion in Pennsylvania

Mall sales in Philadelphia and Pittsburgh SMSAs doubled between 1967 and 1977 (See Table 15). This relatively low growth rate is not surprising since numerous regional malls were already constructed in the two areas between the mid-1950s and mid-1960s. By contrast, mall sales increased by a factor of five in the ten smaller Pennsylvania SMSAs, and their share of the market in 1977 was greater than that of the two largest SMSAs. In nonmetropolitan parts of the state, the mall share of the market also increased rapidly, to almost 20 percent in 1978.[14]

TABLE 11

Shopper Goods Sales and Income, Smaller Pennsylvania SMSAs
(In Millions 1977 Dollars)[1]

Year	Population (In OOO)		Money Income		Shopper Goods Sales		Percent S.G. Sales of Income		
	City	Suburbs	City	Suburbs	City	Suburbs	City	Suburbs	SMSA
1967	783	2024	$3730	$ 9831	$1061	$1344	28.4%	13.2%	17.
1972	756	2590	4033	13483	1055	1948	26.2	14.5	17.
1977	699	2773	3913	14642	774	2240	19.8	15.6	16.
% Change, 1967-1977	-10.7%	37.0	4.9	48.5	-27.0	66.7	-30.3	13.9	- 6.

These areas: Allentown, Altoona, Erie, Harrisburg, Johnstown, Lancaster, Scranton, Reading, York, and Williamsport.

TABLE 12

Expected and Actual Sales in Smaller
Pennsylvania Metropolitan Areas
(*In Millions 1977 Dollars*)

	Central Cities	Suburbs
Actual 1972 Sales	$1,055	$1,948
Expected 1977 Sales:		
Adj. for Consumption Change (-7.3%)	-77	-142
Adj. for Income Change (-2.9%)	-31	155
Expected 1977	947	1961
Actual 1977	774	2240
Percent Change Explained by consumption and income	38%	4%

TABLE 13

Changes in Retail Sales, Central Cities of
Smaller Pennsylvania SMSAs
(*In Millions 1977 Dollars*)

Year	Shopper Goods	All Other Goods	% Shopper of Other
1967	$1061	$2011	52.8
1972	1055	2242	47.1
1977	774	1891	40.9

TABLE 14

Number of Employees in Shopper Goods Stores
Pennsylvania SMSAs
(*In Thousands*)

	1967	1972	1977	% Change 1972-1977
City	21	23	16	-30%
Suburbs	29	40	48	20%

Notes

1. The forthcoming report is being prepared under provisions of a contract between the Urban Institute and the Office of Policy Development and Research at HUD.

2. Shopper goods, as defined by the Bureau of the Census, include general merchandise, apparel, furniture, and a general category of "other miscellaneous shopping goods."

3. Large SMSAs are defined as those with sales exceeding $850 million in 1977.

4. $r = .49$, $n = 16$.

5. Regional malls, for the purpose of our analysis, are defined as centrally managed shopping centers, predominantly enclosed, air-conditioned malls, with 350,000 or more square feet of space, and one or more department stores, with retail stores concentrating in shopper goods. Application of a looser definition in which square feet of space is the only criterion would increase the 1979 proportion of mall sales as a percentage of all shopper goods.

6. As a result of changes in names of shopping centers, the addition or deletion of retail space, and reporting errors, square footage estimates can only be approximate, particularly for 1967.

7. Since the price of shopper goods increased more slowly than for other goods, the quantity of shopper goods purchased did not decline during this time period. However, relatively lower prices apparently have not stimulated additional demand.

8. In addition to malls, some nonmall retail space is also being added by the construction or addition of small neighborhood centers and free-standing retail stores. These additions probably offset reduced square footage resulting from retail stores either converted to other use or demolished.

9. The Worcester CBD is one of the few CBDs in the nation where sales did not decline rapidly between 1972 and 1977. Pittsfield, Massachusetts, and Des Moines, Iowa are among the other exceptions.

10. Median sales in nonenclosed superregional malls based on ULI data in 1977 averaged $85 per square foot, in enclosed malls $96 per square foot.

11. City population declined 6.8 percent or less than income, while the balance of the SMSA population rose more slowly than income. Therefore, population explains less of the sales shifts than does income.

12. Wages of retail workers are among the lowest in the labor force. In addition, wages in real terms have declined between 1972 and 1977.

13. Between 1970 and 1977 total annexations included only 18 square miles, less than .3 percent of the U.S. total.

14. This percentage appears higher than expected and may be attributable to data inconsistencies.

Downtown Malls: Prospects, Design, Constraints

FRANK H. SPINK, JR.

OVERVIEW

The revitalization of the retail core of our cities has become a major strategy for urban revitalization. It is not a new objective, but the perceived feasibility of actually accomplishing this objective has risen dramatically. There has always been a strong group in support of the downtowns of our cities. During the suburban development boom of the postwar years, however, the strategy tended to be one of survival: how do we freeze the deterioration of downtown? How do we stabilize what is there? There was very little emphasis on the idea of trying to turn the downtown around and make it grow. This is the current objective.

The decline of retailing in downtown was to varying degrees a parallel phenomenon to the growth of the suburbs. The more affluent people were moving out of cities into suburbs and with them, their purchasing dollars. Initially, the new suburban retail development looked very much like a small scale downtown. Many of the "new" suburbs immediately after the Second World War were, in fact, built around the smaller streetcar suburbs of the 20s and 30s, or small-town stops on commuter railroads. The main streets or downtowns of these areas grew through incremental expansion in response to new demands, but the pace of residential development outstripped both the physical and business capacity of these retail groupings to meet the demand.

While there were prototypes for contemporary suburban shopping center design developed in the 20s and 30s, the combination of the Great Depression and World War II precluded the application of this concept until after the war was over.[1] The shopping center concept, however, had already been devised and was a clear concept in the minds of many entrepreneurial developers. In 1944, when ULI founded its Community Builders Council, the council was prepared to provide a standardized definition for shopping centers, "a group of architecturally unified commercial establishments built on a site that is planned, developed, owned and managed as an operating unit related in its location, size and type of shops to the trade area that the unit serves. The unit provides on-site parking in definite relationship to the types and total size of the stores."[2] Under this definition, the first wave of shopping center development was neighborhood shopping centers designed to serve the bedroom communities that mushroomed around all of our major cities.

The first regional shopping center was built in 1950 at Northgate in Seattle.[3] Initially, the center had one full-line department store as its anchor tenant at one end of a mall street—an open pedestrian street with shops lining each side. The evolution of Northgate illustrates the maturing of the shopping center concept. Over time, this center has grown from one department store to three department stores and over 1 million square feet of gross leasable area and from an open pedestrian mall to, first, a roofed, and then an enclosed, weather air-conditioned mall.

There has been no development concept that has evolved more rapidly and more effectively than the concept of the shopping center. In 1950 when Northgate opened, the best records available indicate that there were, at most, 100 shopping centers that met the definition I have given and most of those were neighborhood-and community-scale centers. While census taking in the shopping center industry is not very precise, the Shopping Center Directory currently lists almost 20,000 centers. That is a 200-fold increase in numbers of centers in just 30 years. In contrast, the U.S. population during the same period only grew by 45 percent and, in constant dollars, the level of consuming by 130 percent.[4] The suburban shopping center is clearly the dominant form of retailing design and management. It was conceived, applied, and refined in the suburbs and its characteristics are almost totally tied to automobile access. The success of the suburban mall as a business venture is unquestioned. Its evolution from purely a retail, entrepreneurial venture to a new kind of downtown in suburbia, while not without its critics, has been successful and responsive to market demands.

Recently our enthusiasm for suburban growth has been countered by other views that have come to question suburban values and lifestyles. Certainly, those proponents of the back-to-the-city movement have rejected its form and substance in favor of a more urban environment. Interestingly, one of the few design concepts that have evolved in the suburbs that has been identified by the new urbanites as a transferable technology has been the shopping center. The objective of this paper will be to examine that idea and its prospects, design characteristics, and development constraints as applied to the downtowns of our cities.

PROSPECTS

How Big is the Market?

It is reasonable to suggest for purposes of analysis that the shopping center in downtown is equivalent to the regional shopping center in suburbia. There is a strong view that the market for downtown retail is better thought of at a neighborhood or community scale. However, to examine market prospects using the regional scale seems a legitimate starting point. Based on criteria of 350,000 square feet of gross leasable area, one or more department stores, and central ownership and management, there are probably about 1,000 existing centers that can be classified as regional or superregional shopping centers.

ULI's Shopping Center Development Handbook states that a regional center requires a market of 150,000 people within a half-hour radius. There are not more than 200 SMSAs in the U.S. that have a population of 150,000 or more.[5] However, the 50 largest SMSAs contain over 100 million people. These 50 largest SMSAs have provided the market for the majority of the 1,000 regional shopping centers that have been built. They have been carefully arranged in concentric rings, each with its own market area. As these SMSAs grow out further, new markets for new centers are created. But each SMSA has only one downtown, or in some cases two or three. This defines a potential market for downtown centers of somewhat more than 200 centers at the most.

For the purpose of this discussion, let us use 200 potential centers. Within that 200 a certain number of cities are not in a position to absorb a new retail complex of the six of a regional center, so perhaps our realistic potential future market for downtown centers is 150 centers at a maximum. The potential for regional centers in the so-called mid-markets is significantly larger. One recent analysis suggested that there are over 600 potential mid-market locations.[6]

Where is the Market?

Where is the market for regional shopping centers? Downtown? Suburbia? The countryside? It is fair to suggest that there appear to be (within the context of development patterns today) two basic configurations of populations that are responsive to the development of large-scale retail facilities. They are the big cities and their suburbs which we have earlier described as the SMSAs, and the smaller cities and their countrysides. We have suggested there are perhaps 150 markets in big SMSAs. There are perhaps several multiples of that number in the smaller SMSAs, which combined with a hinterland market or by aggregation of several small SMSAs, can support a regional center. These are the so called mid-market opportunities. The competition in these two different configurations is significantly different, as are the implications for public policy.

There is currently a great debate going on about the need to control the development of shopping malls in nondowntown locations in order to enhance the market potential for the location of such centers in the downtowns of cities. Without trying to resolve that controversy, it is reasonable to suggest that there is a significantly different set of characteristics between the big city/suburbs aggregations of population and opportunities for retail shopping facilities and the smaller city/countryside aggregations or so-called mid-market opportunities. It is clearly in these latter locations where the market must be aggregated rather than segmented that the current controversy is so heavily focused. Let us look, then, to the big cities and their suburbs and examine the potential market for a downtown regional mall in competition with suburban malls. Is it either/or competition or carefully considered market segmentation?

Let's go back to the definition of the regional center as it has evolved in the suburbs. It has one or more full-line department stores of at least 100,000 square feet. It has a gross leasable area of approximately 350,000 square feet on average with a range of perhaps 300,000 to over 1 million square feet. It has a market area of 150,000 people or more. The last criteria is the time/distance to the center from customer origination. While there are exceptions to any rules, market analysts essentially agree that the primary trade area for a regional shopping center (the source of 60 percent to 70 percent of ultimate sales) should be residents within ten minutes travel time of the center. The secondary trade area (which may generate 15/20 percent of all sales) should be within fifteen to twenty minutes travel time. And the tertiary or fringe trade area (which is the broadest area from which customers may normally be drawn and from which the roughly 10 to 15 percent remaining sales would come) would be roughly twenty-five to thirty minutes away from the center.[7]

It is quite easy to take almost any major metropolitan area and plot the existing and/or planned regional centers to see that this concept of time/distance from customer to center has been fairly effectively applied in the development of the regional shopping centers in our suburbs. This exercise will also tend to identify downtown as a logical location for a regional center in a network. There are those who would argue, using more traditional central-place theory, that there is a much stronger gravitational pull to the downtown and, therefore, it is or should be superior to all other locations. Tom Black in his ULRF Issue Paper, *The Changing Economic Role of Central Cities*, clearly supports that view if you are talking about office uses and the centrality of financial and corporate development activity.[8] Most central cities, however, have lost their dominant retail role and are more legitimately viewed as one of several retail nodes in a metropolitan region.

An even more extreme counterview sees the downtown in a less than regional context as far as retail trade is concerned and, therefore, more logically the location of a center at a scale suitable to support a downtown neighborhood or community and giving up its regional retail role to other locations. Regardless of any other opportunities for retail trade, downtown is the center of a neighborhood or community. Its residents are those who live in or near downtown, its daytime population, and its hotel/transient population. The retail needs of this kind of neighborhood or community are different than for a traditional neighborhood, but those needs are there regardless of any other larger market opportunities. An evaluation of each particular instance will suggest which perspective is more valid and if that situation can be changed by certain actions.

Resident Markets

What is disheartening in most cities is the examination of the resident population characteristics within the defined trade area for a downtown regional mall. Compared to the market of suburban centers, it is probably a poor market. That is, the amount of disposable dollars available for any particular shopper good is significantly lower per capita in this market area than an equivalent market area around a suburban mall. If we examine the characteristics of resident populations in the downtown market area of most metropolitan cities, we find it is the home of a low-income population. Their resources must be applied to lodging and food, the necessities of life, and there is very little available for consumer goods. Therefore, their purchasing power per capita in support of a regional retail center downtown is dramatically lower than that available to a shopping center development in an equivalent market area in suburbia.

It is interesting to look at the primary, secondary, and tertiary trade area patterns that might be ascribed to a downtown shopping center in comparison to a suburban one. The suburban center expects to generate 60 to 70 percent of its sales from those within ten minutes. In order for the downtown mall to be successful, it is highly likely that what would be the tertiary market for suburban centers, customers twenty to thirty minutes away, must become the primary source of customers for a downtown mall. That is, that downtown malls must be capable of attracting the more affluent customers from its market fringe. In a metropolitan area well served by regional malls, these same customers are probably located in the secondary if not the primary trade area for an *existing* suburban regional mall. *Therefore, it would seem that the competition for dollars resident in the larger metropolitan areas is not between downtown and any future regional malls that might occur in the outer suburbs but rather between downtown and the existing regional malls located either within the central city or in the first tier suburbs. The renovation and expansion of first tier regional malls is the real competition with downtown retail revitalization or new growth.*

It might be interesting to pause and take a look at the characteristics of the existing regional malls that might fall within this area of competition. In many metropolitan areas, they are best described as first-generation regional malls, that is, malls that were designed and built in the 1950s and /or early 60s and do not necessarily have the design quality, range of merchandise, or environmental assets of more recent regional malls further out. This suggests that perhaps downtown can effectively compete with existing regional malls for the customers and dollars they need to be viable. However, many of these first generation malls are rapidly undergoing major renovations in order to maintain and protect their markets, not only from the potential threat of downtown revitalization but also from loss of sales to the more glamorous and newer vintage centers further out in the second and third ring of suburbs. Their primary trade area customers are in the tertiary trade area of these new larger centers. This suggests that downtown must move quickly or be passed by.

The concept presented is merely an application of Riley's Law of Retail Gravitation, formulated nearly fifty years ago, which described the phenomenon differently but has merit in evaluating the market potential for downtown retail centers. He said, "When two cities compete for retail trade from the immediate rural areas, the breaking point for the attraction of such trade will be more or less in direct proportion to the population (size) of the two cities (centers) and in inverse proportion to the

square of the distance from the immediate area of each city (center)."⁹
What this law really said was the people will normally get to the biggest
place they can get to the easiest. If that is true, then the greatest asset to
downtown regeneration and the creation of downtown malls will be the
improvement of easy, quick and convenient transportation access suitable
for use by a shopper to downtown, coupled with a shopping environment
equal to or better than the nearest competition.

Nonresident Markets

Up to date, the discussion of market potential for downtown has
focused on resident population, that is, people whose primary residence is
located within a certain trade area under traditional market concepts.
Downtowns have unique characteristics that give them a competitive
edge in attracting customers for at least portions of the day that are not
available to the typical suburban mall. For example, while the economic
role of many central cities declined as centers of retail trade, to a great extent they have not lost but gained preeminence as the centers of finance
and commerce. While suburban office parks and freestanding office
buildings have proliferated in significant numbers, downtown continues
to remain the location of corporate headquarters and principal offices for
financial, insurance, and other institutions. The employees for this group
of uses are significantly more affluent and have greater disposable incomes than the residents of the downtown primary market area. They are
within the primary trade area of downtown for certain hours of the day.
However, their availability to retailers as customers is limited to lunch
hours, prework and postwork periods prior to the commute trip; it has not
been extended into the evening hours (illustrated by the vast empty can-
yons of most downtown financial streets after 5:30 p.m.) and, therefore
are not available to retail establishments during the evening hours which
have become the prime time shopping hours in suburbia. This becomes
not a problem but an opportunity, which will be illustrated by the next
discussion of the new forms of retailing that have potential for application
in downtown.

New Forms, New Markets

There are many ways to describe the unique opportunities and give
them names, and it is possible to argue with the choices suggested, but
there are five new markets that offer excellent opportunities for the
development of downtown malls. In single words, they are: *tourist, convention, specialty, entertainment,* and *improvement.* Each of these opportunities has unique characteristics and a capacity to understand and

respond to them requires a special skill and talent.

Tourist. For a long time tourist meant countryside, at least in the United States. But with a renewed interest in our historical past, cities have suddenly become a potential magnet for tourists. There are some premier examples of retail developments that attract tourists. Certainly, the most often spoken of in the last year or two is the Faneuil Hall/Quincy Market development of the Rouse Company in Boston. It is interesting how many people you meet who are not in the development community who define Faneuil Hall as a place to go to when you are in Boston and spend some time, almost as much as they define the Smithsonian in Washington as a place to visit and spend some time while you are in that city.

Tourism generates hotel business and overnight accommodation downtown means shoppers downtown—at night. A new term has evolved recently. It is cultural tourism. It is defined as tourist based industry tied to cultural facilities and cultural heritage.

Conventions. The United States has become the country of people going to meetings. Meetings have become a way of professional, business and special interest life. Almost every kind of business development and educational activity revolves around a process of regional, national, and international meetings, conventions, conferences, symposiums, work-shops, forums, etc., where people can get together and address the complexities of our society in relation to their particular area of concern, look at products, exchange ideas, meet and greet.

It would appear that our expanded capacity to distribute the written word via publication and the verbal word via radio, television, and telephone systems has increased rather than decreased the demand for face-to-face contacts to discuss, deliberate, see and learn. Thus, new or upgraded convention facilities present another new market for downtown retailing. This can be a daytime market but, like tourism, it also generates nighttime demand.

Specialty. In our affluent society where mass-produced goods and services have become the necessities of our good life, the demand for the handmade, one-of-a-kind, unique, not-available-elsewhere goods and services and experiences has risen dramatically and is within the reach of a very significant portion of our population. It is within our nature to be willing to travel significantly further and suffer much greater inconveniences to obtain a special good or service. In general, the market area required to support an outlet for specialty goods is much larger than for traditional shopper goods. Downtown with its centrality in a region stands in the unique position to capture this market.

A major characteristic of those specialty centers developed to date is that a much greater percentage of gross leasable area is devoted to food service. Dining out is both a necessity and an event for tourists. To a great extent, *specialty* and *tourist* are closely tied together and, thus, cities may see themselves in competition not with their suburbs but with other cities, both in the United States and internationally, and with destination resort areas, in responding to this market opportunity.[10]

Entertainment. Entertainment has become a major form of recreational expenditure in our society. Movies, theaters, rock concerts, symphonies, the dance—are all enjoying increased box office sales. Most major entertainment and cultural complexes are downtown. The enhancement or expansion of these facilities will create a new market and an important one, since big-ticket entertainment events are in the evening and, therefore, can bring or keep people downtown in the evening.

Entertainment can also be a "fast-food" affair. A quick count of street musicians on Washington, D.C.'s upper Connecticut Avenue during the noon hour of a nice day might include a one-man band, a concert violinist, a harpsicordist, a ragtime piano player working out of the back end of a van, a bagpiper, a steel drummer, a guitarist, a flutist, a mime and a magician, each with hat in hand and each drawing a crowd and presumably contributions large enough at least to keep body and soul together. While street musicians can enhance opportunities for daytime retailing, bringing people out of their offices and into the streets and into shopping malls downtown, the more permanent and substantial forms of entertainment can keep people downtown or bring people downtown after 5:30 p.m., thus attracting significant new markets to downtown. As mentioned in the discussion of tourism, eating out has become a form of entertainment. Entertainment should not be defined too narrowly. Even the disco boom has generated new markets.[11]

Improvement. It is more difficult to relate this category to downtown retail development. But a new phenomenon has occurred in the shopping center industry in suburbia. It is what might be called the home-improvement shopping center. It is community or regional in its service area but it has a completely different tenant mix from the traditional regional mall. Its anchor tenant is the home improvement department store, consisting of lumber yard, garden store, kitchen shop, bath shop, plumbing and electrical supplies, flooring, carpeting, wallcovering, roofing, siding, paving, and any number of other home improvement products and services departmentalized under one roof. Its "mall" tenants are specialty stores that augment and expand the variety of goods and services available in any one of these particular categories. The glass shop, mirror shop, custom-furniture store, upholstery shop, and plumbing contractor as opposed to supply store, and as well as similar other contractors of various types and, possibly, the interior decorator, consumer finance company, etc. Mall tenants may also include some less obvious match-up tenants, family clothes, designer outlet, etc.

Why is this idea mentioned in the context of downtown? Because in downtowns of most cities it is impossible to buy a two-by-four. In many cities we are seeing a resurgence and rehabilitation of neighborhoods near or adjacent to downtowns. Yet the goods and services needed to renovate and remodel are concentrated in the suburbs far from this growing market. To a great extent the downtown neighborhoods are being rehabbed by the children of the suburbs, children born and raised with a do-it-yourself home-improvement experience. It would be very interesting to explore the potential for this kind of retail trade in downtowns that are experiencing nearby residential revitalization.

Separately or in combination, these new opportunities—tourism, conventions, specialty shopping goods, entertainment, and home improvements goods—appear to be the unique foundation upon which a viable market for a downtown mall might be constructed.

DESIGN FOR DOWNTOWN

In discussing the opportunities for the development of downtown retail malls within the context of regional shopping center development experience it is absolutely necessary that we examine the design issues for downtown and how they are different from their suburban counterparts. What should a downtown mall look like and how should it work?

As a starting point first let us take a capsule description of the suburban shopping mall. It is the grouping of small stores lining a pedestrian street with department stores as anchor tenants carefully positioned at the extremeties and intermediate points along the pedestrian street to maximize the convenience of the shopper on foot and his access to the maximum amount of goods and services over the shortest traveling distance. As center size has grown, what was originally a one-level configuration has grown to the two-level and, in some instances, three- and four-level configurations in order to maintain an acceptable distance between anchor tenants and dramatically increase the number of stores that may front on the pedestrian street. It is inward-looking because there is no reason for looking out. It is self-contained and climatized. While primarily a place to buy, it is also a place to eat and be entertained. It is a place to watch people and be watched. It is a place to be freed from the automobile except as a means of access.[12]

Surrounding this little self-contained world is a large parking lot designed to minimize the uninteresting walk from car to the center entrance and to minimize the distance required to carry packages and trundle children. The regional shopping center is clean. It is secure. It is open in the daytime, but, more importantly, at night and on weekends. It is very attractive to the individual and to the family. It offers something for all ages.

Almost all of these characteristics are attributes that would be most desirable to transfer downtown. And most of these characteristics are appropriate to transfer downtown. However, the specifics of design need careful interpretation as does the issue of access. For example, multilevel shopping malls work in suburbia because the center is self-contained and pedestrian traffic is carefully designed within this closed system. In downtown, second- and third-level shops have a tough time unless very carefully conceived because shoppers can get out of the "system" easily. Can we legitimately suggest that we can simply lift and transplant the suburban shopping mall downtown? The answer to that question is yes and no.

First of all, we are probably talking about two basic groups of downtowns, those that grew during and after World War II and those that are much older and had their beginning with our nation. The former are those cities in the Sunbelt and in the West which grew up with the automobile much like the suburbs did. They are auto-oriented. They also grew up with air-conditioning, since most are located in hostile climates—extremes of heat, wind, and humidity. The direct transplanting of the regional mall with its parking lots structured instead of surfaced, with its air-conditioned mall turning its back on the outside but connected to adjacent blocks by climatized pedestrian ways, may be an acceptable design concept. Even so, the overall objectives for downtown revitalization suggest the need for modifications, particularly if there is a desire to create a more urban environment.

In eastern and northern cities, or rather let us say, those cities whose basic design and structure preceded the rise of the automobile as a major means of transportation—that had, in their heydays, downtown retail centers that were pedestrian-oriented, tied in later days to the streetcar or subway or elevated rail systems and not the the automobile—an entirely different approach to downtown mall design must be devised. While the mall must strive to maintain the characteristics described for the suburban mall, including such creature comforts as security and shortness of walking distances, it must also reach out and be a part of the network that is the fabric of a revitalized downtown. It should not turn its back on the rest of downtown. Views of the city around it may be an important part of the ambience of a downtown mall that make it different. Unfortunately, there are some examples of inward-turning, fortresslike projects which were conceived in the 1960s and 70s that illustrate very clearly the lack of overall impact a suburban enclosed mall design can have for downtown revitalization.

One major design problem in downtown mall design is that often the anchor tenants are already there. They are in old, inefficient structures and are poorly located in relationship to each other. Downtown must be prepared to compress itself in order to achieve some of the elements of concentration that have been so carefully structured in suburbia. This may require some radical surgery to rearrange anchor tenants.

To sum up very simply, the shopping center mall downtown must be made to fit into the fabric of the community as it is or will be. It will not be a center surrounded by a sea of parking lots. And, therefore, it logically must reach out and be an integral part of the downtown fabric. However, if it is going to work and be competitive with its suburban counterpart, it must achieve the same objectives that made the suburban shopping center mall successful and pleasant. That is, an appropriate grouping of tenants effectively arranged in an attractive shopping environment with strong central management and excellent access.

In suburbia, one of the phenomena that has occurred with regional mall development has been the development of its peripheral areas. It has been suggested that many shopping center developers earn more profits from the peripheral land that they hold for development after the shopping centers have proven successful than they do directly from the shopping center investment. Without defending that statement, it has been said enough times to give it some credence. It is fair to suggest that a regional mall located in downtown can have a similar impact in its downtown but in a different way. Unfortunately the developer of a downtown mall will probably not be in a position to reap any direct benefits since he will not control adjacent sites as he might in suburbia. That leads me to my final comments about the design of malls in downtown which are to examine four concepts, or phenomena if you will, which should be integral parts of the design process for downtown malls. They are: adaptive use, mixed-use development, joint development, and public/private development.

Adaptive Use. The reuse of existing structures for a use or uses other than that for which they were originally intended. In simplest terms adaptive use is the factory that becomes an apartment building, railroad station that becomes a shopping center, warehouse that becomes an office building, or any other possible combinations of original structures and new uses that have been adapted to new and viable economic use.[13] One of the major constraints against new mall development in downtown is the lack of available unencumbered sites for such development. Clearly the last few years have indicated that wholesale urban renewal and clearance to create such sites is neither politically feasible nor necessarily desirable in maintaining and enchancing our existing downtowns. Existing buldings are now being looked upon as an asset, not a liability. In many cases they are also considered of historical importance and, therefore, are protected to some degree from demolition. They require a creativity and sensitivity that can be most demanding of development and design skills if they are to be adapted to a new use.

What is most encouraging is that there are ample examples of design solutions using adaptive use that are significantly more creative and handsome than those fabricated for an empty landscape.[14] Certainly the early prototype, Ghirardelli Square in San Francisco, has proven the worth of this approach and the success that Faneuil Hall has experienced as mentioned earlier reinforces the feasibility and desirability of this concept. What is so important to recognize in adaptive use is it provides an opportunity that the suburbs cannot provide because they do not have the resources. It can clearly prove to be the competitive edge.

Mixed-Use Development. ULI has defined mixed-use development as a large-scale real estate project characterized by (1) three or more significant revenue-producing uses such as retail/office, residential/hotel-motel, and recreation in which well-planned projects are mutually supporting; (2) significant functional and physical integration of project components (and thus a highly intensive use of land) including uninterrupted pedestrian connections; and (3) development in conformance with a coherent plan (which frequently stipulated the types and scale of uses, permitted densities, and related items).[15]

A survey conducted in conjuction with ULI's publication on mixed use indicated that there were eighty mixed-use development projects existent or under development in the United States and Canada as of 1976. Since that time many more projects of a similar nature that meet the criteria described above have been undertaken. They are not all in downtown and they do not all include significant retail elements in the form of a downtown shopping mall, but they do all represent a unique and logical approach to downtown revitalization.

Most of our downtowns were originally developed as a series of single purpose buildings, offices, theaters, department stores, shops, etc. There were public investments in public activities such as concert halls and convention centers but, again, they tended to be freestanding facilities, totally independent of their neighbors.

One of the prototypes discussed in the mixed-use book is Rockefeller Center in New York. In many ways it is the granddaddy of mixed-use development. It is under single development control. It has, with some exceptions, a well-organized pedestrian network that serves the entire Rockefeller Center area. It has been designed to grow. It is not fixed in time. It has a variety of uses. And, most importantly, its greatest strength is that it has become a place to go. It is in and of itself an attraction.

One of the later modifications in suburban shopping center design has been to make them not just retail centers but places to go, places for people—places where people can congregate, where they can do more than just shop, places to eat, to be entertained, to see, and to be seen. The logical extension of this concept is to go beyond simply the activities related to retailing and suggest that the combining of office, recreation, civic functions, institutional activities and educational facilities into complexes which are very carefully integrated together will result in a magnet that cannot but help to attract new users. Therefore, it is important, in looking at opportunities and prospects for downtown malls, to recognize that they should not be considered independently, as they are so often in suburbia, but rather as a potential element in a much more ambitious and, therefore, mutually supportive mixed-use development proposal.

Joint Development. As defined in ULI's publication, *Joint Development: Making the Real Estate-Transit Connection*, joint development is real estate development that is closely linked to public transportration services and station facilities and relies to a considerable extent on the market and locational advantages provided by the transit facility.[16]

Joint development provides a unique opportunity in the development of downtown shopping malls. Unlike its suburban counterpart, the downtown mall's access could or, perhaps should, be by mass transit. As a result of initiatives to revitalize our downtowns and most specifically as a result of the rising costs of gasoline and the potential for energy shortages at any cost, new mass transit systems have been developed or are proposed and existing systems are undergoing analysis for refurbishment and improvement.

When we described our prototypical downtown market area, we described as one of our major sources of potential customers those that are located in the first tier suburbs and beyond. Mass transit lines reaching out from downtown can dramatically expand the population within thirty minutes travel distance. An argument has been made that this same system can draw customers out of downtown to suburban malls. That is true to the extent that transit stations would be located within existing or proposed shopping centers in suburbia. A quick examination of existing or proposed systems suggests that this is rarely if ever the case.

In contrast, downtown transit stations are almost invariably located

within the existing downtown retail district. The proper proximity exists.
All that remains is to take advantage of that proximity in the planning
and design of downtown malls. The competitive advantage is obvious. If
we think of the transit station as being the parking lot in a suburban mall
and, therefore, the point of access to the center, then the distance from
the transit station to the downtown mall entrances should probably be no
more than 300 to 350 feet, which is the typical furthest distance from the
edge of the suburban center's parking lot to the mall entrance. Obviously,
even closer would be more effective. The access should be convenient and
direct, not inconvenient and indirect. Unfortunately, the two newest
systems in the United States (BART in San Francisco and METRO in
Washington, D.C.) have not effectively taken maximum advantage of
this opportunity. The Gallery in Philadelphia, developed in conjunction
with an existing transit system, is by far the best finished example in this
country.[17] The International Square development in Washington, D.C.,
when it is completed, will be a good example of both joint- and mixed-use
development. Canada to our north, however, has understood this concept
very well and much sooner than we. Examples like Eaton Centre in
Toronto[19] and Place Bonaventure[20] and Place Ville Marie[21] in Montreal
provide good illustrations.

There is an analogy to be made between the need for immediate access from transit to the shopping mall and the problems we have experienced in trying to provide parking downtown as an inducement to
retail revitalization. There are numerous examples where parking has
been provided downtown because it was felt that insufficient parking was
one of the causes of decline of retail sales. There are many examples that
such parking has not provided the kind of immediate and direct access to
a shopping mall that is suggested as necessary for transit to have a positive
impact. Extensive downtown parking has also not been cost-competitive
with free parking at suburban centers and, therefore, did not have the
desired result. A major consideration, therefore, in assuring the success of
a downtown mall will be the provision of access as good or better than
that provided in suburbia. The quantity of parking needed must be
balanced by the availability of transit access but, in all cases, the quality
of parking or transit and its proximity are probably more important.

There is one inherent characteristic of transit-delivered patronage
that has not been effectively addressed. That is the problem of package
handling. At the suburban mall purchases are carried for very short
distances along efficiently designed pedestrian streets. If they become too
burdensome, they can be quickly and conveniently transported to the
automobile parked nearby so that the shopper can continue unimpeded

by heavy or awkwardly shaped packages. If the package is somewhat too heavy or bulky in shape, convenient package pick-up points have been made available.

In our downtowns of yore, package delivery was an accepted part of the cost of doing business for downtown stores. This has all but disappeared except for the most exclusive of retailers. Perhaps one of the new elements that needs to be created in the downtown mall along with joint development with transit is the development of a centralized package receipt and delivery service that would assure same-day or, at worst, overnight delivery of purchases, thus relieving transit passengers from carrying any more than they wish to. This might truly give downtown centers a competitive edge. It's possible that this service plus transit fares could be provided at a cost below that charged for parking as compared with auto access using high cost gasoline. If the improvement center concept were to be applied downtown, a solution to the handling of deliveries would be equally important to success.

Public/Private Development. Another idea alluded to in the mixed-use development discussion and the joint-development discussion is the opportunity in downtown for development that includes both private and public facilities. Any number of communities are looking to the commitment of major amount of public funds in the development of convention centers, civic centers, centers for the performing arts, as the public's contribution to the revitalization of cities. All too often in the past, these facilities have been developed independent of any attempts to integrate them with private development. Here again is a unique opportunity not available to the suburban regional mall. However, it presents a whole new series of problems to the development process. ULI, in its *Downtown Development Handbook*,[22] attempts to address the complexities of public/private development. It is a brand new field in development terms. The range of experience on which we might draw is very limited and, in many cases, too recent in implementation to provide any test over time. It is, however, a concept that must be pursued if public investment is to truly leverage private reinvestment in our downtowns.

CONSTRAINTS ON DOWNTOWN MALLS

Given the new opportunities for creating markets in downtown described above and the new development techniques that might be used to implement it, can the potential for downtown malls be effectively achieved? Can they be developed and be competitive? The outlook for some holds great promise; to others the likelihood of success in all but a few instances would appear questionable.

Sites for downtown malls are tough to come by. When they are available, the cost per square foot of site will be significantly higher than that of a potential site in suburbia. Likewise, construction costs will be much higher than those experienced in suburbia. This will also be true for all operating costs, particularly security and maintenance. Preservation concerns which encourage adaptive use may be a constraint against the use of surgery to rearrange existing elements, anchor tenants, etc. Most probably, government intervention will be needed both to provide the tools necessary to create sites but also to resolve the conflicts of preservation and revitalization.

For a downtown mall to succeed, the rents that it must support must be much higher per square foot than that required in a typical regional mall. There is some evidence that this may be possible and it has been achieved over the short term in several recent examples. Is it sustainable?

The growth of regional malls has been tied to a rising percentage of disposable income. We are now seeing dramatic increases in the cost of housing, food and transportation, with a suggestion that more increases in these areas are yet to come. These increases have significantly eroded the discretionary purchasing power of the average family. What impact will this have on the demand for specialty goods, entertainment, recreation and tourism, and convention and meeting businesses, all of which seem to be those elements that will help support a market for downtown malls? While it has proven desirable and necessary to provide subsidies to downtown development in order to balance out higher costs than developing elsewhere, it is with the assumption that over time these subsidies will be recovered. Statistics indicate that the cost of placing new shopping facilities on line has far outstripped the potential for those centers to provide a sales-income stream to support the capital costs. This has resulted in a slowing down of shopping center development in suburbia. It would appear that it is not the competition between city and suburbs that is the threat to realizing the potential of malls in downtown, but rather the competition for spendable dollars between discretionary consumer goods and the dollars required for shelter, food, transportaiton, and health care.

Summary

Downtown can be the site of a regional mall. Because of its unique location as the central focus of our larger metropolitan areas, as the hub of transit systems, and the destination of tourists, businessmen, and convention and meeting attendees, it would appear it is also possible for it to regain some of its preeminence as the center of retail trade for selected specialty goods and services. It will not be possible to achieve these objectives without a strong public/private partnership. Success will be demanding of the best development talents available.

Notes

1. Urban Land Institute (ULI), *Shopping Center Development Handbook* Washington, D.C. (1977), pp. 12-20.

2. *Ibid*, p. 1.

3. *Ibid*, p.. 15.

4. The *Directory of Shopping Centers in the United States and Canada, 1977*, Burlington, Iowa: National Research Bureau, (1977), and U. S. Department of Commerce, Bureau of the Census, *Statistical Abstract of the United States*, Government Printing Office, Washington, D.C., (1978), p. 141, Table 710 (Gross National Product in Current and Constant [1972] Dollars, 1950 to 1977).

5. U. S. Department of Commerce, Bureau of the Census, *County and City Data Book, 1977*, Table A-2 (Population in 1975 and 1970 of SMSAs in 1975 Population Rank Order), p. 800.

6. Rodney E. Engelen, "What Is The Future Of Downtown Retailing In Middle America?" and Gerald Schwartz, "The Middle Market: An Idea Whose Time Has Come?" *Urban Land* (October 1979).

7. ULI, *Shopping Center Development Handbook*, p. 25.

8. J. Thomas Black, *The Changing Economic Role of Central Cities*, Washington, D.C.: Urban Land Institute, (1978).

9. ULI, *Shopping Center Development Handbook*, p. 29.

10. Nina Gruen, "What is Special About Specialty Shopping Centers?" *Urban Land* (January 1978).

11. Kathy Long, "Disco Draws Dancers, Shoppers to Downtown Cincinnati, Ohio" *National Mall Monitor* (September/October 1979), pp. 28-29.

12. See case studies on shopping malls in *Shopping Center Development Handbook*, pp. 149-248.

13. See *Adaptive Use: Development Economics, Process, and Profiles*, Washington, D.C.: Urban Land Institute, (1978).

14. *Ibid*, pp. 162-240.

15. Robert E. Witherspoon, Jon P. Abbett, and Robert M. Gladstone, *Mixed-Use Developments: New Ways of Land Use*, Washington, D.C.: Urban Land Institute, (1976).

16. ULI Research Division with Gladstone Associates, *Joint Development: Making the Real Estate-Transit Connection*, Washington, D.C.: Urban Land Institute, (1979).

17. "The Gallery," *Project Reference File*, Vol. 8, No. 4 (1978) and *Joint Development*, pp. 33-62.

18. *Joint Development*, pp. 86-98.

19. "Eaton Centre," *Project Reference File*, Vol. 8, No. 14 (1978).

20. *Joint Development*, pp. 99-127.

21. *Ibid*, p. 101 and *Mixed-Use Development*, p. 186.

22. *The Downtown Development Handbook* [ULI, 1980] is the fourth handbook in the Community Builders Handbook series. It focuses on the emerging process for downtown revitalization.

The Preliminary Track Record

PETER D. LEIBOWITS

Compliments have been paid to my partners in Canada, suggesting that their innovative development procedures in downtown projects in Canada would be the basis for their developments in the United States. However, the reason for my partnership with Cadillac Fairview was due to the differences in development procedures between Canadian shopping centers and U.S. shopping centers. There are similarities, but the shopping patterns and the use of mass transportation dictates different approaches from those which would be successful in the United States.

The retail complex in the urban areas of Canada was successful due to the excellent mass transportation which is used by people of all economic levels. This superb transportation network provides easy accessibility to downtown, where major retailers maintain major flagship stores providing downtown with the ability to provide the customer with a greater choice and selection of merchandise and services. In addition, the severe winters in Canada created a unique need to provide climatized shopping areas in the downtown area.

The basic topic of this paper is to define the preliminary track record of downtown shopping malls in the United States. While it is too early to come to a definitive conclusion as to the viability of the few projects that have been built, I do believe that the properly designed and merchandised retail complex in carefully selected downtowns will be successful and will become an increasingly important trend for the shopping center industry.

Each downtown has distinct and different environments and characteristics. Therefore, retail complexes will be designed and developed to blend and meet these differences.

There have been *four* basic types of retail developments that have taken place in downtowns and will continue to take place in downtowns. The *first* was the pedestrian mall created by closing the main retail street between the existing retail structures, and improving the environment with plantings, benches, fountains and other aesthetic amenities. This approach, for some downtown areas, is a satisfactory solution, better than dislodging or relocating the retail district of the central business district.

The *second* current form of downtown retailing is to create substantial retail complexes within the spines of major office and hotel complexes. These projects can be successful if they are merchandised to serve the daytime office population and the new city residents. This form of retailing complements the structures that they are part of.

The *third* type of retail complex is to build enclosed regional malls between existing major department stores or to add major department stores within the urban area. *If department stores maintain flagship stores (defined as significantly larger and better merchandised stores than their suburban counterparts) downtown, and if those stores have maintained their significant market share, chances are there is an opportunity to build additional retail facilities to complement the extant department store(s) and create viable opportunities for additional retailers.*

Obviously the decision to do so will then be dependent on the availability of contiguous properties and the willingness of the political structure in assisting private developers in this plan. Two illustrations of this concept can be viewed in our company's project in White Plains, New York, where we are adding two new department stores to the market in a traditionally designed mall downtown and in Columbus, Ohio where we are planning a major mall connected to a highly successful Lazarus department store.

The *fourth* type of development, and perhaps the most difficult, is the anchorless retail development or the theme center such as Quincy Market in Boston. This project required creative development procedures and merchandising to uniquely fulfill the populations' requirements. Quincy Market is highly successful in Boston due to its easy accessibility from the traditional retail district, the large tourism and the tremendous college population of the city. It is my premise that very few cities could support a project such as the Quincy Market. However, since each city has its own unique characteristics, creative development can perhaps find its own success in specific communities.

The element that seems to be significant in downtown projects has been an emphasis on providing an important food and entertainment environment as part of these projects. In evaluating successful projects such as Quincy Market in Boston, Gallery in Philadelphia, Ghirardelli Square in San Francisco and Citicorp Center in New York, all are uniquely different. However one common denominator is there—food and entertainment components in an architecturally exciting environment.

Our company operates two divisions: one is a suburban mall division developing nine malls in major markets throughout the U.S.; the other division is an urban mall division which is responsible for building, and finding cities within the U.S. where we can build major retail complexes as part of the central business district. Since this paper is focusing on downtown projects, the comments will be limited to our urban division and those factors which created the need for us to have a specialized urban mall division.

The suburban mall came into being some two decades ago due to the vast growth of our suburbs. The major retailer simply followed his customer into the suburbs in order to provide better and more convenient services to his customers. The American public became obsessed with the use of the automobile, and with the growth of the suburbs, the automobile and the expansion of our highway system provided excellent locations for department stores to expand nearer their customers. The shopping center was created to fulfill these needs and has continuously become a more sophisticated and exciting marketplace to fulfill the shoppers' needs. The shopping center started as a small strip of stores, progressing in the last two and one-half decades to in some cases, as large as seven department stores with over two million square feet of retail space under one controlled and planned environment.

The trend and need for the suburban shopping center will continue in the future, fulfilling changing growth patterns and shifting population needs. However, a new downtown trend has emerged because the improving environment in the central business district is creating an exciting place for people to work, shop and live. This trend is creating opportunities in many cities to build significant retail complexes. With proper analysis and planning, developers will find rewarding opportunities in our forgotten downtowns.

The 1980s present, in my opinion, new patterns for the shopping center industry. First, and certainly most important, is the revitalization of existing shopping centers. Some are now approximately twenty years old; with renovation and remerchandising, these centers can continue to maintain their competitive position in their respective markets.

The ability of department stores to merchandise smaller stores is what we define as "middle markets." The middle market can be as small as 150,000 people within a trade area and with properly sized developments these markets can now have and support quality enclosed shopping centers.

The final, and certainly the most dynamic, pattern emerging is the opportunity to build retail complexes in many of our cities throughout this country. The growth of downtown malls will not be stimulated by government restrictions on suburban developments. There are a number of factors emerging in the 1980s that do provide a viable opportunities in our downtowns—these conditions should be the stimulus, not more government or government control. One factor stimulating urban growth is the impact of women in the work force; currently over 50 percent of married women are now working. Women's role outside the home provides for changing development opportunities. Commuting will now be evaluated differently. With a couple traveling thirty to sixty minutes daily, downtown residence has become much more desirable and a realistic alternative to suburban living.

The cost of new single-family housing has now increased to an average of over $70,000. Restoration of older homes, townhouses and brownstones has become very fashionable, and people are discovering them as an excellent investment as well as a fashionable place to live. Apartment living is becoming acceptable to the working family.

The 60s and 70s saw a tremendous slum clearance in our cities. Fountain Square in Cincinnati, for instance, created the need for new and modern office space. Less congestion and more open spaces provided a much more acceptable environment downtown.

Another important factor in the redevelopment of downtown is the concentration of mass transportation in the cities. The department of transportation is making a major commitment to all types of mass transportation, such as bus malls in Portland, Oregon, Columbus, Ohio and subways in Baltimore and Washington. We are convinced that the development of economical and convenient mass transportation will serve to make downtowns more competitive with the suburbs. As a matter of fact, in Washington, Woodward and Lothrop recently completed a 6-million-dollar renovation which tied its store into the recently opened Washington Metro system. They report that customers in the store have increased by 70 percent since that project's completion.

The rising cost of energy is one of the great crises facing our nation in the 1980s. As energy costs continue to escalate, the luxury of suburban living, which is not energy efficient, will become less and less attractive. Coupled with mass transportation and housing, the energy crisis will tend to be a significant factor which will help increase the population of downtown.

The quality of life goals have made dramatic changes in the family of today. Married couples are starting their families later and have been placing more emphasis on dining out and going to theaters. We have also been noticing the emergence of single-person households; this means for urban areas more people will be going and living downtown. Therefore, when downtowns provide housing, entertainment, shopping and convenience in their working place, their viability will continually increase. The 80s will see this new family emerge, creating continuing changing development opportunities to meet the new trends.

What will this all mean to us? It means that the American dream is different today than it was before. Since World War II, the goal of the American has been to have a house, a half acre, a car and a boat. This has changed dramatically. The sons and daughters of this generation are going to be living differently and having different desires than their parents. Their needs, created by the times, have them walking to work, having fewer children, women involved with activities outside the home, involvement in a variety of social and environmental concerns. Creating a desirable alternative in the central city will make for an attractive lifestyle.

Now that we have moved some of the people back into downtown, I am going to tell you some of the problems about going into downtown. Some downtowns have lost their reason for being. This means that the retail development is not their solution and the prevention of suburban growth is not servicing the needs of the population. The developer cannot work within the downtown alone. He needs public assistance. In the five urban projects in which we are involved, we have asked and have received varying degrees of assistance involving federal, state and municipal funds. Without that, our projects would not be economically viable.

We have stated and shown, that in some cities the cost factors in downtown are dramatically greater than in the suburbs; therefore government assistance is required to provide the developer with incentives that would equate the economics of suburban developments.

The approval process of downtown projects is much more complex and time consuming, although the gap is narrowing. Costs are invariably higher, design and construction more complex, security and operating costs are often higher. Tenants will frequently face a different merchandising operation. Socioeconomic problems and federal assistance is complicated by accompanying requirements and red tape.

The pros for going into downtown, however, can be summed up in this manner: For the past several decades there has been a retailing vacuum downtown. Resources now exist to enable developers to create a very competitive retail environment. There now exists a potential to draw from the total market, particularly where the department store operates a flagship unit. Often the anchors need only renovate, as opposed to building new structures, thus giving them lower entry costs into the market. *As the downtown attracts more housing and employment, the primary market will grow faster than the remaining marginal sites in the suburbs, creating more opportunities downtown.*

The downtown development project is able to call upon a new and very significant resource—public financial assistance. While the various programs are often confusing and may be overlapping, the end result can mean the addition of a lot more dollars to enhance economic feasibility. The following is a partial list of the federal programs that are available to assist implementation of downtown projects:

1. *Urban Renewal.* This program has been in existence for many years and is the grandfather of economic development programs. By designating renewal agencies, Urban Renewal provides for land condemnation and at one time provided grants directly to approved projects. While the grants have been transferred to other programs, the condemnation program is a useful tool and in some cases cities may have some urban renewal monies available for existing projects. Phase I of The Gallery in Philadelphia utilized $18 million from this program to pay for the construction of the mall area.

2. *Community Development Block Grants.* CD funds are the result of combining several older programs into one grant given to the city yearly. Downtown development projects seeking this form of assistance compete on a local level with requests for neighborhood playgrounds, social programs and other "people" programs. This usually means a very difficult and risky approval process.

3. *Urban Development Action Grants.* UDAGs are the current method HUD uses to provide direct aid to a specific development project. This program currently provides $400 million per year and has gotten a lot of attention from the development community. HUD talks in terms of providing "equity" money, but most of the funds will be committed only after private financing is secured. Recently they have also been preferring a second loan approach as opposed to a grant. The Albee Square Mall now under construction in Brooklyn has used this program.

4. *Economic Development Administration.* EDA has a number of very successful economic development programs. In addition to libraries, city halls and other public works projects, EDA gives grants and loans for public amenities and private development. In Columbus, Ohio EDA has funded a public plaza/ice rink which will be a major amenity for the Capital South project—a retail, office and hotel development. This agency is very cooperative and has avoided much of the bureaucratic entanglements one finds in HUD.

5. *Urban Mass Transit Administration.* The new UMTA urban initiation program is designed to aid downtown projects that are related to mass

transit. UMTA has become very aware of the opportunities for
economic development in association with mass transit stations and has
just published a book in connection with the Urban Land Institute entitled *Joint Development: Making the Real Estate-Transit Connection*.

6. *Historic Rehabilitation/Adaptive Reuse*. Recent changes in the tax
    laws allow a five-year depreciation schedule for improvements to
    buildings that are certified as historical structures. This excellent tax
    shelter is making reuse projects feasible in older downtown structures.
    Helmesly's Palace Hotel in New York is probably the biggest project in
    the country using this form of assistance.

7. *Industrial Revenue Bonds*. Coupled with a UDAG grant, there is an
    IRS ruling raising the limit on the issuing of industrial revenue bonds
    to $20 million. This makes an attractive vehicle for a project to lower
    the financing constant by utilizing tax free revenue bonds.

On a lesser scale, Interior can finance urban recreational areas, i.e.,
parks and plazas; HUD has a myriad of neighborhood- and housing-
oriented programs, Labor has the CETA programs and even Agriculture
has an economic development capability. While the rules and regulations
change frequently, a city with good federal relations can draw on significant federal aid to make a downtown project economically viable.

There are also a variety of state and local economic development incentives. Tax abatement, zoning changes, the funding of capital improvements from local or state funding sources, and special taxing
districts are often available at the local level to make downtown projects a
reality.

Our urban division is involved in a number of major retail complexes
in the central business district. The first project, which we will open in
the summer of 1980, is in White Plains, New York. And as I looked at this
list I realized my next word was that White Plains was unique, but I
realized that basically every one of these projects has something unique
about it reflecting the characteristics of each city.

In White Plains, the opportunity to build a center was provided by
restrictive zoning throughout Westchester County. These communities,
and not the federal government, decided on the type of environment they
wanted and in doing so dictated that the retail hub for the county would
be in downtown White Plains. Therefore, the obvious solution in this
market of a million people, which currently has no enclosed regional
shopping center, was to build a center in the heart of downtown White
Plains and to complement the existing retail structure of the city.

The White Plains Urban Redevelopment program began in 1958.
Our shopping center, The Galleria, will open in 1980. Even though the
opportunity to build a regional center was clear, the lengthy delay before
the reality of a new center was caused by the reluctance of department

stores to locate in downtowns and the acknowledgement by political officials that, in order to help downtown, they would have to provide amenities and financial assistance to make the economics viable. The key to this project's success was Federated Department Store's and J.C. Penney's willingness to be downtown and the city of White Plains's willingness and ability to build a major parking complex as part of the project.

The next project is in Columbus, Ohio. Columbus has regional malls throughout the suburbs; however Lazarus Department Store, 1 million square feet of retail space with approximately $100 million in sales annually, is in the heart of downtown Columbus. Lazarus has remained the dominant retail force in the greater Columbus area and we, as developers, are going to capitalize on their strength and complement their store and provide an even greater reason to come downtown and elongate the customers' shopping hours.

Our plan is simply to build an exciting environment, which we refer to as our Town Center concept, to encourage the shopper to leave the Lazarus store through the mall, anchoring it with a major food and entertainment court. Additional anchors will be a major Western International hotel and office tower with direct links to the center. Phase II of this project will include adding additional department stores and peripheral store space with one or two office towers above the retail structure.

Kansas City, our next urban project, presented considerations not only of suburban competition but of other retail developments adjacent to downtown. This area not only has adequate suburban malls, but additionally has the Crown Center Development, a retail multi-use project which is about six blocks outside the downtown area, and Country Club Plaza, a substantial retail development, a couple of miles outside the downtown.

However, in the heart of downtown Kansas City two department stores have remained viable and have maintained their market share. It became apparent that by connecting those department stores with a climatized mall a viable retail entity could be successfully developed. With the cooperation of Macy's and Jones Department Store, a division of Mercantile, we proposed a plan to the city that would ensure the continuance of major retail activity in the heart of Kansas City. We are confident that linking Macy's and Jones Department Stores with a supportive mall introducing new small retailers will result in an extremely viable downtown for Kansas City, the merchants, and ourselves as developer.

Cadillac Fairview and our partners, Texas Eastern, have jointly undertaken a development in Houston, Texas consisting of thirty blocks in the heart of the central business district. We recently broke ground for a hotel and are drawing plans for a few million square feet of office space. Analyzing the retail needs of downtown Houston, it became apparent that its huge office population was not being served by any important retail complex. We are planning a 200,000 square foot retail complex with 25 percent food and the balance specialty retail stores to serve this vast office and residential population.

The merchandising and marketing will be geared to the vast population that is in downtown and we will tie our project together with the underground pedestrian system now in Houston. We are planning the project in phases in order to increase the gross leaseable area to continually meet the requirements of the increasing population of Houston and any changing patterns of downtown which will emerge.

In our downtown developments our first step is to determine the strength and needs of the city. We analyze realistically the suburban competitive facilities and the attractiveness of the project to bring people back into downtown. The final decision in developing downtown is to build a project that uniquely fills a void in that market. If you ask me for a single most important factor to have in a downtown retail complex, my initial response is a major flagship store providing goods and services not provided in suburban outlets.

Retail needs can be met downtown in the four ways mentioned earlier. Not every city should try to build a mall in its core, but rather use that retailing which is suited for its downtown. Cities must build on their existing strength and be prepared to be flexible with changing demographics.

A relationship and partnership must be established between the public and private sectors to bring these types of projects to fruition. These relationships will provide opportunities for many types of development. The private and public relationships must be strengthened and reinforced, recognizing the realities both for the public interest's and the private developers' economic requirements. The 80s will present continuing opportunities in downtowns to again reinstate downtown as a major retail market place.

Downtown Pedestrian Malls

MARGARET S. WIRTENBERG

How to revitalize declining downtown areas in central cities has been of increasing concern to businessmen and landowners, politicians and planners for almost three decades. Rejecting radical alternatives, the concerned forces in some cities decided on a conservative (in the sense of preservative) approach: the establishment of a downtown pedestrian mall by closing the main shopping street to vehicular traffic.

Cities in which the mall alternative was carried through from the 1950s to 1974 number forty-nine, according to data compiled by the Downtown Research Association. Of these forty-nine downtown malls,* fifteen occured in traditional census-defined central business district cities. Ten of these are the subject of this study; the other five are excluded for one or more of the following reasons: unavailability of data, very recent creation of the mall, mall location outside of the city's CBD, or mall location within a totally new construction project.

The ten cities studied are Evansville, Indiana; Fresno, California; Knoxville, Tennessee; Lansing, Michigan; Louisville, Kentucky; New Bedford, Massachusetts; Paterson, New Jersey; Providence, Rhode Island;

---

*Malls in smaller cities and towns, while more numerous, are of less interest here as they represent the creation of a center rather than the salvage of existing streets and structures downtown.

Sacramento, California; and Tacoma, Washington.

City directories were used to tabulate numbers and types of businesses by street, before and after the establishment of the mall. In each case it was determined that a considerable majority (approximately 70 percent) of the businesses in the mall vicinity or matrix were located on the mall street, one street parallel to it, and one cross street linking the two. It is these three streets which were analyzed in detail. Businesses were categorized according to the *Standard Industrial Classification Manual*.

Mall cities, like Rome, were not built in a day or in a vacuum. To understand the phenomenon of malls at a particular stage in the urban evolution, it is necessary that mall cities be viewed in the context of population and income trends for city and region, and the trend in business formation for region, city and CBD.

When the Census Bureau introduced the concept called the "Standard Metropolitan Statistical Area" in the early 1900s, it gave official recognition to that amorphous region, which over the years has attracted outward-bound city people and businesses in their wake. It was inevitable, however, that the outward current would flow even farther afield to new amorphous megaregions. The ultimate has now become the penultimate, with the announcement that this year (1980) the Bureau is introducing the concept of "Consolidated Areas," each consisting of two or more SMSAs. The fact that some SMSAs are losing population and income to more distant suburbs is far from reassuring to the cities and their shrinking CBDs.

To some degree, the national centifugal trends are reflected in the population trends in the ten mall cities and nine SMSAs from 1950 to 1970 (Paterson did not have SMSA data for 1950). The growth in the average (mean) population of the SMSAs was greater in 1950-60 than 1960-70. For the cities, the 1950-60 decade showed a slight decline, partially due to outmigration from cities to other parts of their SMSAs. In the 1960-70 decade, the decline was halted and the trend rose slightly. On the average, therefore, it would appear that all is not downhill for the ten mall cities in terms of population.

Since all ten cities came to the same conclusion, to create downtown malls, it would seem correct to conclude that they were equally vulnerable economically. But that was not the case. Five cities had a higher per capita income than their SMSAs and their retail stores were not declining in number. The other five cities were lower in per capita income than their SMSAs and their retail businesses were declining. What made these two apparently opposite groups of cities agree on the decision to create downtown malls?

The question touches on the waning role of the CBDs in respect to the regions. Where CBDs once had regional function, these have largely been taken over by suburban shopping centers (major retail centers) yet other retail shopping needs are still being supplied in the city and its CBD. Downtown, once the mecca where all shopping needs could be filled, is no longer the magnet, and the decentralization of its functions has hastened its decline. Whether a city was richer or poorer, or was gaining or losing population, each of the ten cities had a common Achilles' heel, an economically hobbled downtown.

For the ten subject cities, the growing danger became very real in economic terms in the mid-fifties, when the number of retail stores in the cities started their downtrend and businesses in the CBDs were poised at the edge of a precipitous slide. There was also the insidious danger of creeping obsolescence associated with the CBDs, as reflected in dormant land use unaccommodated to changing business needs, and obsolescence of the physical plant itself. Occupancy of commercial structures dropped off as prospective tenants preferred other locations to downtown.

Beause a mall represents a microcosm of the world of trade, its human scale does not intimidate the investigator who would make quick assumptions and easy generalizations. However, without a detailed examination of the mall matrix and especially its three major streets, it would be different to measure the effects of the establishment of a mall by a street closing.

The creation of a mall, as a deliberate act of containment of a variety of commercial activities within a circumscribed area, exerts a dynamic effect on the business character of the closed street and the other two major streets, the parallel street and the cross street. To a greater or lesser degree among the ten cities, a reordering of types of businesses occurs in each of these streets which indicates a commonality of experience. Comparison of the distribution of types of businesses in each of the three streets before and after the establishment of the mall reveals consistent characteristics of land use change in the mall and adjacent streets.

It can be shown that there are specific characteristics which the major streets in all ten cities have in common. For example, streets located in similar relationship to the mall (and the mall street itself) in the ten cities share a common experience.

In terms of sheer numbers of businesses of all kinds, mall streets were home for more businesses than the other two major streets combined. Generally, it appears axiomatic that mall streets are the dominant ones in a mall matrix. This is not the case in all ten cities; in New Bedford, the major cross street has more tenants than the mall street. Only in Paterson, the smallest and least typical of the ten malls, does the mall street have fewer tenants in general and fewer retail tenants than the parallel or cross streets.

In the mall streets of the ten cities, the retail sector (or two-digit group in the 50s segment in the SIC code) outnumbered the retail sector in both of the other major streets combined by almost their combined total. The yardstick of retail function gives the mall street an even more dominant role in the mall matrix than the yardstick of total of businesses.

The mall street, therefore, as differentiated from the other major streets in the mall matrix, has maintained a strong retail posture in the total business mix. It should be pointed out that the general decline in numbers of business of all kinds (including retail, at a slightly slower rate than the total) prior to the establishment of the mall did not come to a halt with the street closing. The only exception was the government sector, which grew in the mall street and flourished to a greater extent in the major parallel street. As for the major cross street, government offices declined at first, than gained.

The major parallel street, traditionally less important than the mall street in retail activity, was nonetheless a largely retail street before the mall. In the years following the closing of the mall street, this ceased to be the case. Instead the parallel street has increasingly become the site for professional and governmental offices.

This change from secondary retail street to office orientation makes the major parallel street an indirect beneficiary of the street closing. For although it generally declined in numbers of businesses, that decline was at a slightly slower pace than that of the mall street itself. In this regard, the individual cities differed from the average to an extent that this finding seems to lack the overwhelming endorsement as a demonstrable mode of land use change. However, the data offers considerable weight to the preliminary conclusion that major parallel streets have indeed undergone a transition from areas of mostly retail activity to largely office-type businesses as a result of the formation of the mall.

Of the three major streets in the mall matrix, the major cross street was most vulnerable to the disruption of traffic patterns downtown as a result of the closing of the mall street. Before that, the major cross street had the second highest total of businesses among the three major streets. Subsequently, it lost so many businesses that it barely retained its second place. The rate of decline in numbers of businesses in the cross street was approximately 50 percent greater than in either the mall street or the parallel street. Even the government sector declined in the cross street at first, then showed a nominal increase compared with the other major streets.

Summarizing the effects of a downtown mall on the three major streets in its matrix, it is apparent that mall streets have enlarged their role in retail business and parallel streets have become more office oriented, with both of these results occurring, to some degree, at the expense of the cross streets.

For a closer analysis of the business composition of the three major streets, it is necessary to examine the "before" and "after" situations in each of the streets from the perspective of the numbers and percentages of specific types of business (to two digits in the SIC code) in relation to the total number of businesses in each street.

In all ten malls, each major street is made up, to a greater or lesser degree, of all sectors of the broad industrial classifications. In seven of the ten cases, the retail function, quantitatively, is not predominant, in that it does not constitute at least 50 percent of the total number of businesses. It is the service businesses and professional services taken together which have the largest percentage. Retail businesses run a close second in the mall streets, but show a decline in favor of services elsewhere. The only mall street whose retail businesses represent more than half of the total are Knoxville, by an overwhelming proportion; Tacoma, by just barely more than half, and Paterson, where the extremely low proportion of activity in the mall street in relation to the other two major streets reduces its statistical validity for this analysis.

While it has been pointed out that the government services moved counter-trendwise when the total number of businesses was declining in all three major streets, it is interesting to note the percentages. In the mall street, prior to its closing, government offices represented less than 1 percent of all businesses. After the mall street was closed, the share of the government sector rose to 4 percent. In the parallel street, the rise in government offices was markedly greater, going from just over 9 percent to just over 18 percent. Slower growth was evident in the crossstreet, where the government sector rose from 7½ to just over 10 percent.

Thus, government services in total increased from 4.6 percent to 8.4 percent of all business in the three major streets, with the percentage of government offices in each case varying inversely with the prominence of the retail sector in each street.

In view of the great deal of turnover of businesses in pre and postmall years, an effort was made to find where the missing businesses went after they left their former location in the major streets. Toward this end, a demonstration study of the New Bedford experience indicated that the amount of change within the downtown area was indeed impressive, and that replacement business does appear in the mall street and even more so in the parallel street, but not in the cross street.

In the mall street twenty-nine businesses remained in the CBD, yet the fact that there were forty-four businesses in the mall street after the street was closed indicates that fifteen new businesses had moved to the mall. In the parallel street the total number of businesses remained approximately the same, yet the number of old businesses was but half the total. Over forty additional businesses found the parallel street a good location; the same cannot be said for the cross street. Almost all the businesses located there after the mall was established were there before; almost no new businesses were attracted.

These findings also reaffirm the conclusion that closing a street in downtown can be a boon or a bane to business, depending on its location in the matrix, and the probability that changed traffic patterns may inhibit the development of a cross street in particular.

As such enterprises as general merchandise stores in increasing numbers pursued their customers to the suburbs, the central business district, traditionally the home for a complete range of retail businesses, became even more retail oriented. In the streets that housed a miscellany of individual retail establishments before the streets were closed as pedestrian malls, the number of these stores increased later. In the ten mall cities, department stores have been deserting their downtown sites.

For the most part, the changes in land use in the mall and its vicinity have taken place against a background of decline in the total number of businesses. Yet there is a modicum of comfort for the cities in the fact that although the regions are unquestionably in the ascendant over the cities and particularly their business centers, there are hopeful indications in that the cities are losing retail stores more slowly while the regions are gaining them more slowly.

In the effort to determine whether there is a consistency among streets which have become malls, in terms of physical characteristics, such as street dimensions and bulk and distribution of structures, more diversity than consistency was discovered. While there were many extreme contrasts in linear dimensions and other criteria, the contrasts were offset in part by apparent consistencies in the relative bulk and density of structures in the ten malls.

Malls have been criticized because the upper stories of the buildings are largely vacant in contrast to the bustling street level activity. It was Kierkegaard who wrote that life can be viewed as a three-level mansion but most people live in the cellar. To their credit, most of the malls in this study have helped increase the occupancy rate in the street level as well as the first floor in the entire mall matrix, but they did not do as well for the upper stories where the vacancy rate has worsened. Surely the malls, whose bread and butter priority is to attract shoppers, could not be expected to solve the pervasive problem of vacant office space in older downtowns.

There is more to physical characteristics than dimensions of a street and bulk of its buildings. A downtown mall is not built to specifications; it exists, with all the eclectic adornments of individual architects of different decades; it is a *fait accompli*. The American downtown mall, because it constitutes an ad hoc adaptation of brick and mortar already in place, flaunting designs, many of them of doubtful provenance, is light years apart from the simplicity and purity of architectural design characteristic of its hereditary link to ancient Greece. Yet, turning a downtown street in an older city into a mall accentuates its indigenous character so that it may be rediscovered and appreciated from a new perspective. Thus, while the downtown mall may not be able to compete with suburbia, it does present an attractive alternative.

Malls are unique, each attempting to address its problems and priorities in its own way. With due regard for local and regional idiosyncracies, it is fair to assume from the study of the ten mall cities that the synthesis of population trends, per capita income and the time line on numbers of stores takes precedence as a critical and reliable barometer of growth or decline. The readings continue to show a general decline in the central business districts of the ten cities. Obviously, street closings for the creation of pedestrian malls have not been able to reverse the downward trends in older cities.

Although the decline in the ten cities did not come to a halt with the establishment of the malls, the rate of the decline was restrained to some degree, varying with the different cities and individual characteristics of the mall streets and their vicinity. There must be a twinge of disappointment, even for those who did not harbor great expectations, in the realization that the malls have not succeeded in stopping the process of erosion and obsolescence of downtowns. In the Bible, young David, armed only with a sling-shot and five small stones, defeated the fully armed giant Goliath and changed the course of history. Can a single street be expected to stand up to a metropolis and change the course of urban history?

Many older cities have been experiencing a loss in population and income resulting in further attrition in their CBDs. Are the CBDs going to become an endangered species in America's urban ecology? While its track record has been spotty for some time, the central business district is still the economic wheelhorse of the older cities. Its stamina is not what it used to be and its gait is irregular, but it continues to serve within a smaller and more concentrated range.

What can the CBDs do to check the rate of their decline? They can understand from the experiences of these ten mall cities that there is no magic bullet to cure the economic and other ills of downtowns. They can settle for less, in the knowledge that the adjustments which the economy makes to shifts in population and falling incomes have been ameliorated by the political act of closing streets to traffic and transforming them into malls. The creation of malls, initially an immediate political solution, represents a positive and constructive philosophy which cannot harm but only help directly and indirectly in the survival and continued functioning of older downtowns.

SECTION IV

The Merchant's View

Preface

It is the retailers who are the pivotal elements of general merchandise distribution in the United States. Their decisionmaking, rules of the game in store siting and basic game strategy are central to the future. While the role of the shopping center developer per se is of enormous importance—and increasingly so—it is financing which makes development possible. And it is the approval by retailers, in their commitment to long-term leases, which is the *sina qua non* of financing—and with it the realization of the developers' concept.

In the course of our discussions with major institutional investors, the point was made repeatedly that it is the retailers' judgment which is the base rock, certifying the underlying collateral involved in the financial packaging of development. And within the parade of retailers it is the major department stores, with their ability to pull traffic, which are the very epitome of large-scale centers. Complementing the key anchors are the chains which provide the linkages and continuity between them, as well as much of the rent levels, and not uncommonly far higher per-square-foot production than the department stores.

Yet much of the planning for central city revitalization takes place without real insight into the dynamics of the front-line players.

Whether future retail development takes place in central cities, in suburbia or in exurbia depends upon the considered judgment and proven future success of these distributional entrepreneurs. What is their vision of the basic physical environment within which their wares will be displayed in the future? Is it to be an extension of today's trends? Or are there new factors—either of competition or basic setting, particularly demographic elements—which will reshape the future?

In the first paper, Philip Brous, President of Miller-Wohl Company, Inc., illustrates the locational decision-making rationale of a group of retailers-specialty store national chains—who occupy the interior of major shopping malls in the spaces between the anchor tenants (usually department stores).

1. Most of the major national chains presently engaged in specialty retailing emerged concurrently with the advent of regional shopping centers. Most were not in business in any significant way prior to 1960.

2. Several factors spurred their development:
a)   The tremendous expansion of bank credit cards permitted the small merchant to secure the same credibility and advantages as the large department store.
b)   The homogeneous environment of the enclosed regional mall established a retail setting far superior to the limited facilities occupied by chain stores in downtown locations. The sharp differentiation in the quality of space between downtown department and chain stores virtually disappeared within regional mall facilities.

3. Locational choices of chain stores are characterized by short-term planning periods and minimal geographic constraints. Since they are not dependent on a newspaper's advertising umbrella, and they lease their quarters (and have prototype formats for facility design), there is no part of the country they can't enter with seventy-five to ninety days notice.

4. While finances provide little problem (outside funding is usually not required), the major concerns of expansion are logistics (supplying the store), staffing, and knowledge of the market.

5. Market research undertaken by chain stores is not as sophisticated as would commonly be expected. They live parasitically off the research done by the anchor stores in the centers which they enter, and also research done by the major developers themselves.

6. The critical factors for establishing a presence within a center are:

a) Who are the majors (department stores) and will they be able to continue to draw for at least the length of the chain store's lease (twelve to fifteen years)?

b) Are the majors dominant enough to control the market, and what will the mix of small tenants be like inside the mall?

c) Where is the space located within the mall?

7. The chain stores are obviously in business to make a profit by serving their customers. The stores are located where the customers (primary audience) are found most frequently in greatest numbers. They will go wherever their customers go. At present, this is the suburban shopping center, although there are some viable downtown locations that are active.

8. Reliance is placed on the major department stores to bring traffic into mall locations. Inside the shopping center, chains such as Miller-Wohl want to be close to the center of the mall where the highest traffic is found. Newer malls offer more excitement because there are smaller shop fronts—twenty to forty feet versus sixty to eighty feet in older portions— generating more small stores, all vying for a share of the action.

9. In the future, continuance of chain store growth is expected within enclosed shopping centers, both in new and existing ones.

a) In new centers, it is possible to secure the exact store configuration desired; however, sometimes additional customer growth must be waited for.

b) In existing remerchandized centers, while space may have to be taken on a space available basis, the tremendous concentration of people already present is a major advantage. A brand new, well-designed store in an existing mall will pull customers in like a beacon light at an airport.

10. Store space will continue to shrink, not only due to increasing base rents, but also due to escalating extra charges—common area maintenance, heating and air conditioning, etc. Extra charges can easily pass the base rent in magnitude over the duration of the lease period. This is spurring a continuous evaluation in store configuration, shipping, and stocking formats in order to maximize the advantage of increasingly expensive square footage.

Foster Sears, President of the International Retail Institute, Inc., then examines retail trends in the 1980s. Focusing particularly on the large-scale regional facility, the conclusion is reached that—given current social and economic trends—the dominant theme of the 1980s will be the reworking and remerchandizing of extant regional malls.

1. Over the past twenty years, many retailing events have evoked considerable surprise, particularly the growth of suburban centers. Is this surprise due in large part to unpredictable outside forces, or just to a lack of knowledge of market forces?

2. While specific instances and events are almost impossible to predict, the underlying currents and general directions fostering them are relatively apparent to those who are willing to look without bias.

3. If we examine the trends of society and our economy, and the demands being put on it, it is possible to suggest that tomorrow's retail direction is virtually preordained, barring unforeseen events of exceptional magnitude.

4. Major trendlines of considerable import include the following:
   a) The arrival of a new generation of adults with new lifestyles, objectives, opportunities and problems. They will have smaller families, two-worker families,—and they may have difficulty maintaining the rising lifestyle that their parents took for granted.
   b) They are likely to develop new values, keyed more to quality than to quantity—more in keeping with the values of their grandparents than those of their parents. They will have more sophisticated tastes.
   c) Concurrently, the expansion at the periphery of major cities is decelerating rapidly. Rising construction costs, environmental constraints, energy costs and family trends (suggested above) will lead to denser settlement patterns.

5. Under these circumstances, it is not reasonable to expect many more shopping centers of regional character to develop in the coming decades, except in smaller towns, cities, and markets by-passed earlier.

6. The only way that a large number of new centers could be added would be to take business away from existing projects—business that a strong center will fight to keep—since there are few, if any, unserved areas in today's suburbs.

7. Because of the difficulty and cost in financing and building new centers, the existing facilities will have a decided edge in any future competitive battle.

8. Thus the greatest growth in returns for the regional shopping center industry will not come from new "bricks and mortar," but rather from reworking existing centers to more clearly reflect the demographic parameters of their trade areas.

Perspective on the real estate sector of the retailing industry is then provided by Raymond L. Trieger, Vice President of Property Development of R. H. Macy Properties. In particular, the view is that of the department store, which serves as a basic anchor tenant of any large-scale shopping center. The general trendlines of department store locations are reviewed, and the potential of downtowns (or CBDs) are explored.

1. Underlying the locational programming of merchants is the basic premise that retailers are essentially service oriented; they do not create the need for more shopping. They make the desired merchandise available to consumers where they want it—at a convenient location and at the right time.

2. For better or worse, the suburbanization of all aspects of America has been realized. The department store which views the metropolitan area as its natural market will experience a declining share of the market if it serves it only from a CBD locction.

3. It must seek to serve the population where the population wants to be served. The mistakes of merchandizing can be remedied in short order. But the mistakes of real estate—of locational choices—are not easily removed from the landscape.

4. The pattern of present and future department store expansion can be partitioned into the following categories:
   a)   *Market Extensions*—moves into the suburbs of the store's metropolitan area and subsequently into more distant outlying suburbs of that area; or jumps to nearby cities, either into the CBD or into its suburbs directly.
   b)   *Fillers*—moves to a previous low-density population area between existing branches.
   c)   *Smaller Market*—moves to what have been labeled "middle

market" locations, particularly when their (the department store's) own metropolitan areas have become saturated.

d) *Newly Available Sites*—moves to sites not previously available but through ingenuity becoming available; these opportunities are generally found in inlying areas but at the same time generally place reliance on vehicular traffic.

5. In addition, the downtowns (CBDs) will be of considerable interest to department stores. However, many of the exciting new CBD developments in large cities have negative impacts on the downtowns they are designed to serve, particularly on the traditional retailing clusters which are often undermined.

6. Where downtown development presently makes sense it made sense before the rapid escalation in energy costs and before the Conservation Guidelines. However, at least the following six criteria are needed to make downtowns and department stores succeed:

a) An excellent, not just adequate, public transit system,
b) A large employment base,
c) An appropriate retail environment—a conducive, safe atmosphere,
d) The absence of existing major suburban retailing,
e) Regional access, and
f) Supportive local government.

7. Government restrictions on regional centers may create further urban sprawl, and not really assist beleaguered CBDs. If outward-moving populations demand retailing, retailing facilities will be developed to serve them. If regional centers (convenient one-stop shopping facilities) are constrained, they will be replaced by a municipality of strip centers— which are less publicized and meet fewer regulatory obstacles—sprawled across the landscape.

8. The future will show a continued pattern of develpment that will replicate that of the immediate past. Where market thresholds are appropriate, there will be downtowns and there will be suburban shopping centers, with or without federal intervention and with or without energy shortages.

The Chain Store
Looks at the Future

PHILIP BROUS

The purpose of this presentation is to provide an idea of how I, representing the chain store phase of the industry, might look at shopping center development, both presently and in the future.

People ask, "Who is Miller-Wohl, or what is a Miller-Wohl?"

Miller-Wohl is actually a chain of 240 stores. We are in the junior apparel specialty store business and we are located across the entire country from Seattle to New England and from the Texas border to Florida. We are representative of a rather large group of specialty store retailers who occupy the interior of the major shopping malls between the anchor stores. Among the stores in our category are Casual Corner, which has annual receipts in the neighborhood of $350 million; The Gap, which has over $300 million; Limited Stores, which secures in excess of $250 million; Petrie Stores, possibly the most profitable retailer in America, doing over $450 million and netting over 10 percent; Lerner Shops, doing over $600 million; Brooks Fashion Stores, doing over $150 million; and finally our company, Miller-Wohl, which will do just under $200 million this year.

These are just some of the small specialty stores in the apparel sector. Also listed among specialty stores are men's clothing chains, the shoe chains, the sporting goods chains, the record companies, the fast-food companies and all of the small independent merchants who fill out the spaces in large shopping centers.

In our small subsector of the junior and misses apparel market, the

245

group of companies listed above has annual sales well in excess of $2 billion. Most of these companies were not in business in any significant way in 1962. They are all relative newcomers. Most of them are headed by entrepreneurs who are now worth a minimum of $10 million and up to $250 million each. (This is in an era when it is said that nobody could make a lot of money and there are no more frontiers to conquer.) This whole industry is new; these were people with the foresight to get into the enclosed mall business in its infancy. These were people who foresaw the flight of the middle class from many of the inner cities and managed to put their stores where the customers were going to be.

There were several other factors that certainly helped our development. One of these was the tremendous expansion of bank credit cards. These cards allowed the relatively small and unknown merchant to have the same credibility and advantages as the large department store. The Visa, Master Charge or American Express card was equally as good in the small store as in the large department store.

Another major advantage was that the large enclosed shopping center offered a homeogeneous environment since the entire center was built at one time. In downtown locations, the department store had the beautifully done property, while the small store was generally in the run-down, single-story, taxpayer building (with all of the garbage out front and bus stop in the wrong place). Once you get into the enclosed mall, the differences between the big stores and the little stores fade away.

Another interesting thing about our sector of the specialty store business is that we have the ability to move out of a given geographic area. We are not limited to the area covered by a local newspaper's advertising umbrella. There is no part of the country that most of us cannot enter on a minimum of seventy-five to ninety day's notice. It takes us about fifteen days to negotiate a lease and a minimum of sixty days to build a store and fill it with merchandise. We do not have to plan like the large shopping center developers, eight to ten years in advance. We do not have to plan like the major department stores, two to three years in advance. Once we have concluded our negotiations with the landlord, then we use the plans for our prototype stores and we can generally put these into shopping centers in quick order. Most of us have the ability to open at least thirty stores in a single year. Also, most of us sit with significant cash reserves and do not have to look outside for our funding. The cash is not really a big problem. Logistics may be. We question whether we can supply the store--whether we can find the people to run it—and do we know the market?

In the early infancy of the chain store business, our type of store was located in the downtown center city in a 100 percent location immediately adjacent to a major department store. Lerners on 34th Street in Manhattan would be a perfect example of that. Our company has highly successful downtown stores in Chicago, Cleveland, Milwaukee, St. Louis, New Orleans, Miami, Denver, Philadelphia, Houston and many others.

Sometimes, however, these neighborhoods change and then we are forced to reevaluate our own position. At times, we do not even have the option to remain if urban renewal forces us out. From our point of view, there are some viable downtowns that we are very anxious to go into, or to stay in, and there are many downtowns that either we don't want or that do not need us.

This leads us to possibly the most fundamental question, which is, "Why are we in business?"

We are in business to make a profit and to serve our customers and our customers, in the case of our business, are young women whom we think are between fourteen and twenty-five years of age. She is our primary audience and, in our opinion, she is now found more frequently in greater numbers in the suburban shopping center than she is found downtown. As long as that is the case, that's where we want to locate our stores. The moment there is conclusive evidence that enough of our customers are moving back downtown, we will be happy to go back downtown. We will go wherever they are and go wherever there are enough customers to support our stores.

We have found something else interesting that has been touched on by the earlier contributions to this volume. This is the fact that the enclosed shopping center is a whole new sociological world. It has replaced the candy store of our youth as the place for young people to go to congregate. As presented earlier, there has been talk about crime in enclosed shopping centers; there was talk about all kinds of problems in enclosed shopping centers. Very little was made out of the fact that young people like to go there and particularly to show up on Saturday and Sunday. They also like to go there all summer long when school is out. This is now the place when one can go if one lives in the suburbs because there is no other central meeting place to meet in which you may see your friends. When I grew up in New York City, one went to the major department stores like Bloomingdales or Macy's on Saturdays. This was both a place to shop and a place to meet people. In suburbia, there are no dowtowns. The youngsters (whom Bloomingdales calls "the Saturday generation") gravitate toward the enclosed shopping mall. They like nothing better than to arrive early on a Saturday morning and do some shopping, have lunch in one of the fast-food places, do some more shopping or meet friends, and then possibly go to the movies or to an ice skating rink if the mall has one. While in the center, they are likely to visit a record store, look at cosmetics, and, God willing, will spend $10 to $15 on a dress or a skirt or a sweater or something of the sort that we sell. The trip to the mall is easy and there are generally buses to catch if your parents are too busy to drive you there. This is the sociological phenomenon which got to us and encouraged us to put our stores in the shopping centers.

We have recently changed our entire pattern. We have opened up, since 1974, approximately 150 stores in enclosed malls and almost all of them were profitable within the first six months. All were profitable within the first year. There are generally no huge opening expenses necessary. We do not advertise. We pay high rents, or what we think are high rents, to be close to the center of the mall where the highest traffic is found. We do rely on the major department stores to bring traffic into the mall. We do add excitement to the mall. We feel that in many malls which have new wings the new wings offer more excitement because there are more small storekeepers with their twenty, thirty or forty-foot fronts all vying for a share of the action. The older part of the center has may sixty to eighty-foot fronts and by comparison, the traffic on a Saturday looks entirely different.

We have been interested in downtowns also. During the last four years we've opened in Philadelphia on Chestnut Street and we have taken a store in downtown Milwaukee in a version of a renewal of the landmark Plankinton Building. We have also opened in the Gallery in downtown Philadelphia.

Our market research is not quite as sophisticated as many of you would believe. We lie parasitically off the research done by the anchor store in the centers which we go in and also the research done by the major developers themselves. When we try to judge whether to go into a center, it is because of who the majors are and whether we think they will be able to continue to draw for at least the length of our twelve- to fifteen-year lease. We wonder whether they are dominant enough to control the market and then what will the mix of small tenants be like inside the mall? This is relatively important to us. It makes a big difference to us where our forty feet of space are located within the mall. This might influence our decision to go into a mall more than any other factor. We also like to know who our own competition will be and what type of audience the mall itself will bring in. For the most part, we can rely on the research being done by DeBartolo, Taubman, Simon, Jacobs Visconsi or Marshall Field or Federated or the May Company, or Dayton-Hudson. With this knowledge, we can go into Schaumburg in Chicago or Fairlane in Detroit or Sterling Heights in Detroit or Randall Park in Cleveland and do well from day one.

For the future, we see a continuation of our growth in enclosed shopping centers, both in new centers and existing centers. Ideally, we would be looking for half of our stores to be located in new centers and half in remerchandised older ones. In the new centers we can get the exact store configuration that we would like, and this certainly helps us. However, sometimes we must wait for additional customer growth in surround communities. In the older centers, even though we have to take space on a space-available basis, we benefit from the tremendous concentration of people living in or near the center.

Ideally, like Miami Beach real estate, the object in our business is to get as much front footage on the main mall as one can get. We strive to get a store approximately 40 x 150 feet. This is generally easier to do in a new center. In an older center, we may have to settle for a thirty-five or thirty-two-foot front and an "L" in the back.

With reference to the brand new centers, we are just not smart enough to understand fully the impact of $2 and up per gallon gasoline on our business. We can only guess and hope that our customers will reorder their priorities and then perhaps instead of many trips per week, there will be fewer trips but that more money will be spent on each trip. We are finding that our sales have held up much better in malls that are closer to the centers of population than those out in developing areas.

As far as smaller centers in cities of less than 100,000 populations, we are testing a number of enclosed malls that are anchored by a 40,000 or 60,000 foot K-Mart and perhaps a "C" store of J.C. Penney or Sears. We are going into a few of these units. We've opened one or two of them so far with modest reaction. We have not found enough teenagers attracted to these centers. You see, we are not in the convenience business as we are not selling milk or rye bread. We are selling junior fashions at very popular price levels. We are the equivalent of the department store's low-priced main floor or upper-priced basement. These are not discounted clothes and there are no claims that this merchandise was ever any higher priced than what we have it priced at.

Perhaps, you might think of them as copies of famous label designer jeans or copies of a specific ski jacket. Instead of having the famous designer names, we will have a nicely styled pair of pants, frequently made in the same factory in Hong Kong for $19 without the "logo" that the department stores are running for $36. We do not play upon the fact that this is a famous designer copy. The reasonably sophisticated teenager knows that it is similar and well priced and hopefully comes to buy it from us. I want to make that point clear because there is a growing business of selling nationally branded merchandise off price, and that is not the business we are in, nor is it the business of Petrie or Lerner or Limited or Casual Corner. Most of us sell unbranded fashion merchandise that represents good fashion and hopefully, at very good pricing.

We have been shrinking our store space. We started out about nine years ago taking 8,000 to 9,000 square feet of space. Now we have found that we can operate quite successfully in 5,000 to 6,000 feet of space for several reasons.

One is sheer necessity. The price of space kept going up and it wasn't only the rent, but also the extra charges that have gone through the roof from the point of view of the small merchant. The cost of common-area maintenance and all of the HVAC (heating, ventilation and air con-ditioning) and other costs that are charged directly to us on our net leases have escalated to a point where they are frequently up to 50 percent of the base rent figure. There is no cap on these expenses as there might be on the base rent. The extras can easily pass the rent before the term of the lease is up. As a result, we have found that we will have to learn to merchandise in smaller space.

We were among the leaders in our industry in removing the windows from a "window chain" and using every square foot to its maximum advantage. We have shrunk fitting rooms and stock rooms to a point where they occupy less than 15 percent of the total space. We are also trying to find ways to ship to these stores more frequently so that we can significantly increase our stock turnover, within the store. Inventory turnover, to a merchant, is critical and is a good way of retaining your cash and also curtailing markdowns.

One more important thing that we look for is market share rather than population growth. Population growth is very nice to us, and we've heard tales of the Sunbelt's growth and also how fast Phoenix and Tuscon and others are growing, but there are really not an awful lot of people out there yet. Large malls like Ford City in Chicago or Fairlane in Detroit or Roosevelt Field in New York have significantly more people coming through each day than you will find in the Sunbelt cities. If you as a merchant can get your fair share of values and do a creative physical plant, then you stand a good chance of prospering. We admire the job done by Mr. Ed Finkelstein at Macy's in New York and believe that a really attractive-looking store, whether in a new mall or an old mall, will act as a magnet and pull people into it. Particularly in the ten-year old mall, a brand new well-designed store will pull customers in like a beacon light at an airport. If you are a good enough merchant and know how to handle them after they are pulled in, you can really make a lot of money.

I hope that I have given you a little insight as to our thoughts in determining where we should put our stores.

Retail Economics of the 1980s

FOSTER E. SEARS

Where is Retailing Headed in the 80s?

Examining the literature on the future of retailing over the past twenty years makes fascinating reading. Who, for instance, would have predicted the demise of W.T. Grant and Robert Hall? Who would have foreseen the loss of stature of A&S (Abraham and Strauss), the one-time leader in the Federated chain? Who among us can honestly say that the success of the catalogue outlet was preordained, or that K-mart would out-distance all comers in the discount field? Who, indeed—and yet couldn't some of these situations have been foreseen with some degree of accuracy if one had had some honest foresight and an insider's knowledge of the businesses in question?

The magnitude of the growth of suburban centers has surprised many. Is this surprise due in large part to unpredictable outside forces, or just to a lack of knowledge of the forces of the marketplace?

It is always dangerous to make predictions in a world where so many internal and external forces impact on each other in ways that no one can foresee. Perhaps no one could have foreseen the Arab Boycott which caused such discomfort. But does that mean that we couldn't have foreseen the problems that would ensue in a world where petroleum use is growing and world reserves shrinking?

Could not a careful observer of A&S have foreseen the problems that that retailer was likely to have by being so heavily committed to downtown Brooklyn and Hempstead?

Was it realistic to assume that W.T. Grant could prosper, in a world growing increasingly competitive in second-rate locations, with third-rate merchandising?

K-Mart would have been harder to predict—success usually is—not because its approach was not obviously successful almost from the start, but because none of the other merchants appeared to understand the reasons for their success early enough to offer them a strong challenge—permitting them, as it were, to dominate this form of retailing after a late start in the discount field.

While domestic and world economic and political events are almost impossible to predict—from the standpoint of *specific* events—their general directions are relatively apparent to those who are willing to look without bias. Unpredictable events will continue to surprise us daily, but those events are made possible by the general directions that domestic and international societies dictate.

Would, for example, a weak and divided Iran be likely to have challenged a powerful and preeminent power that was the United States of twenty years ago in a world that was not that dependent on their oil? If this indignity hadn't occurred in Iran other similar events would have—and are still likely to happen elsewhere—because of the current state of the universe.

I'm amazed at the gullibility of the public when our political leaders express surprise and confusion over the rate of inflation, while a restrictive and confused bureaucracy speeds up the money presses to keep up with the government's new spending programs. Again, events may be unpredictable, but their general direction should be obvious to those who have any knowledge whatsoever of economic history.

I wonder, therefore, if we look at the trends of society, our economy, and the demands that are being put on it, if tomorrow's retail direction is not preordained, barring an economic collapse or major war? (Both of these events would obviously occasion a major change in direction.)

We have seen in a score of years a complete change in the structure of our cities—brought on by many forces—following the Second World War. For 200 years our cities grew on a relatively steady basis, street by street, block by block, the perimeters extending out to the limits of the bus and streetcar lines.

Then, with the migration from the country to the city, the marriage and baby boom, the proliferation of automobiles and highways, the G.I.

Bill, the FHA and the flood of the rural poor into the center city, an explosion occurred spreading the population over millions of acres, as well as increasing the already populated areas of the city many-fold. We all know the results: millions of single-family free-standing houses served by new schools, shopping centers, larger and larger suburban city services of all kinds, until many of the suburban areas around the larger cities developed a life of their own, no longer depending on the center cities that sired them.

Now a new generation of adults have arrived with new life-styles, objectives, opportunities and problems. They will have smaller families, the woman is likely to be working and they may have difficulty in maintaining the rising lifestyle that their parents took for granted.

They are likely to develop new values, keyed more to quality than to quantity, more in keeping with the values of their grandparents than those of their parents. They will be better educated, have more sophisticated tastes, be better informed—perhaps less well read—and their information will come more and more from television and other developing information sources.

The expanding periphery of major cities is decelerating rapidly and in some cases has stopped. Rising construction costs, environmental constraints, energy costs, denser housing patterns and family requirements are likely to accelerate this trend over the next decade in spite of the fact that the postwar baby boom is now in the nest building period.

Under these circumstances, is it reasonable to expect many more shopping centers of regional character to develop in the coming decade, except in smaller cities and towns that were bypassed in the 60s and 70s.?

The only way that a large number of new centers could be added, in my opinion, would be to take business away from existing projects—business that a strong center will fight to keep. And because of the difficulty and cost in financing and building new centers, the existing projects will have a decided advantage in that battle. This situation can be clarified by the use of some simple arithmetic.

Let's look at it from the department store's point of view. Department stores in the major cities currently account for between 30 and 35 percent of all DSTM (Department Store Type Merchandise) expenditures. There are likely to be between six and eight department store organizations in a city with a metropolitan population of 2.5 million, or a suburban population of about 2 million.

Per capita DSTM expenditures in the country naturally vary substantially by income, and to some extent by region, but on an average basis, they are in the neighborhood of $1,000 per capita. Per capita department store type merchandise expenditures multiplied by 30 percent to 35 percent (midpoint: 32.5 percent) means that the average consumer will spend approximately $325 in department stores.

$$\$1,000 \times 32.5\% = \$325 \text{ per capita}$$

If we are to assume that the average suburban department store totals about 200,000 square feet and requires between $18 and $20 million to have a reasonable bottom line profit, it is simple arithmetic to measure the amount of such space that can be supported in any given market. This, of course, doesn't mean that other stores can't or won't be built, or that individual circumstances won't favor a specific new center on occasion.

Let's take some examples of cities in this size classification to see how many *suburban* department store units can be supported at $18 million per store.

Area	Metropolitan Population	Suburban Population	Supportable Number of Department Stores
Cleveland	2,200,000	1,900,000	34
Houston	2,465,000	2,100,000	38
Minneapolis/ St. Paul	2,100,000	1,600,000	29

By now you may have guessed that the markets in question already have the supportable number of stores. In fact, my count indicates that Cleveland currently has thirty-three units represented by six companies, Houston has thirty representing eight companies, and Minneapolis/St. Paul twenty-six, representing six firms.

Looking at it from another point of view—regional centers normally attract about 50 percent of the DSTM potential—if we were to assume that the average center contained 800,000 square feet and should have a sales volume of $80 million, we are able to determine the extent to which these metropolitan markets are saturated by regional shopping centers.

Area	Regional Potential (millions)	Supportable Number of Centers	Actual
Cleveland	$ 950	12	13
Houston	$1,050	13	13
Minneapolis/ St. Paul	$ 800	10	10

Even though there is a degree of balance in these markets, there is nothing to preclude the additional developments, if an aggressive developer or outside department store organization comes to the market.

The problem is that there are few, if any, unserved areas in today's suburbs. The existing center has a great incentive to fight new competition aggressively to retain its position in merchandising, marketing and design programs. Because the old center has a tremendous cost advantage, it can easily defend its position against the newcomer in most cases.

Where is the Growth Coming From?

We at the Retail Institute believe that the greatest growth in returns for the regional shopping center will not come from "bricks and mortar," but rather from reworking the center to more clearly reflect the demographic characteristics of the center's trade area.

We are assisting center owners and managers to cope with this opportunity by lending assistance in the areas of merchandising, marketing, store operations, design, etc. We believe that both the economic and demographic conditions of the 80s will create major opportunities for growth where it counts: *at the bottom line*.

The Department Store Perspective

RAYMOND TRIEGER

"The Merchants View," as the title of this section, doesn't suppose that merchants know what is best for society, but it does give us the right to at least express our own opinion as to what we intend to program for our respective companies. As a citizen, and as a former planner, I enjoy the intellectual and the philosophical debate about downtowns and the suburbs, but I have a primary responsibility (and I'll speak more to this point a little bit later) to think about our stockholders' equity, return on sales, return on investment and so forth. But I do think, as naive as I might be, that there is a great deal of similarity between that point of view and what might be best for society in the long term.

I would like to digress for another moment and point out something that also is probably very elemental to everybody. Retailers are essentially service oriented; we do not create the need for more shopping. We satisfy a need. Retailers are creating what economists call time and place utility, making desired merchandise available to the consumer where he or she wants it, at a convenient location and at the right time. The Federal Highway Program is pretty much in place. The outlying factories and office buildings have moved the employment base to the suburbs. Now, perhaps from an urban policy standpoint, the Federal Highway Program was wrong. I said "perhaps," I don't know that, and I don't think that this is what we're here to discuss, but the highways are in place, and the people have moved out to the suburbs, and their jobs have moved out, as well.

The department store which views the metropolitan area as its natural market will experience a declining share of the market if it serves it only from a CBD location. It must seek to serve the population where the population wants to be served. The merchants in our company, and in every department store, have a unique and interesting ability. They can move merchandise very easily: if its not the right thing, they mark it down, and they mark it down again, and they mark it down again, until they get rid of it. Their mistakes are buried. They've gotten rid of it.

But the real estate executive's decision is there forever. He can't hide his mistakes, and so our job is to make the merchant look good, to make it easy for him.

Now, we have heard a great deal of interest being expressed in where and what form new retail developments will take in the 80s, particularly because of two factors: the increasing cost of fuel, or perhaps the greater difficulty of obtaining fuel, and greater restrictions and impediments by government on traditional retail developments. There has been a lot of talk during the last couple of days and the last couple of months, and there are a lot of generalizations that have been expressed—downtowns are "good," downtowns will "work," they won't work, and so forth. To a certain extent we at Macy's have had more experience in downtown and similar redevelopments than almost any other department store. Perhaps that gives us some right to claim an expert's mantle, but I believe it also proves that we don't know all of the answers yet—what will work and what won't work. There is a presumption in the question about the nature of the future retail developments that they will be different than those in the past, so although Peter Leibowits made a list of the types of shopping centers in his talk earlier, I'd like to describe my own categorization, at least as a point of departure as for where we're going in the future.

Generally speaking, department stores first began their branch program in the middle 40s by developing free-standing stores in established business districts with or without parking. For those of you who know New York and New Jersey, (I'm going to use them as some examples) the Macy stores in the Flatbush section of Brooklyn, in White Plains, in Parkchester, in Jamaica, and the Bamberger stores in Morristown and Plainfield are examples. I understand that the Hecht and Woodward & Lathrop early branches in Washington, D.C. followed the same pattern. I think that's probably the case generally everywhere, in established business districts, free-standing stores.

In the 50s, of course, came the birth of the regional shopping center. However, even during the last three decades, characterized by the spread of the shopping center, a great number of downtown and other urban projects were also undertaken for branch development, generally in connection with urban renewal and similar revitalization programs. I believe that most new department store locations fit into one, or in some cases, a combination of a number of categories.

The *first* of these are market extensions, generally of two types:
a. moves into the suburbs of the store's metropolitan area, and subsequently, into more distant, outlying suburbs of that area, or
b. jumps to nearby cities, either into the CBD or into the suburbs of that city disregarding the traditional need for a CBD location. Bamberger's ring of branch stores around Philadelphia, soon probably to be followed by Bloomingdale's and A&S doing pretty much the same thing at least in Philadelphia.

The Macy developments in New Haven, Connecticut and Sacramento, California, were cases of the latter illustration, by jumping to an outlying city and going downtown and downtown only initially.

A *second* general category would be a "filler," a previous low-density population area between existing branches, where suddenly population growth fills in and you decide there's room enough here and you put another store into a market that was previusly served from two existing units, and you put in a third one in between them.

The *third* category would be a smaller market, categorized previously in this volume as a "middle market." As major department stores feel that their own metropolitan areas have become saturated, many of them have jumped many miles away, without regard to their traditional advertising or market penetrations and without regard even to servicing and warehousing. They have just jumped into new cities, generally to locations which are large multistore, dominant highway-oriented regional shopping centers serving very very widespread areas—fifty or more miles. What Macy's did up in Albany would be that category, and there are dozens of examples all over the country.

The *fourth* general category is something we call a newly available site, generally through somebody's ingenuity. It might be urban renewal, also. It generally is a close-in site, but it is taking a site that was not previously available, and through ingenuity or urban renewal, all of a sudden making it "available." Our own Kings Plaza in Brooklyn was a brickyard, an auto agency and the Atlantic Ocean, and we made it into a shopping center. You've heard talk about the Brickyard in Chicago, and the Willow Grove Amusement Park in suburban Philadelphia where Federated has announced its intent to create a shopping center. The Queens Center on Queens Boulevard in New York would be another illustration. Generally, these are categorized by a reliance on vehicular traffic just as a suburban shopping center would be.

Now, against that background, what do I look for in terms of new retailing developments (barring an absolute prohibition by the Federal Government on anything except downtown developments, and I don't think they've come to that conclusion yet)?

Now, a great deal has been said about the comeback of the downtown. And there have been a number of very, very exciting projects that have been and are being developed: Toronto's Eaton Square, the second phase just being completed; the Renaissance Center in Detroit; the Gallery in Philadelphia; Faneuil Hall in Boston; Water Tower in Chicago; Crown Center in Kansas City; and The Gallery, Peter Leibowits development in White Plains. While each of these differs a little bit from one another, there is no doubt in my mind that the creation of apartments, and hotels and offices all have a synergistic reaction and they all help retailing facilities.

But an interesting factor to consider is that many of these development have a negative impact on the downtowns that they are being created to serve. Consider for a minute the old Detroit business center and what has happened to it as a result, partially, of Renaissance, or the part of downtown Philadelphia near Wanamaker's, or the split in Kansas City's retailing created by Crown Center, or the impending split in Oakland between the new Bullock's, Liberty House-Penney's development and the traditional retailing center where Weinstocks and I. Magnin are located. I think that in some respects it will be a disaster for downtown Oakland. Consider also our own store in downtown Sacramento, where we opened in an urban renewal fifteen years ago, fourteen or fifteen blocks away from the traditional retailing core where Weinstock's and Penney's were located. Last month, Weinstock's finally ended up abandoning its store and building and opening new store at our end of the downtown, leaving the old to further deterioration and blight, and the need for further redevelopment in another direction, probably nonretailing. And I believe, that the new project that is being built in White Plains will have a negative effect on many portions of the White Plains business district. Not the Macy's store or Saks Fifth Avenue or the Bloomingdale's stores, but on Mamaroneck Avenue, the traditional business street.

Recently Macy's opened a new store in the business district of Sunnyvale, California, an urban renewal site, created through tax incremental financing. A number of these kinds of projects have been created in California, but these are not downtown projects in the traditional sense that we are all talking about. These are really suburban locations in the context of the San Francisco or the Los Angeles metropolitan areas, which happen to be located in that small town's downtown. They are suburban shopping centers and they function that way. I think that they will succeed, and I think that in nearly every one of these cases they will solidify the retailing base of the community and there will be community-wide benefits.

I think, however, that such projects are few. As exciting as some of the other new retailing projects are, I've tried to indicate that downtown redevelopments have been around for many, many years. Think about the Chapel Square in New Haven—two department stores, a huge garage, a hotel on top of it, office buildings all around it and regional access—or Bridgeport's Lafayette Mall, the Sacramento project that I have just mentioned. There are varying degrees of success and nobody knows the formula that will make it work or not.

What I am suggesting is that where downtown development makes sense, it made sense before the sheiks increased the costs of oil and before HUD said that the suburbs were a "no-no." It made sense before and makes sense now, and it doesn't take UDAG grants to make it successful. Although I think that UDAG grants are providing a very, very beneficial impact for projects that might have gone or might not have gone, they won't make a project succeed that doesn't make sense from a market standpoint. To use other examples, we have Herald Square in New York and Union Square in San Francisco that have become two of the most exciting retailing locations in the country. Neither of them are planned developments by a developer or by a city. Neither has federal or city funds invested, and yet both of them work, basically because of a merchandising job being done there.

I would like to comment upon the State Street example that was used earlier. We put up a project in Kings Plaza in Brooklyn. It was not a slum, it was, and is, a good area, in fact. But this was private capital. We created what at the time was the largest garage in America, 3,600 cars. We created a marina, we widened streets to such an extent—these are city streets and highways—that traffic going to the beaches of Brooklyn works better on a Saturday in the summer now, going right by the shopping center, than it did before the shopping center was built. And we filled in 80 feet of the Atlantic Ocean. We did all of this with our own funds because we thought that it would work—no federal grants, no city grants. And we had a city government that cooperated with us, because they thought that it would work—the City Planning Department and the Board of Estimate of the City of New York.

Now downtowns, I think, need at least the following six criteria in order to make them succeed. *First*, an excellent public transit system—not just an adequate one—but it has to be so good that it will be used for shopping; *second*, a heavy employment base; *third*, this is something that I can't fully describe, it is something that we call an appropriate retail environment; *fourth*, the absence of existing major suburban retailing; *fifth*, regional access, and *sixth*, local government that really wants to make it work and not just to pay lip service to the idea of downtown development. A new office building or two, a new hotel or two, a convention center, the widening of a road or two, a garage or two—these are not sufficient. The average woman in a metropolitan area does not want to shop downtown if she has a real choice. Shopping has become a family experience: it's done at night, it's done on Saturdays, it's done on Saturday nights when the whole family goes shopping. And unless it is very, very conducive, downtown is not the place where people want to go in most cases. The CBD has got to have more going for it than a suburban shopping center, unfortunately. It is appropriate at this point to comment on the HUD program. I believe that the government restrictions on regional centers may create further urban sprawl. I really believe that. As long as population will continue to move outward, it will need retailing facilities and retailing facilities will be developed to serve them. Now if it can't be regional shopping center, convenient one-stop shopping centers, then it is going to be more of the ugly sprawl that we have seen from the early 50s on and continue to see today. Because these kinds of strips really don't get the publicity that the regional shopping center does, so they get approved faster and they get moved through the processes. I think that these will continue to be built, and as a result, I think that you are going to have the same percentages of shopping facilities in the CBD versus the suburbs as we have seen. I think that the society at large will not be the beneficiary of it.

I would like to use two examples, if I may of what I am trying to say. We've got one case in downtown Santa Rosa where six years ago a developer decided that he was going to try to put together an urban renewal project. The city government wanted it; Macy's and the much maligned Sears Roebuck—maligned by every urbanist in the country—were committed to the site. A couple of suburban shopping center owners have been suing ever since the CBD project was annouced, keeping the development from taking place, and claiming everything you can think of from antitrust and environmental rationales to everything else. This is a case of zoning being a monopolistic feature or attempted to being used for monopolistic purposes.

One other example is worth mentioning: we came to Fresno, California three years ago, a very pleasant city. There is one regional shopping center in all of greater Fresno, with three department stores, and it is very successful. It was zoned and built about twelve to thirteen years ago.

About ten years ago a pedestrian mall was created downtown. There is not much retailing left downtown, but the mall is there. Also during the last ten years, a tremendous amount of office space has been built in the suburbs, lovely single or two-story office space all over the suburbs. There is little employment base left downtown, and there is no shopping downtown. We came along and wanted to put a store out next to that existing shopping center. Low and behold, the planning board said "yes," and they passed it. The City Council said "no, come downtown." This is a case of the barn having been burned after the horse was stolen. The politicians all said, "Gosh we can't vote for you downtown, because that will destroy all chances of there ever being a downtown retailing." We said, "Okay we'll wait, we'll give you a year," and we sat back with our investment and we waited. A year later, nothing, the politicians still said "No, we are not going to allow you to go to the suburbs." We said, "Okay," and we made a commitment to the next suburban town outside of Fresno. At that point, the city council met for our zoning.

I think that this shows something about the municipal planning difficulties with the Conservation Guidelines. I want to end by saying that I think that the future will show a continued pattern of development that we have seen during the last twenty years; there will be downtowns and there will be suburban shopping centers. The downtowns will be rebuilt where they make sense and where they have been making sense in the past, with or without federal intervention, and with or without energy shortages.

SECTION V

Are We
Overbuilding?

Preface

The state-of-the art in long-term forecasting has rarely been put to the test as forcefully as is currently the case. Declining real incomes, energy costs and the possibilities of future constraints in supply—changing demographics long in the making but suddenly yielding a whole new conceptualization of household function and configuration—all impose limits on the use of the past as a guide to the future. The very maturing of the industry, its coming into investment primacy, has imposed conditions of market risk, yet at the very same time unparalleled high prices are being paid for extant centers—and certainly for the construction of new ones. The period of inflation which we are involved in accounts for this latter element, but virgin areas for center development are seemingly few and far between.

How do we adjudicate the risk/reward elements? What forms and configurations (and most strikingly-locations) hold the key to the future? The declining appeal of the long-term fixed mortgage in the face of the falling value of the dollar has left an investment vacuum. The shopping center, once a novelty requiring high rates of yield in order to secure financing, has, within the last several years, become a preferred vehicle both to lenders and investors. Will this continue?

In a relatively brief period of time, we have seen the supermarket industry move from a high growth, high rate of return activity to a much more prosaic, clearly matured area of investment. In this industry real estate costs have soared; sales per square foot are relatively stagnant. Stock market evaluations have relegated even the best of the regional chains to low values. Increasingly, competition has led merchants to protect their share of the market at the detriment of investors. Is the lifeline of the shopping industry going to parallel this earlier commercial form? What are the opinions of prime lenders and investors?

In the initial contribution to this section, Claude Ballard, Vice President, Real Estate Investment Department of Prudential Insurance Company, focuses on four specific trends in retail development for the 1980s and beyond.

1. An urban retailing revival can become a major reality in the 1980s. However, the development process must be refined in a fashion similar to that in suburban locations.

   a)   The old flagship department stores in CBD locations are operating properties characterized by severe problems—lack of depreciation and high energy-related costs. These may have to be replaced, although conflicts with historic preservation will arise.

   b)   The market for new urban retail projects will consist of city residents (50 percent), the daytime workforce/office population (25 percent) and tourists/suburban visitors (25 percent). The latter two market segments have already demonstrated significant growth while the revival of urban living appears to be gaining momentum.

2. Concurrently, traditional suburban retail development will continue, dominated by large multidepartment store shopping centers.

   a)   What has not been addressed adequately by retail strategists is the effect of takeovers by major chains of regional department store operations. Suburban opportunities will continue to be great in those areas where there are weak regional chains.

   b)   Opportunities will also be present where major department store branches occupy pre-1960 type facilities. Their operating problems are beginning to replicate those of downtown flagship facilities.

   c)   The impact of shifts of major stores to new markets (e.g., Bloomingdales to the Washington, D.C. market) will stimulate new regional center development or the revitalization of older suburban shopping centers. Market saturation has not yet been reached.

   d)   And there will be a further concentration of office, hotel and residential uses around those suburban centers which are well located and well developed.

3. The major department store chains may have opportunities for profits which are currently being ignored. They have been particularly unrealistic in dealing with their flagship stores in central business districts. The "rules of the game" in dealing with these facilities have yet to be formulated. In suburban areas, there is the need for department store operators to better manage their constantly shifting market areas. And this must be viewed both in geographic and demographic terms.

4. The latter reflect emerging demographic contours which will have substantial impact on the spatial distribution of American society and its expenditure and consumption patterns.

Bruce P. Hayden, President of Hayden Associates, further elaborates on the trendlines which may lead to overbuilding:

1. The day of the superregional—the five and six-department store center of 1.5 million square feet or more—has come, is here, and is starting to wane.
2. While there are still market areas appropriate in scale for superregional centers—underserved and rapidly growing market territories—too many forces are gathering to oppose them.
3. The smart developers (and the smart money) who are thinking regional at all are thinking about a different shopping center format—the miniregional—which will be concentrated not in major metropolitan areas but in the markets of smaller and intermediate-sized cities largely passed over the first time around. This is where demand is often unsatisfied.
4. Not only is the pace of creation of new superregionals slowing substantially, but stores of all kinds (and, therefore, the centers in which they are located), downtown or suburban, are getting smaller.
5. The latter tendency is based on one primary factor—cost:
   a) All space users are having to cut back in order to be able to afford new construction. Merchants are finding that they can more effectively use their sales space and sales personnel in smaller units.
   b) Developers more and more are delivering shell space to their tenants, with the latter responsible for all levels of finishing.

6. Costs are hitting major department stores as well. They are tending to think these days not in terms of "bigger is better," but in terms of "less is more." As a consequence they are turning to smaller facilities that do not secure quite as much volume, but take a lot less capital and

generate a better return on investment.

7. Thus smaller stores in smaller centers in smaller market areas will be a major trend. A clear yes must be the answer to the question, "Are we overbuilding?" But the shopping center industry is headed for salvation not of its own choice—not because it's smart, not because it's unselfish, not because it exercises any self-restraint—but by the fact that the cost and availability of money will tend to keep its greed and stupidities under control.

Martin Cleary, Vice President, Teachers Insurance and Amenity Association, then offers a lender's perspective on the shopping center in the coming decade:

1. To place lenders in context, it must be realized that we are followers and not leaders; we do not instigate projects. Not being innovators, we followed the shopping center industry from its community-based origins to its progression to the superregional focus.

2. At the earlier stage of center evolution, the shopping center was not accepted as an investment vehicle by the insurance companies. Now the lender mentality has changed and the shopping center has become the "Cadillac" of the lending industry. There have been fewer defaults and problems with the regional shopping center than with any other type of mortgage.

3. However, "amateur lenders" are now entering this highly sophisticated business and perhaps making shopping center loans without the prudence of their predecessors.

4. One major factor prevented overbuilding in the past. Unlike office, industrial and apartments, which can be built as long as a developer and a lender agree, the shopping center developers will not go forward without the department stores. The latter have a different motivation than just building and lending and have provided the basic regulation of the market. However, this safeguard may not hold in the future.

5. But any change in lending will be evolutionary, piecemeal and long term. And it will continue to again follow the developers.

 a) The middle, medium or mid-market location or mall will continue as a major element of shopping center development. While lenders were initially reluctant to provide financing—due to misgivings about the market—this concern has now been dispelled. In fact, the middle markets may represent a lower degree of risk, since department stores are usually part of the security—i.e. collaterization of the anchor tenant. This is not the case in larger regional centers.

b) The downtown regional center—often a multiple-use project—will also receive greater lender aceptance.

c) A third trend that we will see in conventional lending—again following the developer—is the specialty center. This particular type of development is bothersome, because it doesn't have anchors, it lacks the discipline that we have had in shopping centers in the past, and it doesn't have the foundation of the department stores. But developers will build wherever they see a good project and we poor sheep (lenders) will probably follow them and make some large mistakes.

6. The money market conditions today are as confused as any period in history. The permanent loan rates for shopping centers range through as broad a spectrum as I have ever seen.

7. While loan periods can still have a payout of thirty to thirty-five years—dependent on department store lease lengths or agreements on operating periods—a great number of companies are using call provisions. The latter are the result of the institutional perception of continuing inflation.

8. Inflation is also generating more institutional ownership, joint ventures between institutions and developers and short-term (five-year) renewable mortgages. But I still predict a return to normalcy.

Michael Kelly, President of Dayton Hudson properties, provides an alternative perspective—from a classic department store institution rapidly diversifying into other retailing activities:

1. From a strategic standpoint, Dayton-Hudson has positioned itself as a pure retailer, diversifying within the industry and serving a wide spectrum of customer needs.

2. The key to the future of retailing is flexibility and it is manifested in many ways:

a) Stores must be sized to meet a variety of market opportunities.

b) Flexibility also means the ability to follow and serve customers as their lifestyles and demographics change, and catering to new opportunities in downtown mixed use specialty centers, mid-market, small market and other market segments that may have been missed in the suburban land rush.

c) It also means coping with the complex challenges of market segmentation arising from demographic trendlines. One dimension of this segmentation is the partitioning of the retail business into necessities and "ego" goods.

3. The process of managing flexibility in nontraditional market responses will inevitably lead to a fallout and vulnerability of a number of retailers, particularly as margins are stretched paper-thin by a combination of inflation, increased operating costs, taxes and the extraordinary cost of money.

4. It is no secret to anyone in the shopping center industry that it has reached maturity. The number of large shopping center opportunities is diminishing and most developers who concentrated only on regional shopping centers are diversifying both inside and outside the real estate industry. The era of the specialist is giving way to the era of the generalist.

5. Despite middle age, the shopping center industry will still have a full plate for most developers. The trends and opportunities will be revitalized facilities, smaller centers, and mid-markets, and downtown. While the last represents a genuine growth opportunity for creative development, it contains substantial risks, far above those of suburban development.

6. The locations of existing regional centers will be a strength, not a weakness in the future. The restructuring of the regional shopping center offers a number of possibilities:

   a) A true center for all forms of merchandising,
   b) Renovation and reuse of facilities and peripheral land to meet the needs of a true central market place,
   c) A focal point for transportation alternatives and a focal point transcending traditional retail shopping.

7. We are not overbuilding—yet, in select areas a novel competition is emerging, as certain department stores begin to move interregionally. This new drive may well result in some competitive problems. But in most cases, the market dictates development, development does not dictate the market.

8. Can mass retailing be revived in the central city? If the market is there, the retailer may find a way to do it. However, it may be several smaller stores in the first tier of suburbs that responds to market needs rather than a big new store built downtown.

9. It must be remembered that the central city is just another market for the retailer—its success or failure will depend on basic economics and the desire of the consumer in that specific market.

Stephen H. Cowen, Vice President for Retail Development, Hartz Mountain Industries, Inc., then outlines the attributes of the inner-ring territories of metropolitan areas as potential sites for retail development in 1980s. It is this geographic area which is earlier suggested as a potential market for new shopping center construction.

1. The inner ring lies between the CBD and the suburban ring highway (low-density suburbia), and consists of older higher density suburbs and business/industrial zones. It is generally an area bypassed by the waves of regional shopping center development.

2. The demographic profile of the residential population of the inner ring typically is an aging one. However, due to generally low housing costs—and despite below-average median incomes—relatively high disposable incomes are present. In addition, the inner ring also shows an influx of younger, higher-incomed, two-worker families.

3. Within the inner ring, most of the aging commercial centers—small older downtowns which were dominated by the CBD—have been stripped of their major retailing functions over the past twenty years as suburban regional malls proliferated. As a result, most inner ring households patronize outlying regional shopping centers, i.e., personal expenditure streams are exported to more distant suburban locations.

4. Thus a substantial market potential for major retailing activity may be present within the inner ring. The infrastructure requirements and attributes may make the inner ring an easier location for development than the CBD over the next decade. Facilities located in the inner ring, however, will mainly be in competition with older suburban facilities; the core has already been pruned.

Trends in Retail Development: The 1980s and Beyond

CLAUDE BALLARD

This paper will focus on four specific trends in retail development for the 1980s:

1. Revival of urban retailing,
2. Selective suburban expansion,
3. Opportunities for profit being ignored by major cities, and
4. Demographic shifts allowing the revival of urban living, i.e., new households and new housing in urban cores.

Revival of Urban Retailing

Urban retailing, which is defined as new or structured retail entities in traditional central business districts, will become a reality in the 1980s. The demand for these projects is far outstripping the capability of national developers to produce them. There is inevitable conflict, however, between federal policies such as preservation of historic buildings and other stated goals, i.e., the improvement of mass transit and the creation of subways in low-density metropolitan areas conflict with each other in this sense. Wholesale preservation of "historic landmarks" does little or nothing to solve the basic problem. The basic problem remains the provision of cheap transportation to concentrated nodes of retail and office complexes. These office complexes have to be built in the traditional core areas of the city and will generate a demand for additional retailing. This is happening already in places like Washington, D.C., to some degree in New York, to a lesser degree in Detroit because of Renaissance Center and prime projects there, and to a lesser degree in major West Coast cities.

The problem with the concentration of federal policies in a small area is inevitable. This is a war in which federal agencies prevail; it begins to look like there is no opportunity to refine the development process into a deliberative procedure wherein the retail development game can be played in a manner similar to how it has been played in suburban locations for the last fifteen years.

One obvious question is: Why should we preserve buildings which have negligible historic value when we're concentrating so much effort on improving transit to the same areas that we are preserving with low-density forms of development?

Detroit stands as a prime example. Within a one mile square CBD, it has approximately 135 buildings which may be dedicated by the national trust for historic preservation. Virtually all the building owners are willing to have their buildings registered, simply to take advantage of excessive depreciation writeoffs which are available when a building is declared a historic structure. The basic underlying problem still remains—this policy is in conflict with the announced goal of building a subway into the CBD from the outlying portions of the city of Detroit. Some areas of the city, for example, have experienced a great turnaround in residential housing. These homes are being rebuilt and used by middle to upper-income professionals as permanent residences, freeing them from the commuting syndrome.

The second underlying problem is the fact that most of the current ownership of older buildings in urban cores is really in the hands of long-term owners who have fully depreciated their properties. Again, as far as individual ownership of this type of property is concerned, the buildings themselves are, on an average, almost fully depreciated. A related problem is the corporate ownership of massive buildings such as retail structures: operating costs are escalating rapidly, far in excess of sales gains. Another problem is that these old flagship stores, in most major eastern cities, account for 15 percent to 25 percent of the chain's sales in that particular metropolitan area. For example: Hudson's in Detroit, Rich's in Atlanta, and other major flagship stores in older metropolitan areas. What are these building owners going to do?

If the sales transfer from the downtown store is imputed back by logic (and perhaps by practice) to the next closest outboard store from the CBD location, approximately 50 to 60 percent of the sales will be lost to the chain, resulting in a further collapse of the urban core. What needs to be done? The federal government should take a realistic look at the opportunities for redevelopment of larger retail structures. It should seek another alternative to provide depreciation coverage to building owners who have buildings which are capable of being renovated.

It should be federal policy to formulate a cabinet-level position dealing with urban development problems, i.e., there should be someone who has veto power over other regulatory agencies so that the conflicts noted above could be avoided in the future. The nation is headed for a very serious energy crunch and it must not force abandonment of structures which should be maintained. Similarly, it should not create artificial restraints on total redevelopment of areas that have approved transit in place.

A great deal remains to be done about rebuilding the housing stock within the core areas of major metropolitan areas. This will be done only because there is a tremendous demand for this type of housing as energy and transportation costs generally escalate beyond the growth of individual income. There is a huge desire for "urban housing" in areas which have seen tremendous losses of population partially through migration to suburban areas. What needs to be done? The housing industry has yet to realize the impact of large-scale shifts in consumer desires. Many young professionals and young married couples have the potential to live in an urban setting. Schools need to be improved at the same time that the housing stock is being made available. What really needs to be done is for the housing industry itself to develop a financial medium which allows development of new housing in urban cores. Traditionally, the housing industry's approach has been to avoid building single-family or detached housing of any kind in these areas. The simple fact is that presently there is so much land available within five to eight miles of large urban area cores that this process could go on for the next five to eight years without either:

a)   absorbing all the land; or
b)   absorbing all the utility capacity, which increasingly is being constrained in suburban areas.

Why does this housing need to be built? A main reason why it needs to be built is that no matter what kind of mass transit system is built, it is terribly expensive to build and maintain it in an operating condition acceptable to middle- and upper-income groups. Wouldn't it be easier to take the load off this system by creating incentives to build housing in core areas? It would save a tremendous amount of energy.

Type of Urban Redevelopment
Possible for Retailing

Retail infrasturcture development or rebuilding will be concentrated in the cores of major urban areas, i.e., new department stores will be built. These stores will be, over the long term, replacements of existing operating properties which have tremendous problems due to the lack of depreciation and high energy-related costs which are escalating at the rate of 20 to 30 percent per annum while sales are remaining flat compared to inflation. If a particular property is fully depreciated, the escalation in operating costs is especially harmful. For example, a utility bill of $1.3 million for water, steam, gas and electricity in a major, old urban department store without depreciation is actually twice that amount when the effect of the earnings of that store are washed through the corporate books. There is absolutely no incentive when sales are flat or declining to maintain an operating presence in that store. Most of the major urban retailers are already at the point where they have done all the possible things, i.e., lower temperature and humidity controls; attempts to sublet space to other users; and attempts to close off a portion of the building. All of these things have been done. The stores are retreating into their own space and still cannot remain profitable because of the escalation of costs in maintaining that space.

Who will be the Customers
for the New Urban Retail Projects?

They will be composed of the following groups:

1. Approximately half the sales will come from the areas within major metropolitan areas, i.e, the whole city or community will be responsible for producing approximately half of the sales. Everyone knows what the income characteristics of this population are.
2. Approximately 25 percent of the sales will come from office populations working in buildings that have been, or are being built within the cores.
3. The remainder of the sales will come from tourists and visitors to the core from the suburbs who are attracted by the unique presentation of merchandise as well as downtown entertainment possibilities.

Up to 50 percent of the customers (higher on certain shopping days) will use mass transit. This is already happening. The importance of subways to initially reach high-income populations which are not presently in the CBD cannot be overstated. Express bus systems and so forth also need to be improved.

These particular kind of retail projects imply, but need not be, multi-use projects which are dependent upon other uses. But it makes little sense for a major retail developer to put residential, hotel, and office uses into the same project because he is multiplying his risk. However, these uses do need to be built within a reasonable distance of the retail project itself. For instance, within five miles a tremendous amount of housing should be built. One area where this has already happened is the north "Gold" Coast of Chicago where Water Tower Place was placed in relation to it. The effect of Water Tower and the North Michigan Avenue development on further residential development has been very favorable. The basic problem residential developers still have, however, is how to test the market in an area where there is no track record of development and no rent thresholds to work against. These problems have to be solved. They cannot be solved by a retail developer any more capably than a residential developer doing high-rise housing can produce a complicated retail project.

The federal government could do a lot to solve the whole problem by providing assistance to housing developers and retail developers, i.e., no tax on the earnings from the projects for the first ten years, etc. A number of these things could be forced-drafted into the development program. Then there would be heavy lender support provided that the decks are cleared for this type of work. It makes no sense to have 30 to 40 percent of an urban core (which is the subject of so much attention in terms of transportation delivery systems, etc.) *declared historic*, thirty to forty percent of the land mass devoted to wide roads (which are no longer needed) or historic buildings which are of such a low density that they cannot support the daytime office worker population or the retail uses which are required by the size of the transit (delivery) system. An example of an area where constraints have not prohibited redevelopment in another time frame (prior to EPA and Preservation) is the effect of the subway on the District of Columbia Office Development. This office development is proceeding so rapidly that it is literally forcing rents for land (i.e., land costs) so high that retailing no longer works profitably without some kind of support or subsidy.

In other words, the market development segment called *office development* is proceeding much more rapidly than the economics of retail development are allowing retail development itself to occur (in D.C.). No retail developer can afford to pay $25 per square foot for land while an office-building developer in the district apparently can do so at the present time and still produce a building that is viable.

Both residential and office construction, however, need to be built in core areas. It is more efficient and it is more reasonable to expect this to occur than it is to expect, over the long term, people to commute from far suburban locations to work in these core areas. Of course, at the same time, a countervailing trend will be occurring:

1.   Fractionalization of the urban office market: The people living in the suburbs are constantly greeted by opportunities to work in the suburbs. As this is occurring, there is improvement of the transit system bringing people who are living midway between the suburban office complexes and the core area out to the suburban office complexes. These developments are occurring very rapidly today because they are able to compete in terms of price and effectiveness against "urban core" projects which normally are massive structures on considerably less land. The fact is that in the areas which have not started to redevelop, the core area is difficult to make go for any type of use, *even if the land is free*.

    On the other hand, suburban office rents which are essentially the same as core area rents reflect higher profitability because of the demand for office space convenient in time and cost to the residence of the daytime office worker (suburbanization of the office function).

2.   During the last twenty years, a tremendous number of hotel rooms have been built at freeway nodes throughout suburban locations while the total hotel industry has not concentrated on urban locations. Increasingly, the market for well-placed hotel facilities in urban cores will grow. There should be a great deal of lender attention to this issue.

The best argument for urban redevelopment is simply that the energy cost and the *lack of certainty* of supply will make it difficult to ignore these *opportunities no matter what the problems are*.

In many locations throughout the country, the high cost of suburban housing is forcing people to move back into a lower cost, existing urban housing stock, originally of high quality construction.

What Does All of the Above Mean?

There is a huge demand for housing close to jobs, i.e., a large number of households that have the potential to move back and reoccupy overlooked values in housing. To some degree this started happening after the first Arab oil embargo in 1973. We, of course, are now in the second oil embargo which is more subtle—it is determined by price.

Higher population density implies less risk for any kind of retailer provided he can shift his merchandise and store image to meet shifting age groupings and income groupings within that population density. One way in which this has already happened is in the fast-food business. Some of the fast-food people saw, in the early 1970s that the population density of the area halfway between the suburbs and urban cores would allow them to place units on a one- or one and a half-mile radius basis rather than the three- to four-mile radius basis traditional to the suburbs. They found, to their surprise, that these densities supported volumes two and three times what they had been used to on twice the spacing in suburban units.

They did not anticipate this kind of volume and have now almost totally developed their capability in urban strips and have now gone to urban cores to some degree to work off the potential of the daytime office worker population as well as the evening night shifts and maintenance forces etc. When you think about it, suburban developments are "manufacturing" a density through the use of the automobile. For example a regional shopping center of 1 million square feet needs approximately 300,000 to 350,000 people within twenty-minutes driving time to make it work. If one half, or 150,000 people lived beyond ten minutes, it is difficult to underwrite (with today's energy costs) the success of this project because of the uncertainty of fuel supply and ever-rising fuel costs.

SELECTIVE SUBURBAN EXPANSION

There will continue to be traditional suburban retail development. This will occur for several reasons. Quite overlooked in the above discussion is the fact that a large percentage of retail shopping will have to be done within twenty minutes of the place of residence. There will not be the opportunity to do a terribly great amount of comparison shopping, especially when the shopping facilities are not concentrated. For example, many of the early centers had only one or two department stores. These centers are still existing but increasingly they are subject to competition from four- to-six department store centers. The latter will survive because they are terribly efficient in producing customers for sales productivity and have modern mechanical plants which allow economies of scale in operations at low operating costs overall against sales. To a lesser degree, the older centers which were built in the early 1960s still have the same kind of operating problems that the older urban core facilities have, i.e., they are no longer competitive because they are functionally obsolete and to some degree there is economic obsolesence caused by the development of multi department stores shopping facilities further out suburban areas.

Four to five years ago, it was my opinion that the first area to redevleop rapidly in terms of urban retailing would be the inner ring of shopping centers around the urban core. Actual sales levels in the last twelve months, however, have shown that many of these stores, even when they are new, are not responding to that theory. In fact, they are experiencing sales declines in many cases while far suburban and existing urban-core stores have enjoyed increases against inflation.

In the first case, far suburban stores have benefited from the localizing of shopping patterns and the dominance of multi department store selection opportunities available to the consumers. In some cases, the core stores in selected markets have benefited from the huge increase in office construction which results in huge daytime office worker populations. The existing retail facility which is operating within this mass of daytime population will obviously be very successful. Suburban office complexes are supporting retail function in much the same way, where there is a concentration of suburban office space.

Some people are saying that regional retail development effected a concentration of shopping patterns which had not previously existed either because of the lack of residential population in sufficient size to merit large scale development or because retail practice and theory was so widely divergent as to the needs of the consumers. It took a tremendous amount of time—and don't forget this—to get retailers to combine within one retail project in numbers greater than two. There was a fear that the addition of a third and fourth department store would seriously affect the potential volume for each individual store. Actually, of course, the opposite occurs in a regional facility. There is no known limit to the potential for growth as long as new department store units do not present similar merchandise in great depth parallel to (an existing or) another department store in the same development.

All of these things relate totally to expansion in both urban and suburban markets. What has not been addressed sufficiently by retail strategists is the effect of takeover of existing department store chains of a regional nature by major chains, such as the takeover of Rich's by Federated; the takeover of Hudson's by Dayton's; the takeover of Wanamakers by Carter, Hawley, Hale; the takeover of Neiman-Marcus by Carter, Hawley, Hale; and the merger of Saks Fifth Avenue with Brown and Williamson Tobacco Company, etc. All of these chains are well capitalized and capable of expanding the regional operations into other regions.

The shopping center industry per se is less than twenty years old; as we have described it immediately above, it is less than five years old. The opportunities for development in the suburbs will continue to be great in those areas where there are weak regional chains or where national chains are in pre-1960 type facilities. For example, many of the pre-1960 type facilities which are owned by Penney's and Sears Roebuck are essentially free-standing facilities which have had a strip added on to them. All of these facilities are now in need of major redevelopment and also are in need of the addition of one or more department stores. The projects themselves are possible targets for takeover by shrewd developers who understand the marketing patterns of the future and who can create enough space, either in terms of parking or retail pads, for a second or third department store.

Retail strategists cannot ignore, nor should developers, the impact of the shifts of major stores in the various markets. For example, it is an unwritten law that Marshall Fields does not expand beyond a certain geographic area. The same is true for Wanamaker's versus other regional stores in the East. To a large degree, none of the stores in the early 70s and throughout the 60s, which now plan to make vast moves within the U.S., would have jumped territories like they are currently planning. An exception, of course, is Macy's, which went to California and which may take its units to other parts of the country. It would have been inconceivable several years ago to anticipate that Wanamakers might move as a regional store. Another case is the expansion by Carter, Hawley, Hale into East Coast cities. It is logically possible to assume this will happen now. Market saturation, therefore, in terms of the opportunity to do retail development has not been reached. Saks Fifth Avenue has to build approximately three stores a year for the next twenty years in order to meet its expansion goals. It is extremely difficult to find locations for this kind of development program in existing regional centers, largely because they have not been planned properly to allow the inclusion of Saks and because most of the existing retail centers are not of the multi-department store type. This will cause the development of new regional centers with multiple department stores in suburban locations. All this will happen at the same time urban redevelopment is also occurring in the retail sector.

There will be a further concentration of office, hotel and residential uses in areas around the suburban centers which are well located and well developed. This story has not even begun to be written. For example, many large developers have large inventories of land around suburban centers. This inventory has not been addressed in terms of market demand based on existing energy costs. These centers are located by and large near major transit or freeway nodes. They are superbly effective in dominating a region up to thirty minutes in time distance from it and they are well recognized as focal points of development.

Older centers (those built before 1970) have to some degree seen a recycling of the areas around them. Many of the office uses have been complimented by hotel uses, a third stage of suburban redevelopment. This certainly would not have occurred if the shopping center had not been placed there initially. This kind of second- and third-phase development after the shopping center—office and hotel construction—will be paralleled in the future by increased residential densities around the total project (which need not be restricted to the shopping center site). What cannot be overlooked is the fact that the shopping center industry is not even, at this point, twenty years old.

Other Suburban Opportunities

The market is demanding far more department store space than presently exists. Department stores are capturing a higher percentage of the potential department store type goods in their sales levels. However, what is overlooked is that there is a tremendous amount of discount store space which in the long view has to be viewed as an alternative form of retailing until adequate department store and multi-tenant shop space can be built in urban centers. For example, in any large metropolitan area today, department stores have finally reached total sales volumes approaching that of areas that have discount stores spaced at one and one-half to two-mile radii from each other. In effect, lower sales production on a square foot basis at the discount stores is gradually eating into the operating returns of these stores. These stores are especially vulnerable to a well-placed regional shopping center. A considerable amount of sales transfer occurs out of the discount stores and into the comparison shopping oriented regional centers. I know this is happening because department stores that are located in suburban centers outboard of a large mass of discount store space have found out that when they built the new store, of possibly a larger size, they did not have the transfer that they anticipated out of their original store. However, we know that sales did drop off in the discount store space between the two stores, i.e., old and new stores. This leads me to believe that the department stores have great expansion potential as they operate to give a much broader presentation of merchandise to the American consumer. To some degree, you can see this is the organization of the Kresge Company, which for the first time is being headed by a man out of merchandising and not operational expansion.

Other opportunities in the suburbs which are not being addressed in retail development include the need for department store operators to better manage their market areas in relation to their penetration of them against various market characteristics *which are constantly shifting*. A good many department stores still have no idea of where their customers are coming from every day. They only have a rough idea. They need to identify the source of their sales by geographic location. They need to pinpoint their advertising to get the maximum penetration of what is a reasonable drawing area for that store. Very little is known about the effect of advertising on retail shopping patterns. The answer to the retail advertising problem has always been to throw money at it and to shift media around enough so that there is some response from the buying public. There has to be a great deal more analysis directed at the store level toward finding out where these customers come from, to developing a loyalty on their behalf and to meeting their needs. There are a considerable number of regional chains, such as Broadway, which have not fully exploited this opportunity either in suburban or urban store locations. At the same time, many of these older stores are in need of recycling either through new or rebuilt facilities. These stores are often experiencing declining sales volumes. It is my opinion that many of these stores will be abandoned at the same time they should have been recycled.

What is Being Ignored by the Chains?

The chains have been very unrealistic in dealing with their own flagship stores in central business districts. Most have acceptable sales levels and most are producing 15 to 20 percent of total sales in a metropolitan area that they have expanded into. For instance, a flagship store might be complimented by as much as ten more stores in suburban locations. However, the flagship store still accounts 15 to 20 percent of the total sales for that particular department store in that particular metropolitan area.

The profitability of the store due to the reasons discussed above and below, however, is affected by its age and the deteriorating trade area in which it is located. The latter are offset to some degree by economies of scale which have been achieved by cutting down on operating expenses wherever possible, and by upward shifts in office and residential construction activity. It is not acceptable to say that a clear rule can be made with any downtown flagship store or any downtown in the country. Each downtown has its own unique characteristics; it started in a unique way based on a particular form of transit system.

For instance, downtown Detroit was not started by the railroads; it was started by its relation to the Detroit River. The earliest form of transportation on the Detroit River was canoe, and then larger boats which were reflected in warehouse construction along the river to store goods from these boats. Last, in the development stage prior to the automobile, the construction of railroads was undertaken to get goods from the docks out into the outlying areas away from the riverfront. Next, railroad stations were constructed around these areas, or in them, i.e., two or three railroad stations were constructed and then there developed a large downtown office and hotel complex independent of each other unit. The last thing that happened was the full-scale development of retailing, which did not take place until approximately 250 years after the first canoe hit the shore. And, the largest retail facility was not really fully constructed until World War II.

Realistically, we are looking at the effect of approximately 300 years of development from wilderness to large retail store. When the largest retail store in the Detroit CBD was being constructed, energy costs were considerably different than they are today, i.e., it was cheap to heat a building with coal and steam, so the downtown Hudson's store, like many other stores, had a steam boiler and a central plant of its own. It had at one time the capability of generating some electricity. Each building that was added onto the main building added more pipes, valves, fittings, pumps, circulators of air, etc., until the thing became a mechanical nightmare. The steam heat generated by coal was abandoned to steam purchased from a utility. Meanwhile, because of the evolution of the use of coal to heat and the relative expense at the time of electricity, and the desire of many retailers to have windows to show their goods in natural light, each floor that was added, moving upward, had $4' \times 7'$ windows approximately every five feet on center or on spacing, resulting in approximately 130 windows per floor with a window area of single pane glass of four by seven feet. This particular building is now the subject of urban preservationists' attention.

The facts are that this building cannot be preserved because of the heat loss and the escalating cost of steam purchased from a public utility which recently announced it was raising its steam prices 22 percent. The steam bill on this particular store last year was $850,000, or approximately $2. per square foot of operating retail space. The heat bill for a similar sized unit producing approximately two-thirds of the volume of the downtown (Hudson's store in Fairlane) was approximately $5,000. No one can ignore these costs when the recycling of buildings is concerned. When the facts are such that high costs outpace declining sales levels (even through very high in real numbers against total volume in the metropolitan area), it is very difficult to justify keeping this particular store open. This is true for most major downtown chains: Federated, with A & S in Brooklyn or Hempstead, Long Island, has problems like this. It also has problems with Rich's in Atlanta and most major chains have similar problems in downtown store locations.

When coupled with a lack of depreciation or the end of the depreciable life of the building, there is a phenomenon which I call the depreciation bomb. This bomb doubles the operating costs of the building and will actually force the closing of many of these historic structures. The combined effect of operating costs and no depreciation means that ef-

fectively the profitability is the same as a well-located suburban store doing 20 percent of the volume projected for that suburban store, which
would actually mean it would have to be closed. So, increasingly, you
find department store executives saying, "Our suburban stores are doing
well, but our downtown store is doing x," which is usually 20 percent of
the real volume of that store.

In many cases known to me, the first suburban store that was built by
a major regional chain is running fairly close to the volume of the CBD
store. Over the last several years many of them have been very close in
terms of actual volume, but, of course, in terms of profitability, the CBD
store was a disaster.

If you will look at the earnings of department store chains, you will
find that chains which have a high percentage of space in older stores are
experiencing severe drags on earnings. Most of the concentration of the
stores has been on more rapid expansion which is, of course, more difficult to achieve because of longer time frames required to bring projects
on stream and they have also concentrated on expansion into other
retailers via acquisition. This is a fond hope until you run out of money,
which will increasingly be true as this process continues faster and faster
without the basic problems being addressed.

These stores will find it increasingly necessary, if you look at their
earnings picture, to address these problems realistically and solve them.
For instance, Dayton Hudson, which is located primarily in newer cities
of the Midwest and Far West, has very good earnings, largely because it
does not have the overhanging, huge inventory of older, obsolete space
which is connected with retailing in East Coast oriented chains. For instance, Federated's operating problems have not been addressed by its
management nor will they continue to be under their present mindset.
Most department store executives do not have the technical expertise, conceptual background or the inclination to seriously talk to their building
operating people and attempt to solve the problems which are so apparent. For instance, in the case of Hudson's in downtown Detroit, there
is no choice but to tear down the building because the cost of rebuilding
the building with the existing store in it on an operating basis is one reason
this cannot be conceived of without a huge profit penalty to the chain. Second, the store was designed to do something totally different. A new
store—and these are economies which should be discussed—can be built
for $38 to $40 per square foot for the shell. This space would be airtight
and could be the subject of a new mechanical system. Many of the older
department stores have mechanical systems that are so ancient they could
have been twinned on the titantic.

For example, there are twenty-five-horse-power motors which are large enough to fill a small size room and are over fifty years old, steam generating systems or steam movement systems which are terribly ineffi- cient, and various kinds of vacuum pumps, electrical transmission facilities which are totally antiquated. In addition, very little or no air- conditioning—at least to the level required by modern computers—air- cooling systems in substitution for air-conditioning through the use of chilled water, and constant repairs required on vulcanized mechanical systems all make these buildings almost impossible to rebuild.

When you rebuild, if you do, you have to replace the floors which normally are wooden sleepers in old department stores in core areas.

DEMOGRAPHIC SHIFTS

Several startling things have happened in the last ten to fifteen years in terms of demographics. The most remarkable and well-known effect of the shifting demographics of the country is the decline in average house- holds size from 3.3 persons in 1960 to 2.81 in 1978.

Recently released data shows that only slightly more than one-half of the nation's 57.2 million families contain one or more children under the age of eighteen.

One-parent families accounted for about 7 percent of all households in 1978, up from 4 percent in 1960.

More startling is the fact that the porportion of all households not maintained by families increased from one in every seven in 1960 to one of every four in 1978.

In 1978, there were 76 million households in the United States. This constitutes an increase of 23.2 households since 1960 when there were 52.8 million households.

As noted above, some household types have increased more rapidly than others and they consequently now constitute a greater relative pro- portion of the household total they occupied in 1960.

Average Household Size

Given the increase since 1960, the proportion of nonfamily house- holds and the fact that they rarely contain more than one person, the size of the average household has declined. Other factors, which include com- paratively low birthrates, have also contributed to the scarcity of large households.

In 1960, the average household size was 3.3 persons. The most com- mon household size was two persons (28 percent of all households); a slightly higher proportion of households had three persons (19 percent) than had four persons (18 percent). The percentage of one-person house-holds was 13 percent, a little larger than the percentage of five-person households, which was 12 percent. Finally, the largest households, those with six or more members, constituted only 11 percent of the total.

By 1978, average household size had declined to 2.81 persons. The most common household size was still two persons, 31 percent, but the next most typical size was the one-person household, 22 percent. As in 1960, the proportion of households in 1978 with three persons was 17 per-cent (slightly larger than a proportion with four persons, 16 percent). About 8 percent of the households contained five persons and households with six or more persons comprised only 6 percent.

This is an incredible shift because of the numbers involved over the larger base of total households.

As long as people continue to show a preference for small families, and housing shortages or economic conditions do not force substantial numbers of unmarried persons and families to double up, average house-hold size is likely to remain relatively low. This trend shows strong underlying support for the revival of urban living throughout the United States. It is no longer necessary to have a large home in the suburbs with several rooms to accommodate children. These same households could much more efficiently live within the urban cores or near office complexes built (or to be built) in high-density suburban locations.

Families and the Presence of Children

Over the last ten years, the number of families has increased by 7.4 million to a total of 57.2 millon. About 57 million of the total were "primary" families maintaining their own households. A small additional number, about 250,000 were secondary families—living in a household which is maintained by another person or family group to which they were not related. In 1978, 53 percent of the families included at least one child under 18, 23 percent had a child under six, and 13 percent had a child under three. These percentages are somewhat lower than the com-parable proportions of families with children in each respective age group category in 1968.

Not only have the percentages of families with children under eigh-teen, six and three years of age declined as a proportion of all families, but the average number of children in families which have children has also declined. In 1968, families with children under eighteen were likely to have an average of 2.4 such children; those with children under the age of six had 1.55 children; and those with children under the age of three had an average of 1.2 such children. The corresponding averages for 1978 were: 1.96 children under eighteen; 1.31 children under age six; and 1.10 under age three.

Where these families live is of critical importance in determining the future of retail development. Increasingly, these families or households were maintained in and supporting areas quite dissimilar to the areas they are supporting today. Many of these families are living rather inefficiently in large homes and they are frustrated by their commuting and the cost of transportation, etc. It is only natural for the market, reacting to a demand for closer housing, to support full-scale regionalization of the location of these families close to their jobs and close to their preferred place of shopping, if possible.

Other demographic factors which are interesting are as follows: certain segments of the retail industry are headed for disaster because they are relying on a customer base which is going to be eroding in the future. For example, the fast-food industry is totally dependent on the eighteen- to thirty-four-year-old age group. This is reputed to be the fastest growing segment of the U.S. population. All this has been true (between 1960 and mid-1978, the 18- to 34-year-old age segment of the population increased from 39.0 million to 62.9 million, an average annual compound rate of 2.7 percent and more than twice the 1.1 percent average gain in total population). This growth will persist through to 1980 when this group will number 65.6 million or 4.3 percent more than it did in 1978. After that, however, there will be zero growth in this age group. This trend, coupled with the way people are making adjustments for higher fuel and energy costs (by eating out less) will spell disaster for this segment of retailing in the same way this group currently shops at retail stores better known as discount stores. Those stores will be similarly affected.

Looked at another way, in 1980 this group will constitute 30 percent of the total population, up from 22 percent in 1960, but by 1990, they will decrease to approximately 25 percent of the population. Thus there will be an absolute decline in this important age group in the 1980s.

Another interesting demographic factor is the coming of age of the children of the post-World War II baby boom, translated into a big increase in working women. By 1979, the total number of working women was approximately 43 million. This is up from a 1960 level of approximately 21 million.

There is every indication that this trend is also flattening out, and that the new number of additional women entering the work force has peaked. This has huge implications for the ready-to-wear industry which is supplying this market segment with clothing suitable for a work situation.

Are We Overbuilding?
Is Large Gobbling Up Small?

BRUCE P. HAYDEN

At the time this volume was put together, the word "is" was certainly good and appropriate. By December 13, 1979, two months after Paul Volcker and the Fed changed their whole attack on inflation and in the process substantially dried up the long-term mortgage market, the question might better have been asked, "Will large gobble up small?" As for "is"—currently "is" is not. As Dan Rose says, "Money is the one building material for which there is no known substitute."

This country seems to have a profound fear of the "big" whether we are referring to big oil, big labor, big corporations, or big shopping centers. I happen not to share that fear in general, feeling personally that on the one side of the coin continued growth to mammoth size can be most accurately regarded as the ability of an enterprise to serve its market well— and that on the other side, the bigger the operation gets, the more vulnerable it becomes to the younger, the smaller, the faster afoot, quicker to respond and less well tied up in red tape.

Looking specifically at shopping centers, however, I happen to think that the day of the supperregional has come, is here, and is starting to wane. I do not think we are going to see a great many new superregionals created. To be successful, the five-and-six department store center of 1.5 million square feet more or less needs to find an underserved and rapidly growing market area. There will continue to be such areas, and there will continue to be new superregionals created, but today the smart developers and the smart money who are thinking regional at all are thinking about a category that ULI has not invented yet—the miniregional. These miniregionals, incidentally, are not going into Houston, Los Angeles, Chicago, and northern New Jersey. They are going into Columbia, South Carolina; Danville, Virginia; Eugene, Oregon; Springfield, Missouri; Temple, Texas; and other good smaller to intermediate-sized cities that were largely passed over the first time around. This is where you will find the Mike Kellys, the Mel Simons, the Jim Wilsons, Strouse-Greenbergs, and others concentrating their efforts. This is where the demand and the market are often unsatisfied.

The big regional, and in some cases even the small regional, seems to have strikes going against it in all directions. They are a pet hate of the environmentalists, for example—as are the superhighways at whose intersections the superregionals have tended to develop. They are feared and detested by the big city mayors—not necessarily the biggest city mayors, but the mayors of Hartford, Lansing, Fort Wayne, Toledo, Des Moines—all of whom see further development of such centers as further nails in the coffin of their hope for downtown renewal.

And, for the present Administration at least, these mayors have new influence—witness the recent White House paper on the federal role in shopping center development in the future issued under the heading, "An Urban Conservation Policy."

In accordance with Executive Order 12044, the major agencies are ordered to subject major programs and activities to new urban impact analyses aimed directly at strengthening the Central Business Districts by preventing the development of outlying competition. An interagency coordinating committee is to create a task force composed of representatives of HUD, EDA, DOT, the Treasury, and the Small Business Administration. Its efforts are directly to support revitalization of efforts, retail and otherwise, in downtown U.S.A.—and, probably more important,—indirectly, under the guise of fighting urban sprawl, to do everything reasonably possible to discourage regional shopping center development that might threaten or seem to threaten established Central-City Business Districts in distressed communities. Everything from highway programs, sewer programs, mass transportation agencies, etc., will be involved with the required urban impact analysis. It will be generated at the request of any city that feels itself threatened, with strong encouragement in the direction of almost a veto power in the hands of the existing city against new centers outside its limits or outside its CBD.

There may be a strong hand of "big brother knows best" in all of this. After all, the suburban shopping center age has blossomed and prospered not because developers had any power to make people come to their doors, but because they were smart enough to know what the public, particularly the woman shopper, wanted, and they made it available. Even before World War II, in the late 30s, the president of the lending institution with which I was long connected came to the conclusion that, "Women do not want to go downtown to shop. They want to shop closer to home. Get us into the shopping center business." These were his instructions to the Mortgage Loan Department and wise ones they were.

Let me disgress for a minute and comment on what I call "the law of unintended consequences." This law can be stated: "In important measures of federal policy, decisions made always generate unintended consequences. These consequences are always serious and usually counterproductive."

You can find example after example. In the particular instance of this proposed federal policy, of which Marshall Kaplan, one of the contributors to this volume, is the principal author, the unintended consequence in my opinion is that, to the extent the President's policy is successful, the major beneficiaries will not be the central cities but will be the owners of existing shopping centers.

For reasons I will set forth in a minute, the American woman is not going to return en masse to do her buying downtown no matter how good an idea Marshall Kaplan and Jimmy Carter think this might be. To the extent that new centers cannot be created, volumes will go up in the existing centers. As a trustee of and shareholder in Corporate Property Investors with major holdings in something like forty regional centers at the moment, I ought to be overjoyed. As one who still believes that America has been built on freedom of choice and the market system, I am dismayed.

Of course, this "big brother knows best" approach is not unusual for government. The public does not like the Susan B. Anthony dollars, for example, and will not have anything to do with them. The Federal answer is, "We will give them out as change in the Post Offices and you will take them whether you want them or not. Then if they are still not acceptable, we will just quit making dollar bills." Most of the women I know—from coast to coast—deplore the fact that there is not much good shopping downtown anymore; but, with even fewer exceptions, they would not use it if it were there. Al Taubman's West Farms Mall on the southwest corner of West Hartford, for example, has practically destroyed retailing in New Britain, seriously harmed the older West Hartford center, and been a major deterrent to retail revival in downtown Hartford. With few exceptions, women say they do not like West Farms Mall because it is so big, hard to find stores there due to the lack of mall directories, and tiring to walk in but they find there what they want—and the convenience of one-stop shopping.

There are a variety of reasons why shoppers tend not to go to Downtown U.S.A. anymore—traffic congestion, paid parking, perceived threats to personal safety—but the federal answer to all of this is similar to the federal attempts to force the Susan B. Anthonys on the public: "We will just give them no alternative. Big brother knows best."

Is there a retail future for Downtown U.S.A.? I think Downtown has been doing a good job recently of finding out what its future is and should be for the last two decades of the twentieth century and the first three of the twenty-first. Successful downtowns are not trying to recreate the downtown retail dominance of the 1920s. Our central cities are finding new roles—as centers for community, cultural, recreation, and meeting activities, as governmental and major corporate business centers, with the clubs, the good restaurants, the specialized retail, and the main department store that, much more so than its suburban branches, still carries the flag.

Not only is the pace of creation of new superregionals slowing substantially, but stores of all kinds and, therefore, the centers in which they are located, downtown or suburban, are getting smaller.

The most excellent reason for this is a very simple one—cost. Construction costs have long been leading the cost-of-living index and continue to—and all space users are having to cut back in order to be able to afford new construction. Merchants are finding that they can more effectively use their sales space and sales personnel in smaller units—and a 50 percent bigger store which may or may not generate 10 percent more business is a very expensive thing.

In an effort to keep costs in line and to keep lending institutions happy, developers of centers big and small are more and more turning over shell space to their tenants, with the tenant responsible for storefront, floors, ceilings, mechanical and lighting distribution, and even the demising walls and their finishes. After this, the merchant has to fixture his store, get his inventory, and provide the working captial necessary to get the whole thing going. It is getting harder and harder to do not only for the little guys, but for the national chains. Today's money rates, if long continued, change "harder" to "damn nigh impossible."

Costs are hitting the major department stores as well. They tend to think these days not in terms of "bigger is better" but in terms of "less is more." They are going back to 80,000- and 120,000-square-foot stores, whereas before they were thinking of 140,000 to 180,000 square feet. They do not do quite as much volume, but they take a lot less capital and generate a better return on investment. Also even the major department stores chains find their resources for expansion are severely limited. They may be able to find money for five major stores and ten small ones scattered nationwide in a given year—and most of them have priority lists going several years into the future on things they would like to do, but from which they must each year select the most promising, putting the rest over.

Aggravating the cost problem, of course, is the increasing cost of regulation and approvals for all types of construction. It is a foregone conclusion today that a zoning application will be bitterly fought with the nearby neighbors who do not want it *here* and the environmentalists who do not want it at all—noisy allies before the zoning board and the courts. Environmental impact statements—which should be but are not as yet accompanied by economic impact statements—are time consuming, expensive, and again subject to challenge.

How do the neighborhood strip centers, new and old, compete with the regionals? Very well, by and large. It has long been apparent to students of the shopping center industry that the regionals and superregionals, as a rule, do not affect the neighborhood strip centers too much—unless the latter allow themselves to get out of control and get too big. It has been twenty years or more since the regional center generally included a supermarket—earlier they used to have two or three. There may be a CVS or superdrug operation, but the neighborhood style drugstore which still does a huge business across the country, located as it is near a good supermarket, is not found in the regional center. The tailor, the shoe repair shop, the small gift store, Carvels, Friendly Ice Cream may or may not appear in the superregional or regional center, but they are the service facilities which, together with the market and the drugstore, keep people coming back to the neighborhood strips.

The centers I would worry about are those in the metropolitan areas that are classified as community centers—200,000 or 300,000 square feet, probably with a supermarket or two, and probably with a discounter or two. If the mass merchandiser is K-Mart and the center is not very large—as the K-Mart centers seldom are—it will probably do fine. When it gets up to 200,000 or 300,000 square feet though, it is far too big to hold its own against the neighborhood center for the everyday needs—and far too small and weak to lock horns effectively with a regional.

On balance, though, if I had to own and could run them myself, I would rather have a series of good neighborhood centers—good corners, strong neighborhoods, each with an excellent supermarket and a darn good drug store—and let the Al Taubmans, the Ernie Hahns, and the Rouses have their regionals. I think I would have more fun, make more money, and live longer.

In conclusion, let me report on discussions I had with two of the most knowledgeable people in the shopping center industry that I know. The first one limited his comments to the general subject of "Are we over-building?" to saying, "I have been asking myself that for the last forty years, and I think at last the answer is clearly yes—but the big are not going to swallow the small."

The second was the late Sidney Greenberg, a fellow trustee of Corporate Property Investors. At a trustee's meeting a few hours before he died, he said, "Smaller stores and smaller centers, generally in smaller cities, are the clear trend." He went on to say, "I think our shopping center industry is headed for salvation, not of its own choice. We are going to be saved not because we are smart, not because we are unselfish, not because we exercise any self-restraint, but by the fact that the cost and lack of availability of money will tend to keep our greed and stupidities under close control."

Shopping Center:
A Lender's Perspective

MARTIN CLEARY

We have been the unsuccessful bidder for any number of shopping center packages recently.

To put lenders in perspective it must be realized that we are followers and not leaders—we don't instigate projects, we don't innovate, and we rarely even have architectural input. Our vote is a negative one and all we can say is we won't finance unless certain changes are made. I wanted to set that as a tone and also to go back a little bit in history. I think that TIAA is a very good example of a lender's history in the shopping center business. It is a fast-growing insurance company (we grow at the rate of about 15 or 16 percent a year). We have a very dependable cash flow. It is essentially a retirement fund for college teachers and because of our size (we are the eleventh largest insurance company in the United States), we can get involved in major projects.

TIAA went into the mortgage business in about 1934. From the pre-World War II and early post-World War II periods we had invested primarily in apartments, office buildings, some industrial, some downtown retail and then in an assortment of motels and a couple of bowling alleys towards the end of that time frame. In the early 1950s we moved to doing deals in small cities. Essentially, downtown, primarily taxpayers, downtown strip stores, consisting of women's wear, shoe stores

297

and the like. There was no parking except on the street and some municipal parking. And then came the first wave of the shopping center developers and the names are almost legend today. (For some reason or other, most of the developers came out of Ohio, which I never really understood, except Foster Sear's comments about Cleveland might be that they built malls around Ohio originally.) They were developing what we call today community shopping centers which are anchored by a junior department store, usually L-shaped. Foster probably used to put most of the J.C. Penney stores right into the apex of the L. It was very easy for a lender to finance because 70 to 80 percent of the tenants were credit worthy. We didn't have to worry too much about location and the deal was an easy one to put to bed.

At that point in time the shopping center was not accepted as an investment vehicle by the insurance industry and those of us who made the decision to go into it really were in a fairly attractive position. The rates were higher and we thought that the risks were lower. If you look around, Connecticut General, Equitable and TIAA were probably the three major early lenders.

Again, not being innovators, we followed the developer in his progress. The developer went from community and neighborhood shopping centers in the early to mid-50s, to small two department store centers and later on to the superregionals. I've really hestitated to impose a history on you but I think that it is important to do this in order to understand where we are today and really where we will go from there.

Now the lender mentality has changed and the shopping center has now become the Cadillac of the lending industry. There have been fewer defaults and problems with the regional shopping center than with any other type of mortgage. And I think that this became much more noticable during the recession of 1973-74. The shopping center which carried a premium rate, that is a slightly higher rate, making it a more attractive loan, now commands the prime rate of the lender.

I use the word in quotes but "amateur lenders" are now entering this highly sophisticated business and perhaps making shopping center loans without the prudence of their predecessors. That to me is a major problem because we all tend to sink to the lowest common denominator. One major factor, to some extent, (which) has prevented shopping center overbuilding was clarified by the preceding papers. Unlike office, industrial and apartments, which can be built as long as a developer and a lender agree, the shopping center developer will not go forward without the department stores. And the department stores have a different motivation than just building or lending. I am not sure that these safeguards will hold in the future.

You have also heard in the previous panel of filling in. I think some of the department store concept of today is that this is not necessarily where we can go in and make a lot of money, but rather this is a market where we must be, we must have a presence with a store, though it may not be financially attractive.

Now that I've set up the history and the caveats, let's look at the lender's thinking of today in terms of the future. Any changes will be evolutionary. It is going to be piecemeal, and it probably is going to be long term and will again follow the developers. For several years, it was the middle or medium market that we have been talking about. A number of us have different definitions of that and I believe that the J.C. Penney Company really instigated the term "medium market mall" and that is the word that caught on. To me a medium market mall is really a small regional center that is reduced only in degree. The anchor tenants are between 70,000 and 100,000 square feet rather than 150-200,000 for regional. The total shopping center area, the selling area, is between 200 and maybe 350,000 square feet, sometimes up to 500,000 depending upon the size of the market, but that is relatively rare. And the market that we are talking about is from 50-100,000 persons. The trade area covers a much greater territory. You've got driving times from thirty minutes to an hour, which you would not (and no one would) put up with in any major metropolitan area.

First moves into this market were made by Bob Congel of Pyramid, throughout New England and New York State. Again, J.C. Penney was probably one of the leaders going into it, and initially the lenders were reluctant to finance it. They had a great many misgivings about. the market. I think in the intervening five years this has been dispelled and the middle market mall is an accepted and attractive vehicle for lenders. One difference in the middle market mall, from a lender's standpoint, is that when you lend on a regional shopping center, typically the anchor department stores are not part of your security. All they do is enter into an agreement with the developer to operate a store and for reciprocal parking. In the middle markets the stores are smaller and most of the department stores are part of the security. So when you are lending on it you have the collateralization of your anchor tenant and you can swing off that to a much lower degree of risk.

There was an important difference between this wave and previous shopping center development. Previously, the developer was responding to or anticipating market growth. When he gets into the middle markets he is replacing downtown, he's not necessarily anticipating any growth. Frankly, from a lender's standpoint, the middle market is easier to look at because he can understand and see it. It is there and, if he has got the right horses, it works. When you are anticipating growth there can be mistakes. The middle markets are replacements for inadequate parking, unorganized development and, really, lack of security in shopping downtown. And whether we like it or not the middle market is a major factor, because the developers have built out of most of the major metropolitan areas in the United States.

The second type of development is the downtown regional center and quite often multiple-use project. The early developments of these really were not looked upon favorably by lenders, and, frankly, having done a few I think that we were right. Those of us who did go downtown early forgot some of our own rules. We adapted sites to a particular configuration. One contributor to this volume, who shall remain nameless, jointly loaned with us on a particular center and the configuration required that the department stores be on either side of the mall as opposed to being on either end of the mall. We would have never have done that in a suburban development. But we did it in this particular center and as a result the center was not quite as successful as we would have anticipated. I think that we have learned and that you are going to see a greater lender acceptance of downtown and hopefully we will profit by our previous mistakes.

Just to give you a concept of how heavily our development is in the downtown areas, TIAA has financed some of the names you may have heard earlier—Queens Center, Brickyard in Chicago, Fairlane Center in Dearborn and Galleria in White Plans. Another is downtown Louisville. Some of these are combinations of regional shopping centers and office complexes and parking garages.

The third trend in shopping center development that we see today is the specialty center. Faneuil Hall Marketplace, which we also financed in Boston, or the proposed Harborplace in Baltimore on which we have a commitment. Both of these were developed by the Rouse Company. This particular type of set-up bothers me because it doesn't have anchors, not because it is not successful. Faneuil Hall may have been too successful. This particular type of center lacks the discipline that we have had in shopping centers in the past. It doesn't have the discipline of the department stores. Developers will build wherever they see a good project and we poor sheep will probably follow them and make some large mistakes.

I think that the market conditions today are confused enough that I probably should discuss them. Let's talk about interest rates and money availability. The developer right now, in our opinion, is doing one of several things. He is delaying his project or he is proceeding with his construction without a long-term take-out, but working with his construction loan only. Or he is proceeding with development and he has a window to come for finance for a six-month period and he is dragging his feet to come to the lender for financing because he is looking for lower interest rates.

The permanent loan rates for shopping centers today are as broad a spectrum as I have ever seen them in the time that I have been in the business. You can see shopping centers being financed at 11 to 12 percent. I have never seen an extreme of 1 percent in terms of offers being made to finance shopping centers. There are major differences in money availability among companies because of policy loans and other factors. So there are some companies that really do have the money available. The term of loans are really dependent on how long the department stores leases are or for what period of time they have agreed to operate. But in the main loans being done today have a payout of thirty to thirty-five years. A great number of companies, about 50 percent of all life companies, are using what is called a call provision or a due data in about fifteen years. They want to relook at the interest rate at some future point in time; they are betting on a long term continuance of inflation.

Recently I moderated a panel on which a gentleman from a British firm, (actually an international firm but headquartered out of Great Britain) participated. I asked him about the conventional mortgage market there. He said that there was none. I asked how you develop projects and he said that you build a project and you sell it free and clear with a yield someplace between 4 and 6 percent. And I asked how do you make sense out of that and he said, "Well, if you are assuming a 9 percent inflation rate, we can buy a project and earn 12 to 14 percent on our money." And he added, "If you fellows don't watch it you are going to be there very soon."

I think that if we have a continuance of inflation or the institutional perception of a continuance of inflation you are going to see several things. One is, as represented by this panel, more institutional ownership. I think the second item you will see, that may not be as satisfactory, is a lot of joint ventures between institutions and developers. You all know what a joint venture is. The insurance company puts up the money and the developer puts up the experience and you can always tell when it is done because the developer has the money and the insurance company has the experience. The third area you will see is short-term mortgages. You will have five-year renewable mortgages. A lot of major institutions are currently contemplating this, so they will have a relook at interest rates, but again it is that same perception that Great Britain moved to.

This is enough straight line extrapolation. I still predict a return to normalcy. I think the old saw, as it has in the past, works. It is "neither a borrower or a lender be, the broker makes all the money."

Are We Overbuilding?

MICHAEL F. KELLY

I count myself as a developer although I also represent a major retailer in the midwest, Dayton-Hudson Corporation. In exploring the current trends of the shopping center industry, the parameters of our company may provide substantial insights. They establish virtually a census of the retailing field and also what we are doing in our business. I would also like to discuss the changes in demographics that make the shopping center in the 1980s our opportunity.

Dayton-Hudson is the eighth largest nonfood retailer in the United States, with operations in forty-four states, and had a projected 1979 sales level in excess of $3 billion. It has four distinct divisions. In the department store division, it has J.L. Hudson, Co., Dayton's J.A. Brown and Diamonds, which cover mostly the midsection of the country in the department store field. It has a low-margin division-Target stores and Lechmere in Boston. Target again covers the central part of the country. We have a specialty store division, comprising Dayton Hudson Jewelers and B. Dalton Books. We also have Mervyn's, a limited-lines promotional store on the West Coast.

From a strategic standpoint, Dayton-Hudson has positioned itself as a pure retailer, diversifying within the retail industry and serving a wide spectrum of customer needs. It might be of interest to you to indicate where the growth is, as we see it in 1984. This growth process serves to emphasize the changing nature of retailing. Target stores plan to grow from sixty-eight to over 150 stores, B. Dalton to over 700 stores, and Mervyn's from fifty to 102 units. The department store group will add only nineteen stores. From a revenue standpoint, that means that 30 percent of the retail revenues will be in department stores, down from about 60 percent five years ago. Approximately 39 percent of revenues will be in low-margin stores, 22 percent in Mervyn's and 9 percent in specialty stores.

This is a new balance in retailing for Dayton-Hudson. It provides the flexibility to locate a number of stores in a variety of situations, both in shopping centers and free standing, and permits the opening of freestanding stores in both Target and Mervyn's cases. It emphasizes the growth of both Target and Mervyn's as the key to corporate growth.

Dayton-Hudson has put its money in the diversification process and on low-margin stores and promotional department stores, and is in the process of modifying its department store allocation program. The key to the future of retailing is flexibility and it is manifested in many ways. You must size your stores to meet a variety of market opportunities. Macy's talked about an inability, at the present time, to go below a 200,000 or 150,000 square foot store. Our department stores vary in size from 40,000 square feet to over 700,000 square feet. We also intend to diversify within retailing by internally growing or acquiring specialty stores. Note in this context the Allied Stores acquisition of Bonwit Teller, Dayton-Hudson internally developing B. Dalton and Target, Penney's acquisition of a Wendy's franchise overseas and K-Mart experimenting with staple foods (I understand that they tossed that out). Retailers are testing the transportability of certain stores with strong names. Saks, Neiman-Marcus, Lord & Taylor and Marshall Field all suggest an aggressive regional expansion of stores which were historically held in home markets. We also see the growing variety of specialty stores ranging from those operating a narrow line of merchandise to catalog and specialty discount stores.

Flexibility in retailing means the ability to follow and serve customers as their lifestyles and demographics change and catering to new opportunities in downtown mixed use specialty centers, mid-market, small market, and other market segments that may have been missed in the suburban land rush. The process of managing flexibility in nontraditional market responses will inevitably lead to a fall-out and vulnerability of a number of retailers, particularly as margins are stretched paper-thin by a combination of inflation, increased operating costs, taxes and the extraordinary cost of money.

In the past several months our industry has seen an increase in Chapter 11's (bankruptcies) and a weakness in some traditionally strong retailers even though sales volumes remain at high levels. The retailers, however, are a resilient group and despite short term pauses, they will contine to expand wherever the opportunities are presented.

In the shopping center area, Dayton-Hudson Properties currently manages seventeen regional shopping centers in eight states. We will be managing 20 million square feet of retail space by 1980. We control over twenty-two future sites for regional shopping centers and we are very optimistic for the future and our ability to live in our specialized industry. (Incidently, two of the twenty-two future sites are in CBDs.) The developers who have the staff, track record and staying power to remain a factor will be progressive. Our strategy involves an expansion of our management busines and a continued aggressive development of large and small centers as well as ancillary peripheral commercial development.

It is no secret to anyone in the shopping center industry that it has reached maturity. Harry Newman, an astute developer from California, points out that at this stage comes low back pains, outmoded ideas, slower reaction times, too little exercise and too big a waistline. The number of large shopping center opportunities is diminishing and most developers who concentrated only on regional shopping centers are diversifying, both within the real estate industry and outside the industry. Remember, as flexibility is the key to retailing, flexibility in the 1980s is going to be the key for the developers as well. In the past several years we have seen traditional shopping center developers moving into hotels, office buildings, industrial parks, housing, fast food franchises, retailing, movies and professional sports. The era of the specialist is giving way to the era of the generalist.

Over the past twenty-five years, shopping centers have become the dominant force in retailing, generating over 60 percent of all retail sales in over 18,000 locations. The new forces that we are now seeing concern environmental issues, energy shortages, historical preservation, inflation, new lifestyles and a shift of governmental policy to favor the heart of our cities. Does all of this mean a new era for our downtowns? I happen to think so, although it will be slow and selective. When one can blend the excitement of culture, entertainment, physical amenities, housing, hotels, shops, and offices, it represents real estate development at its very best. While downtowns represent a genuine growth opportunity for creative development, they are not without substantial risks far above suburban developments. For developers, the risks begin with an undefined development time, political indecision, the lack of clear comprehensive land planning, difficult construction processes and a lack of expertise in mixed use projects. For retailers, the risks involve extraordinary operating and construction costs. They involve specialized customers, modified store hours, and in many cases a nonstandardized merchandise mix. Local, state and federal governments are quite properly focusing attention on the central cities and providing creative financing assistance to make development economic and attractive. But the problems are clear.

Despite middle age, the shopping center industry will still have a full plate for most flexible developers. The trends and opportunities will be in smaller centers, mid-markets, downtowns and revitilization. The larger malls, however, which must have average rents in the range from $13 to $15 per square foot, plus $4 to $5 in other charges, and average in excess of $175 per square foot in sales, will selectively be developed by developers and financial partners with much patience and much fortitude. I just looked at some of the numbers that we had for our 1984 regional center projects. They came in with total project costs in the range of a $100 to $110 per square foot. The challenge to a professional developer with those kinds of costs is obvious.

As we look toward the next twenty years, it becomes critical that we all recognize the dramatic changes in demographics and lifestyles. Dayton-Hudson does a great deal of in-house economic prognostication and I have done my best to listen to them as long as they are optimistic. During the 1975 to 1985 period, 85 percent of our population growth will be in age groups between twenty-five and forty-four years. This is our general target retail population. The trend is to smaller families—better educated, nonsaving and with changing taste levels. The birth rate peaked in 1957 and was at half that level in 1979. In the year 2000, the average age of the population will be forty-two if we retain our current birth rates.

There is also the growing importance of working women; 50 percent of all women currently work outside the home. Another 20 percent intend to work soon. Dual incomes will form a greater amount of spendable income; 75 percent of households over $15,000 have dual incomes, and thus, more wage earners. We are seeing new levels of discretionary spending power. The $25,000-and-over income levels represented 14.1 percent of the population in 1975. By 1985, the $25,000-and-over income levels will represent 30.1 percent of the population and will command 60 percent of the total spending power.

The phenomenal growth of the Sunbelt will continue, with over 50 percent of the nation's growth over the next twenty years being in that area. I would comment, however, that the upper Midwest appears to be very stable and, from a real estate development standpoint, getting an increasing share of attention in recycling, inner-ring development, condo conversions and the like as they become more important. In addition to key demographic trends, we are experiencing a material change in lifestyles, as traditional values are changing to more individualism, a philosophy of entitlement and greater tolerance of values of others.

Interestingly, the diversity of values presents retailing with some real challenges in market segmentation. High-priced, quality merchandise has been selling extremely well. In the candy business, our general candy business is down. The specialized candy business, however, such as Godiva candies, selling at $12.00 a pound, were doing extremely well. Low-priced, quality merchandise of a wide variety has also been selling. The common ingredient is quality and perceived value by the customer. There are penalties for our new values and lifestyles. Children haven't turned out as expected, there is a high divorce rate, lack of ambition, less job satisfaction and a growing skepticism about the future. Prosperity may not be a given. Inflation and energy shortages are long-term problems and government represents an uncontrollable burden. There is a blurring of blue-collar and white-collar distinctions as individual incomes increase. There are increasing time pressures and time choices with dual careers and more leisure time.

Recognizing these changes, what do you do about them? It may mean that you categorize the retail business as a necessity—such as food, staples, and a quick one-stop shopping or home service—and separate ego goods that require the feeling of the merchandise, more personal services, entertainment and leisure. It highlights the need for more sophisticated services and more variety, because of higher disposable income. It may mean a restructuring of the regional shopping center into a true center for all forms of merchandising. We will see greater use of electronics in ordering, especially staple goods. Department-type stores and other stores may be divided into sections, providing ego-oriented merchandise that can be selected in the store, and providing an ordering mechanism for preorders and pick-up of staple merchandise while at the store location. It will mean a critical examination of renovation and reuse of facilities and peripheral land to meet the needs of a true central market place.

It is also important to note that the locations of existing regional centers will be a strength, not a weakness, in charting future change. Regional centers have become the focal point for transportation alternatives that can be a key ingredient in conserving energy, in shortening shopping trips and in providing an activity focal point within an area that transcends the traditional retail shopping. The changes also suggest a greater variety of housing choices, a decline in the affordability of single detached housing and a variety of entertainment and travel choices. On the high-growth scale, medical care, recreation and finance all rate well. It may be that spending for food and beverages and clothing and personal care goods will not grow as fast in the coming years. It won't be as meaningful.

Are we overbuilding? I don't believe so. In certain areas competition from certain department stores challenging a new market may well result in some competitive problems. But in most cases the market dictates development. Development does not dictate the market. The second question asks, is there too much shopping center investment hunger for good financial business decision? I would say that the hunger is real because the values are there. It is probably true that price competition has caused extremely high prices to be paid for shopping centers. But if we believe in inflation as a constant factor in our economic life, the high prices of today may be a bargain. The test is what the buyers do with the property. Left alone, no commercial property will retain its value.

I might comment as an aside that we have recently sold a major part of our shopping center portfolio, and we operate and manage centers for the Equitable and Shell Pension fund, a foreign investor, and we have been at it for about two years with Equitable and one with the Shell Pension fund. Believe me, they are anxious and eager for us, as managers, to manage the malls just as if we were an owner and have been very willing to pay the costs of doing things to the centers that kept them up to date and ahead of the market.

So I think that as far as the institutional buyers, they may not be the original developers, but they are certainly interested in enhancing and protecting their investments. There seems to be a suggestion that the shopping center developers are unloading their centers because they know that they are becoming obsolete. I read in the *Shopping Center World* that by the year 2000 there won't be any shopping centers, so the astute developers are not selling them because they know that they are not going to be around in the year 2000. I would suggest to you that the real reason that the sales are being made in today's market is that there are individual owners who have potential estate problems and wish to get out of the business; additionally, there are public companies who own real estate, like ourselves, and for proper business reasons are selling out. You may be interested in some of the reasons why we sold. We decided to discontinue our real estate business for two basic business reasons: 1) a tremendous need for capital for retail expansion, and 2) the recognition that the nature of the real estate business is not compatible with market valuation for a public corporation. For over five years the corporation had attempted, by separately identifying its real estate business and financial statements, to convince the retail stock market analysts that real estate had a distinct and different set of values, to no avail. These analysts were not prepared to separate the real estate business from retail and gave us no credit for the values that were inherent in a portfolio of assets that had been building for over twenty years.

Our development business was always a substantial producer of cash, but it generated minimum earnings. Indeed, if you run a growth real estate development business properly, utilizing the deductions permitted by the tax laws, you should not generate taxable earnings. Effective shopping center ownership thus has a tendency to increase a public company's asset base, but it also increases its long-term debt and provides very little in the way of earning. It was an indisputable fact that the shareholders were getting no stock-price benefit from real estate assets being held. The argument runs that selling such assets reduces debt ratio and provides capital for retail reinvestment, which earns a return on investment in excess of 14 percent, which in turn produces a higher stock price. While conventional wisdom may say that this is a proper and analytical way to approach it, I still think that as time passes, perhaps the production of cash for a major public company will be more important than an accounting method that stresses earnings per share.

The last question was, "Are the restrictions against shopping centers in governmental areas affecting decisions in building location?" Developers are using extreme care in locational choice. Developers who are professional in their outlook can meet all governmental concerns, but I do say that no amount of force or coercion is going to make any retailer or developer locate a project in an area that doesn't make long term economic sense.

The other question was can mass retailing be revived in the central city? This is a tough issue, but I suspect that the answer is "yes," if the market is there the retailers will find a way to do it. It may be several smaller stores in the first tier of suburbs that respond to the market needs rather than a big new store built downtown. Target has tried to serve inner-city areas and has done so quite effectively in some selected areas by that strategy.

A great deal of time in this volume was spent in discussing shopping centers in a central-city context. Shopping Centers U.S.A. is *not* central cities. Let us not forget that retailing and shopping centers serve people. They serve their needs and desires. Retailing has never been a leader, it has always been a follower in the market place. The suburbs, however you define them, are still the overwhelming choice for housing, industry and jobs. Central cities are still losing population and the suburbs are still growing as people seek a less structured lifestyle. The automobile is a necessity, not a luxury. The energy shortage will change some of our thinking on many things, but the people will still adjust without a massive relocation. The United States is a decentralized economy and in our lifetime this decentralization will not be materially reversed. The central city is just another market for the retailer; its success or failure will depend on basic economics and the desire of the consumer in that specific market. In the past twenty years customers have voted overwhelmingly to shop in suburban locations versus downtowns. As an example, in 1979, 94 percent of the business done by Dayton-Hudson Corporation was down in suburban locations. I fully expect that this percentage will not materially change during the next ten years.

Overlooked Opportunities in Shopping Center Development

STEPHEN H. COWEN

During the last twenty years, retail development has flourished concurrently with the growth of suburbia, and has generally followed freeway and interstate highway construction. The Central Business District (CBD) and its related submarket—defined as the inner ring—have been left untouched by retail developers and department stores. The focus had been almost completely on suburban areas, which offered growing populations characterized by higher disposal incomes. More recently, now that suburbia has been malled, developers and retailers seeking new opportunities have been forced to develop and/or redevelop markets which have been passed over during the earlier wave of suburban shopping center development.

We are all familiar with the retail developments in the CBD and the pluses and minuses associated with new retail developments in core-area locations. The specific objective of this paper, however, is the overlooked market defined as the inner ring. This geographic focus may become increasingly important for retail development in the 1980s.

Definition of the Inner Ring

Situated between the CBD and the suburban ring highway, the inner ring generally consists of older neighborhoods which contain high-density business and industrial activities, and residential and other related uses. In contrast to the typical suburban community, this subsector of an urban area has a higher density of residential development and more business and commercial development. However, the inner ring has lower densities of commercial and residential development than typically found in the CBD.

The inner ring is frequently not serviced as well by major highway development as suburban areas, which in most cases grew as a result of highway access. However, the inner-ring area may be serviced by mass transit of various types.

The New Jersey Meadowlands District is a prime example of an inner-ring market. It is located a short distance from the CBDs of New York City, Jersey City, Hackensack, Paterson and Newark. It draws from high-density residential developments located along the Palisades of New Jersey and has an inordinately high density of industrial and commercial developments in its market area. It is served by a highway system which is primarily designed to handle commuter transit and has not undergone substantial improvements during the past twenty years.

It is currently served by a commuter mass transit system, which has the capability of being upgraded to serve developments in the Meadowlands District. The importance of mass transit in the Meadowlands is less significant for major retail developments than for commercial and residential uses. However, its primary importance lies with the reduction of vehicular traffic on the highway system in general.

Who Lives There?

Frequently, the demographics of the inner ring show a higher proportion of older residents who settled in an area adjacent to a CBD and who, for varying reasons, never made the move to suburbia. Initially, the inner ring offered reasonably convenient access to the CBD and in many instances, it still offers the same convenience to the CBD, where the major source of employment exists. The residents of the inner ring continue to enjoy good access to the city and the activities that occur there, yet have some of the freedoms offered by suburbia.

The population which is presently moving to the inner ring for their primary residence frequently desires to be closer to their primary place of employment, with easy access to the amenities offered by the CBD, and with a minimum of travel time. Housing costs are generally lower in the inner ring than those in the CBD and offer amenities and quality than cannot be found in the CBD. Given the lower cost of housing, the inner-ring population may contain a broad cross-section of younger families with two workers employed in the CBD who do not require the larger residential square footages available in suburbia.

Energy costs have placed a severe constraint on suburban living with the cost of travel to and from employment sources and other services. This constraint should cause a reverse trend back to the inner ring.

With regard to the Meadowlands District, the inner ring consists of that population that lives between the Meadowlands and the Hudson River, from Jersey City to Fort Lee. In general, the population is characterized by an older-age profile and below-average median incomes. However, our residential development at Harmon Cove as indicated that given a convenient location close to the CBD with access to mass transit, people are willing to pay relatively high prices for residential units.

With regard to the demographics of the retail market—in addition to the higher income of new luxury condominium or apartment dwellers—we have found that a great deal of those residents in the older residential districts have relatively high disposable incomes in comparison to national averages. This is probably attributable to a relatively low occupancy cost for housing units.

Challenges of Inner-Ring Development

Land in the inner ring is generally more available and/or more easily developable than in the CBD. The inner ring frequently caters to modified suburban shopping centers whereas the CBD calls for a totally different concept in retail development than found in the suburban shopping center.

Parking is usually more available and at a lower cost than would be found in the CBD. There is frequently less need for 100 percent deck parking and there is less congestion on the roadways and access points surrounding the site.

Mass transit is generally available in limited quantities and frequently oriented towards vehicular types of mass transit. To the extent that rail mass transit is available, studies have indicated that this type of mass transit has little value in bringing customers to and from retail-type developments.

The Meadowlands District is a prime example of what I would term the inner ring in terms of infrastructure. While large land masses are available, inordinately high development costs and limited highway capacity require that developments be clustered and contain densities far in excess of those found in suburban retail developments.

Multi-use type developments are becoming more frequent in the Meadowlands District, which include office, residential and commercial uses. Given the limited highway capacity of the district, projects need be located where automobile access is available today and where mass transit can ultimately be substituted.

This is not to say that mass transit will, in the near future, or even in the distant future, become a viable alternative to the automobile in access to shopping centers. However, mass transit will become a viable alternative to bring workers to and from their residences in the Meadowlands District, which will optimize the limited highway systems.

Political and Social

The development of new retail facilities in the inner ring is primarily a replacement of older shopping districts, which have, to a large degree, been pruned of their major retail functions as suburban shopping centers developed. Our survey studies show that those persons who stop or reside in what I have previously defined as the inner ring of the Meadowlands District do the majority of their shopping in the suburban shopping centers lying substantial distances outboard of their primary place of residence. These people have either not found it convenient to travel to the CBD for their shopping trips, or have found that the CBD does not offer the kinds of goods and services which these people find available at regional shopping centers.

Opposition of local merchants to competition from the newer, bigger and better type of retail facility is probably one of the most difficult items which the developer must overcome in inner-ring development. Modern retail development will offer the consumer the convenience and availability of the suburban type shopping center without the need to travel great distances. In addition, the frequency of shopping trips will probably increase.

The major fallacy in terms of the merchant opposition is that the impact of the suburban mall has already been felt by the merchants in the inner ring. Our surveys of the older shopping districts adjacent to the Meadowlands indicate that the majority of better merchants have fled to regional shopping centers, and those that remain serve only a convenience shopping goods function. Thus, the merchant's arguments that the new shopping center will result in the loss of their primary source of income are frequently without substance.

In fact, local merchants may find their situation improved, as a result of increased employment of revenues generated as a result of the shopping center and the other forms of development, which it encourages.

Conclusion

Despite such potential problems, the inner ring will become increasingly attractive to retailers and developers over the coming decade, particularly if energy costs continue to escalate at rapid rates. It will be a much less complex undertaking to build a major retailing facilities at an inner ring site compared to a CBD location. However, such a location will not be so much in competition with the CBD as it will with existing suburban centers.

Bibliography

EDWARD DUENSING

This bibliography attempts to gather the current (post-1974) material on the subject of shopping centers in order to aid involved persons in acquiring the information they need to make informed decisions.

Alexander, Laurence A. (ed.), *Downtown Mall Annual and Urban Design Report*. Downtown Research and Dev't Center, New York, 1979.

Alsop, Ronald, "High-Hat Malls Lure Highbrow Shoppers to High-Priced Goods: Stores in Cleveland Suburbs Use Valet Parking, Balls Beethoven Birthday Party," *Wall St. Journal*. 192:1+ Dc. 20, '78.

Analysis and Valuation of Retail Locations. Reston Pub., Reston, VA., 1976.

"Anti-Trust Action in the Shopping Malls" *Business Week*. p. 51, Dc 8 '75.

"Are Center Go-Go Years Over" *Chain Store Age Executive Edition*. 53:51-55 My '77.

(Atlanta, GA). Dept. of Community and Human Development. *Heart of Atlanta Shopping District Study: A Plan to Regenerate Atlanta's Historic Business District*. 1977 (prepared by Toombs, Amisan, & Wells et.al.).

Ball, H. "Cureless Justice: The U.S. Supreme Courts Shopping Center Opinions, 1946-1976" *Polity* 11(2):200-228, 1978.

Barnekov, T.K. & D. Rich, "Privatism and Urban Development: An Analysis of the Organized Influence of Local Business Elites" *Urban Affairs Q.* 12:431-74 Je '77.

Beardon, W.O., "Determinant Attributes of Store Patronage: Downtown versus Outlying Shopping Centers" *Journal of Retailing*. 53:15-22 Summer '77.

Beavon, K. & A. Hay, "Consumer Choice of Shopping Center" *Environment* & *Planning*. 9(12):1375-1393 '77.

Bellenger, D.N. et.al. "Shopping Center Patronage Motives" *Journal of Retailing*. 53:29-38, Summer '77.

Berk, Emanuel, *Downtown Improvement Manual*. Chicago ASPO Press, 1976.

Berry, David et.al. "Downtown Redevelopment in Five Cities" *Planning and Public Policy*. 5(2): May '79.

"Big Stores Vote For Downtown Again" *Business Week*. p. 38, Sp 20 '76.

Black, Thomas J., *The Changing Economic Role of Central Cities*. Urban League Institute, Washington, D.C., 1978.

(Boston, MA) Redevelopment Authority: Back Bay. *Boyston & Newbury Streets: A Shoppers Profile. 1978.*

(Boston, MA) Redevelopment Authority: Environmental Review Section. Lafayette Place: Final Environmental Impact Statement 1978.

(Boston, MA) Redevelopment Authority: Research Department. *Study of Boston's Captive Retail Market of Office Employees and High-Rise Apartment Dwellers: Where They Shop and Why.* 1974. (prepared by Marie Kentmann).

Breckenfeld, G., "Jim Rouse Shows How to Give Downtown Retailing New Life." *Fortune.* 97:84-6 Ap 10 '78.

Calif. Planning and Inspection Dept. *Regional Commercial Center Process for the Roosevelt Community Plan Area.* City Hall, '78.

Census Data - "tool for retailers" *CPA Journal* 48:85-6 Je '78.

"Charles Kober Assoc. - Unlike Usual Enclosed Shopping Malls, This one is designed to Reactivate Main Street with New Shops on the Outside." *Progressive Arch.* (Pasadena) p. 92, Ja '79.

(Chicago, IL) Dept. of Urban Renewal. *Report to the Department of Urban Renewal on an Evaluation of Shopping Centers in Urban Renewal Areas.* 1974. (prepared by Urban Associates of Chicago).

(Cleveland) City Planning Commission. *Patterns of Commercial Activity in the Cleveland Area*: 1950-1974. 1977. (prepared by Joanne Layarz).

Concentration in U.S. Retail Trade - 1967. Hofstra University School of Business, 1975.

Cunningham, Michael. "Can Downtown Be Reinvented?" *Ekistics.* 43(256) 159-164 1977.

Davis, J.M., "Component Depreciation for a Shopping Center," *Appraisal Journal.* 47(2): 204-217, Ap '79.

Dent, Borden D., "The Challenge to Downtown Shopping" (Atlanta, GA). *Atlanta Eco R*, 28:29-33 Ja/Fb '78.

Downtown Malls: An Annual Overview. V2. Downtown Res. and Development Center, '78.

Downtown Mall Annual & Urban Design Report. Downtown Res. and Development Center, 1978 (Annual).

Doyle, Ron Shopsteding: Local Merchants Invest in the City. *HUD Challenge.* 10:22-23. May '79.

Ducca, F.W. "Model of Shopping Center Location" *Environment & Planning.* 8(6): 613-623 '76.

Edwards, A. "Let Them Eat Stale Cake," *Black Enterprise.* 8:39-43 Jl '78.

Farmer, R.N. "Business Prospects in the Inner City," *Intellect.* 105:263-4 F '77.

Freeman, Allen "Evaluation: A Shopping Center As Main Street," *AIA Journal.* p. 46-49, July '78.

Gentry, G.W. & A.C. Burns, "How Important are Evaluative Criteria in Shopping Center Patronage?" *Journal of Retailing.* 53(4):73 '78.

Gern, R.C., "Parking Demand at the Regionals," *ITE Journal.* 48:19-24 S '78.

Guest, A.M., "Central City/Suburban Status Differences: Fifty Years of Change," *Sociological Quart.* 19:17-23 Wint '78.

Harris, Neil, "American Space: Spaced Out at the Shopping Center," *New Republic.* 173:23-6 D' 13 '75.

"How Downtowns are Being Brought Back to Life: Views of Officials," *American City & County.* 91:8 Nv '78.

Huxtable, A.L., "Fall and Rise of Main Street," *N.Y. Times Mag.* pp. 12-14, My 30 '76.

(Inglewood, California) Planning & Development Department. *Proposal to Participate in a Business Reinvestment Program.* '77.

"Inner Suburbs, Cities Get Closer Look," *Chain Store Age Executive Edition.* 51: 27-8 My '75.

International Council of Shopping Centers *Shopping Centers 1988: Answers For the Next Decade.* New York: ICSC, '79.

(Jersey City) Hudson County Planning Board. *Economic Base Study.* 1974.

Joardor, S.D. and J.W. Neill "The Subtle Differences in Configuration of Small Public Space," *Landscape Architecture.* 68(6):487-91 NV '79.

Kanigel, R., "Stores Analyzes What's Happening in Downtown Baltimore and Who is Doing What to Rejuvenate the Central City" *Stores.* 59:18-20+ Mr '77.

Kober, Charles, "Regrowth For Existing Shopping Centers," *Urban Land.* pp. 3-9 Fb '77.

Krumholz, Norman and Susan Hoffman, "Revitalizing Urban Centers: Business and Neighborhoods," *National Civic Review.* 68(3):130-135 Mr '79.

(Lake Charles, L.A.). Lake Charles - McNeese Urban Observatory. *Business Inducement and Economic Development in the Downtown Lake Charles Area.* 1977. (prepared by J.J. Champeaux).

Lamm, Robert R. "Marketing Shopping Centers," *Urban Land.* 37:11-16 Nv '78.

Larry Smith & Co., *Copley Place Retail Impact Analysis.* Boston, Massachusetts Redevelopment Authority, 1978.

(Lexington, Kentucky) Downtown Development Comm., *Analysis of Development Potentials in Downtown Lexington.* 1976. (prepared by Economics Research Assoc.).

Levatino, Adrienne, *Neighborhood Commercial Rehabilitation.* NAHRO, Washington, D.C., 1978.

Linden, Fabian, "The Economics of Cities and Suburbs," *Conference Board Record.* 13(3) pp. 42-45, Mr '76.

Lion, E. *Shopping Centers.* John Wiley & Sons, New York, 1976.

Lipton, Gregory S., "Evidence of a Central City Revival," *Journal of the American Institute of Planners.* 43(2):136-47 Ap '77.

Mackenzie, Janis., "Downtown Retail," *San Francisco Business.* pp. 6-8, Dec. '76.

McCahill, Ed., "Downtowns Welcome Back Small Shopping Centers," *Planning.* (ASPO): 42(5): 15-18, 1976.

McKeever, J.R. et.al., *Shopping Center Development Handbooks.* Urban League Institute, 1977.

Melton, R.B., "Downtown—the Road Back" *Stores.* 58:3-5, July '76.

Miller, Ted R., "*Strategies for Revitalizing Neighborhood Commercial Areas: The Role, Application and Impact of Public and Private Resources.*" Nat'l. Institute for Advanced Studies, Washington, D.C., 1977.

Miller, Tracy and Bryan Shuler, "Commercial Revitalization: Four Case Studies," *Challenge.* 10:2, 12-18.

(Minneapolis) Downtown Council, *Nicollet Mall: The Upper Midwest's Largest Shopping Center.* (1974). (Prepared by Levander, Partridge, and Anderson, Inc. et.al.).

"Most People Like Urban Malls," *American City and County.* 90:92 Oct. '75.

Murray, Raphel, "The Gordon's Alley Story; or How to Rebuild a Fading Central City Retail Section into an Exciting Place to Shop," *Challenge.* pp. 22-25, April '79

Nairn, Janet, "Shopping Malls in the Inner City," *Architectural Record.* 163(3): 117- 32 March '78.

National Council for Urban Economic Development, *Neighborhood Commercial Revitalization.* National Council for Urban Economic Development, Washington, D.C., 1979.

(New York, N.Y.) Midtown Task Force. *Times Square Action Plan.* 1978.

(New York, N.Y.) Dept. of City Planning. *Jamaica Avenue Revitalization Program: Richmond Hill,* 1978.

(Newark, De.) Planning Dept. *Identification of Central Business District Parking Problems,* 1974. (Prepared by Margaret Hagerman Hayes.).

Newman, Harry & Ernest Hahn, "The Shopping Center Industry: A Middle-Aged Giant," *Buildings.* pp. 69-71, Jan. '79.

Nichols, L.L. and Jones, R.S., "Leisure in the Modern Market Place; Recreation and Entertainment Facilities," *Parks & Recreation.* 11:8-11 Dec. '76.

O'Hara, D.J., "Location of Firms Within A Square CBD," *Journal of Political Economy.* 85: 1189-207 Dec. '77.

Onibokum, A., "Comprehensive Evaluation of Pedestrian Malls in the United States," *Appraisal Journal.* 43:202-18 April '75.

"A Poll Over the Suburban Mall: Burlington, Vt. Defeats a Competing Shopping Center," *Time.* p. 116, NV 13 '78.

Potter, R.B., "Directional Bias Within the Usage and Perceptual Fields of Urban Consumers," *Psychological Reports.* 38: 988-90 June '76.

Public Attitudes Toward Downtown Malls. Downtown Res. & Dev. Center, New York, 1975.

Redstone, Louis G., *The New Downtowns: Rebuilding Business Districts.* New York: McGraw-Hill, 1976.

Redstone, Louis, "Shopping Provision in the USA," *Forma.* 4(3): 159-161, 1976.

"Retailing Downtown: Amsterdam NY's Downtown Mall," *Stores.* 59: 43-5 Sept. '77.

"Revitalizing Downtown Shopping Requires More than Cosmetification," *Journal of Marketing.* 42: 13 Jan. '78.

Rosenzweig, P., "Promoting the Central Business District," *Buildings: The Construction and Building Management Journal.* 71:62-4 Ap. '77.

Rubenstein, Harvey M., *Central City Malls.* John Wiley & Sons, New York.

(Sacramento, CA) City Planning Comm. *Sacramento Central Business District: Economic and Market Analysis: Final Draft, 1976.* (prepared by Real Estate Research Corp.).

(Salt Lake City, VT) Redevelopment Agency. *Analysis of Market Potential, Block 58, Sale Lake City Business District.* (prepared by Genge/Call Engineering, Inc.) '76.

(Seattle, Washington) Office of Policy Planning. *Seattle's Retail Sector: Trends Implications and Policy Recommendations.* (Growth Management Policy Paper No. 3), '77.

"Shopping Center Outlook," *National Real Estate Investor.* 21(5): 39-58 May '79.

"Shopping Malls in the Center City," Building Types Study, *Architectural Records.* 163: 117-32 March '78.

"Shopping Malls: Introversion in the Urban Context," *Progressive Architecture.* pp. 49-69, Dec. '78.

"Shopping/Office Centers Offer Opportunity," *Builder.* p. 34, Sept. 4 '78.

(South Bend, Indiana). Urban Observatory. *Downtown Development in South Bend.* 1977.

Spanbock, Marion H. ed., *Where is Downtown Going: Twelve Expert Opinions.* New York: Downtown Research and Development Center, 1979.

"Spurt in Shopping Centers," *Business Week.* 92 + Jan. 15, 1979.

Stango, Janice. "Commercial Revitalization: A Key to Neighborhood and Downtown Redevelopment," *Mortgage Banker.* 39(9): 51-56. Jan. '79.

Steele, Michael A. "Fiscal Impact of Regional Shopping Centers," *Planning Where We Live.* University of Illinois at Urbana Champaign: Bureau of Urban and Regional Planning Research.

(Tacoma, WA) Dept. of Community Development. *Tacoma Urban Renewal Area, Wash. R-14, Downtown Economic Study.* 1975.

(Tulsa, Oklahoma) Metropolitan Area Planning Commission. *Utica Square: Special Study,* 1977.

Underberg, Neil (Chairman), *"Shopping Centers 1976"* (Real Estate Law and Practice Handbook Ser. 129). Practicing Law Institute, 1976. (95-1).

U.S. House. (95-1) Committee on Small Business, *Revitalization of Business Districts: Hearings Before the Committee.* GPO, Washington, D.C., Oct. 18 '77.

U.S. Congress Joint Economic Committee, *"Central City Businesses: Plans and Problems: A Study"* GPO, Washington, D.C., 1979.

U.S. Congress (95-2) Joint Economic Committee. *Keeping Business in the City: Hearings before the Subcomm. on Fiscal and Intergovernmental Policy.* March 6-7 '78.

U.S. Department of Health, Education and Welfare, *Challenge.* 10(2) Feb. '79 (Commercial Revitalization-whole issue).

Walmsley, D.J., "Congruence of Overt Behavior with Preference Structures," *Psychological Reports.* 41: 1082 Dec. (pt 2) '77.

Warner, E., "Suburbia's Gift to the Cities," *Horizon.* 20:14-25 Sept. '77.

Watson, B.M. Jr., "Downtown Core Development and Redevelopment," *Public Management.* 58:13-17 July '76.

Weaver, Clifford L. and Duerkson, Christopher J. "Central Business District Control of Outlying Shopping Centers," *Urban Law Annual.* 14: 57-79, 1977.

White House and the Presidents Interagency. Coordinating Council *Federal Programs for Urban Businesses.* GPO, Washington, D.C., 1979. (on order).

"Why Shopping Centers Rode Out the Storm" *Forbes.* 117:35-36+ June 1, 1976.

Winslow, J.B. "Mass Transit, Parking: Two Keys to Shopping Center Success," *American City.* 90:64 Jan. '75.

Winslow, J.B., "Suburban Competition Won't Kill this City: Canopied Mall in Allentown, Pa." *American City and County.* 91:30-2 Feb. '76.

Witherspoon, R.E. et.al., *Mixed Use Developments.* Urban League Institute, Washington, D.C., 1976.

Woodard, Lynn, N., "Modern Shopping Center Design: Psychology Made Concrete," *Real Estate Review*, pp. 52-55, Summer '78.

Young, W.J., "Distance Decay Values and Shopping Center Size," *Professional Geographer.* 27(3): 304-309 Aug. '75.

Index